Innovative Assessment in Higher Education

Throughout higher education, assessment is changing, driven by increased class size, changing curricula, and the need to support students better. At the same time assessment regulations and external quality assurance demands are constraining assessment options, driven by worries about standards, reliability and plagiarism. This book is about the difficult process of changing assessment in sometimes unhelpful contexts. More than a 'how to do it' manual, *Innovative Assessment in Higher Education* offers a unique mix of useful pragmatism and scholarship.

Key features include:

- exploration of the rationales behind different kinds of innovation in assessment
- discussion of the complex assessment contexts in which teachers attempt to innovate
- contextualisation of innovation in assessment within a range of academic settings
- theoretical and empirical support for innovations within higher education
- case studies illustrating the problems encountered with traditional assessment methods

Innovative Assessment in Higher Education is an enquiry into how and why we innovate in assessment and what practices 'work' in different contexts and cultures. A vital resource for higher education teachers and their educational advisors, it provides a fundamental analysis of the role and purpose of assessment and how change can realistically be managed without compromising standards.

Cordelia Bryan is a freelance higher education consultant. She has led four successful UK higher education projects, is a registered practitioner of the Higher Education Academy and is an external evaluator for several projects. She also co-edited *Speaking Your Mind* in Longman's *Speak-Write* series and has lectured and published widely on educational development within higher education.

Karen Clegg is Senior Adviser for Academic Practice and Director of the Graduate Training Unit within Professional and Organisational Development at the University of York. She is also a registered practitioner of the Higher Education Academy and an external consultant for the Oxford Centre for Staff and Learning Development. Previously, Dr Clegg worked as an academic developer for the UK Centre for Legal Education at the University of Warwick.

Innovative Assessment in Higher Education

Edited by
Cordelia Bryan and Karen Clegg

Routledge
Taylor & Francis Group

LONDON AND NEW YORK

First published 2006
by Routledge
2 Park Square, Milton Park, Abingdon, Oxon OX14 4RN

Simultaneously published in the USA and Canada
by Routledge
270 Madison Avenue, New York, NY10016

Routledge is an imprint of the Taylor and Francis Group

Typeset in Times by
Keystroke, Jacaranda Lodge, Wolverhampton
Printed and bound in Great Britain by
The Cromwell Press, Trowbridge, Wiltshire

British Library Cataloguing in Publication Data
A catalogue record for this book is available from the British Library

Library of Congress Cataloging in Publication Data
Innovative assessment in higher education / edited by Cordelia Bryan and Karen Clegg.
p. cm.
Includes bibliographical references and index.
ISBN 0–415–35642–3 (pbk.) – ISBN 0–415–35641–5 (hardback)
1. Universities and colleges–Great Britain–Examinations. 2. Education, Higher–
Great Britain–Evaluation. 3. Educational evaluation–Great Britain. I. Bryan, Cordelia.
II. Clegg, Karen.
LB2367.G7I56 2006
378.1′662–dc22
2005020737

ISBN 0–415–35641–5 (hbk)
ISBN 0–415–35642–3 (pbk)

Contents

Figures

Tables

Contributors

Mairead Boohan is a lecturer in Medical Education at Queen's University, Belfast. Her main interests are curriculum development and assessment. She holds a Queen's University Teaching Award for work in IPE. She has extensive experience of teaching and educational development for undergraduate and postgraduate medical education. In 1997 she introduced a Masters in Education for the Healthcare Professions at Queen's University, Belfast.
m.boohan@qub.ac.uk

Philip Bradley is Sub-Dean for Teaching, Learning and Assessment, for the undergraduate Medical programme at the University of Newcastle. He has played a leading role in implementing portfolios in the Medical curriculum at Newcastle.
p.m.bradley@ncl.ac.uk

Evelyn Brown was an associate dean in the Faculty of Science at the Open University, responsible for the quality assurance of courses and modules in presentation. She also had a twenty-year association with the university's Assessment Policy section, acting as Deputy Chair of the Examinations and Assessment Committee for several years and chairing the committee for nearly six years. Since retiring in July 2004, she has maintained her involvement with the HEFCE FDTL4 (Fund for the Development of Teaching and Learning) funded 'Formative Assessment in Science Teaching' (FAST) project as a consultant.
evelynbrown102000@yahoo.co.uk

Cordelia Bryan is a freelance higher education consultant with broad experience as a teacher and education developer in the secondary, FE and HE sectors. Over the past twelve years she has led four successful UK higher education projects enhancing different aspects of learning and teaching. She co-edited *Speaking Your Mind* in Longman's *Speak-Write* series, and has lectured and published widely on educational development within HE. She is a registered practitioner of the Higher Education Academy and external evaluator for several HE projects.
cordeliavbryan@aol.com

Philip Butcher is a computer-assisted learning specialist with over thirty years' experience in developing interactive applications to support the teaching and learning of science and technology.

Karen Clegg is Senior Adviser for Academic Practice and Director of the Graduate Training Unit within Professional and Organisational Development at the University of York. She heads a team providing development and training for postgraduate research students and research staff. Previously, she worked as an academic developer for the UK Centre for Legal Education (LTSN Law) at the University of Warwick and co-managed an FDTL project on Self and Peer Assessment in Professional and Higher Education (Saphe) at the University of Bristol. Her research and publications are in the areas of assessment, reflection and learning and teaching in higher education. She is a registered practitioner of the Higher Education Academy and an external consultant for the Oxford Centre for Staff and Learning Development.
kvc500@york.ac.uk

Simon Cotterill is a senior research associate in the School of Medical Education Development, University of Newcastle. He has played a leading role in a number of collaborative projects developing and evaluating ePortfolios.
s.j.cotterill@ncl.ac.uk

Christine Curle is Academic Director of the Doctorate in Clinical and Community Psychology at the University of Exeter and Co-Director of the FDTL4 PBL project. She previously worked full time in the National Health Service as a chartered clinical psychologist and maintains one day a week of clinical practice, working in paediatrics.
c.curle@exeter.ac.uk

Lewis Elton is Professor of Higher Education, University College London (Honorary since December 2003) and Professor Emeritus of Higher Education, University of Surrey. He is a fellow of the American Institute of Physics and of the Society for Research into Higher Education, an Honorary Life Member of the Staff and Educational Development Association, and he holds doctorates (*honoris causa*) of the University of Kent at Canterbury and of the University of Gloucestershire. His main research interests are in innovations in higher education and in change processes.
l.elton@pcps.ucl.ac.uk

Sean Gammon is currently a senior lecturer in Sport and Leisure Studies at the University of Luton. In the last few years he has been a departmental senior teaching fellow, a co-organiser of the university's Teaching and Learning Annual Conference and a member of Luton Business School's Teaching and Learning Committee. An international award-winner for leadership in curriculum design, his main research interest in teaching and learning relates to facilitating the student assessment process, having been involved in an LTSN subject centre-funded project on improving student confidence in the assessment process.
sean.gammon@luton.ac.uk

Tony Gardner-Medwin is Professor of Physiology at UCL, with an interest in neural mechanisms of memory, inference and decision-making. He has pioneered many sophisticated innovations in computer-based teaching since 1983, with an emphasis on the exploitation of simulations, practicals and exercises in critical thinking. His work on confidence-based assessment started in the context of teaching quantitative methods to biomedical students.
a.gardner-medwin@ucl.ac.uk

Graham Gibbs is Professor of Learning and Teaching in Higher Education, and Director of the Institute for the Advancement of University Learning, at the University of Oxford. He has written books and papers about assessment practices for over twenty years. Recently he has examined the strategic use of assessment to support student learning, developed the Assessment Experience Questionnaire and studied students' learning responses to different assessment regimes. His ideas about assessment derive in part from having worked in institutions with approaches to assessment that differ in many respects: the Open University, Oxford Brookes University and the University of Oxford.
graham.gibbs@learning-advancement.oxford.ac.uk

Chris Glover is currently working as a researcher in the Research and Evaluation Team at Sheffield Hallam University's Learning and Teaching Institute, where he has been engaged in a number of projects which support the university's learning, teaching and assessment strategy. His main area of interest is assessment, with specific involvement in the FDTL4 'Formative Assessment in Science Teaching' project. Before undertaking research work, he had taught and was Deputy Headteacher in primary schools in South Yorkshire, with a particular interest in mathematics teaching, language development and special needs education.

Geoff Hammond is the Head of School of Medical Education Development, University of Newcastle. His background is in physiology and he has a long-standing interest in educational technologies.
g.r.hammond@ncl.ac.uk

Katherine Harrington manages Assessment Plus and has published on assessment and support for student learning. **Lin Norton** is a chartered psychologist and Professor of Pedagogical Research and has published widely on improving student writing. **James Elander** is a health psychologist and 2004 National Teaching Fellow. **Jo Lusher** is a health psychologist with a pedagogical research interest in using assessment to support students. At the time of writing, **Olaojo Aiyegbayo**, **Edd Pitt**, and **Hannah Robinson** were research assistants with Assessment Plus. **Peter Reddy** is a psychologist and teaching fellow who has published on assessment and supporting dyslexic students.
k.harrington@londonmet.ac.uk

Catherine Haslam is the Research Director of the Doctorate in Clinical and Community Psychology Programme at the University of Exeter. She has worked in various health settings as a clinical psychologist in Australia. In addition to her responsibility as Co-Director for the FDTL4 PBL project, she maintains an active research programme in her specialty of neuropsychology.

Sally Jordan is Science Staff Tutor and Chair of the course Maths for Science at the Open University. She is particularly interested in students' mathematical misconceptions and in the role of feedback in assessment.
s.e.jordan@dsl.pipex.com

Lesley Lawrence is Head of the Corporate Academic Advisory and Counselling Services at the University of Luton. Previously she was Sub-Dean (Teaching and Learning) in Luton Business School and a principal lecturer. Current and recent interest in teaching and learning research and development include: engaging students with assessment feedback through involvement in an FDTL5 project; improving student confidence in the assessment process, an LTSN subject centre-funded project; and enhancing the student experience through optimising support mechanisms.
Lesley.lawrence@luton.ac.uk

Liz McDowell is Director of Northumbria University's Centre for Excellence in Teaching and Learning: Assessment for Learning. She has worked as an educational developer for a number of years and this work was recognised by a National Teaching Fellowship in 2004. Her research interests are in student learning and assessment and she initiated the international Northumbria/ EARLI Assessment Conferences. She has managed or acted as advisor to many developmental projects in the HE sector.

Marcia Mentkowski received her MA and Ph.D. from the University of Wisconsin, Madison in Educational Psychology. As Professor of Psychology at Alverno College, she directs the Educational Research and Evaluation Department, chairs the Multidisciplinary Research and Evaluation Council, and serves on the Council for Student Assessment and the Educational Policies Committee. *Learning That Lasts* (Mentkowski and Associates, Jossey-Bass, 2000) and *Higher Education Assessment and National Goals for Education* (American Psychological Association, 1998) were named outstanding research publications by the American Educational Research Association (AERA). She now serves on AERA's council and executive board. An APA fellow, she serves on editorial boards, has been an invited visiting scholar/fellow at Harvard (1975) and Oxford (2003), and speaks regularly at conferences on issues about learning and assessment.
Marcia.Mentkowski@alverno.edu

Colin Milligan is an eLearning specialist with expertise in designing, authoring and evaluating online learning materials. An overall theme in his work has been the appropriate use of technology and the importance of supporting all online teaching on sound pedagogical principles. Current work is focused on the educational use of simulations, the opportunities for integration of learning and assessment afforded by online delivery methods, and the role that learning technology standards can play in enhancing the learning process.

Sue Morison is a lecturer in Education in the School of Dentistry, Queen's University Belfast. She was responsible for developing and managing the introduction of interprofessional education (IPE) in undergraduate programmes in the Faculty of Medicine and Health Sciences at Queen's. She holds a University Teaching Award for her work in IPE and is the Director of the CETL (NI) for IPE: Curriculum and Assessment Development.
s.morison@qub.ac.uk

Roger Murphy is Professor of Education at the University of Nottingham, where he directs two research centres (CDELL and IRLTHE). He is Co-Director of the Visual LearningLab, a HEFCE-funded Centre for Excellence in Teaching and Learning, and a past President of the British Educational Research Association. He has explored creative and more effective ways in which educational assessment can help promote effective learning rather than hinder good education, as is too often the case. He is the author of a large number of books and articles, and has acted as a consultant to government departments and education ministries throughout the world.
Roger.Murphy@nottingham.ac.uk

David Nicol is the Director of eLearning Research and Development within the Centre for Academic Practice, University of Strathclyde. He works with departments/faculties on educational improvement projects in teaching, learning and assessment in both online and face-to-face environments. He is also the Director of a £1-million development project on eAssessment involving three Scottish universities. Recent research publications have focused on the social dimensions of eLearning, learning objects, formative feedback including electronic feedback systems, shared workspaces and on risk and cost–benefit analysis in relation to elearning.
d.j.nicol@strath.ac.uk

Berry O'Donovan is a principal lecturer in Learning and Teaching in the Business School, Oxford Brookes University. She is a university teaching fellow and currently Assistant Director of the ASKE Centre for Excellence. Her research interests focus on assessment and the transfer of tacit knowledge in organisations.

Margaret Price is Professor and Head of Learning and Teaching at the Business School, Oxford Brookes University. She is a National Teaching Fellow (2002) and currently Director of ASKE (Assessment Standards Knowledge Exchange), one of the nationally funded Centres for Excellence in Teaching and Learning. Her research interests focus on assessment, and recent research and publications relate to assessment processes and standards.
meprice@brookes.ac.uk

Alan Robinson is the Associate Dean (Academic Operations) for the Faculty of Technology at Southampton Solent University. His research interests include: transition and retention issues; identifying students at risk and associated intervention strategies; promoting and supporting student learning through aligned

learning, teaching and assessment strategies; and developing the independent learner.
Alan.robinson@solent.ac.uk

Shelagh Ross is a physicist who has worked on many types of learning materials for Open University science courses. Her research interests include the use of online conferencing for small group work, computer-mediated forms of assessment, and problem-solving strategies for physics students.
s.m.ross@open.ac.uk

Sheila Ryan was Senior Lecturer in Human Resource Management and Organisational Behaviour in the Gloucestershire Business School and taught on the MBA, MA: HRM and MA: PD programmes. Her research interests are in CPD, management self-development and the use of learning journals for professional and personal development. She has contributed to the CPD initiatives of the Royal College of Speech and Language Therapists, as part of the DfEE Lifelong Learning project.

Alistair Sambell is Dean of the School of Informatics, Engineering and Technology Engineering at Northumbria University. He has a background in electronic engineering, and has been involved with a number of projects investigating the use of innovative assessment to enhance student learning in engineering, including a national TLTP3 project on computer-aided learning.

Kay Sambell holds a Chair in Learning and Teaching, Childhood Studies at Northumbria University. She has published widely on research studies that explore students' views of assessment and has been involved in a number of university, national and international projects which have sought to improve student learning by innovating in assessment. In 2002 she won a National Teaching Fellowship. She is currently Associate Director of Northumbria University's Centre for Excellence in Teaching and Learning: Assessment for Learning.
Kay.sambell@unn.ac.uk

Jacqui Stedmon is Academic Director of the doctoral programme in Clinical Psychology, University of Plymouth, and Co-Director of the FDTL4 PBL project. She works clinically as a paediatric clinical psychologist and has a special interest in family therapy.

Mark Udall is Principal Lecturer in Computing and Educational Developer for the Faculty of Technology at Southampton Solent University. His research interests currently include outcome-based assessment, formative assessment and the related issues of student engagement. The focus of his educational development role is promoting change in pedagogic practice, particularly in the development of facilitator skills in enquiry and activity-based learning.

Sue Williams is Principal Lecturer in Human Resource Management Development and Organisational Behaviour in the Gloucestershire Business School. She teaches on undergraduate, postgraduate and professional programmes. Her doctoral thesis investigated the use of action learning in higher education specifically as a personal skills development vehicle. As programme leader for the Chartered Institute of Personnel and Development she ensures the CIPD's expectations concerning continuing professional development are met. She is also a member of HEA and has written a number of articles on reflective practice. scwilliams@glos.ac.uk

Jim Wood is Project Administrator of the FDTL4 PBL project in the School of Psychology, University of Exeter. He has worked in professional education and training in the HE sector and across health and social care.

Foreword

Assessment probably provokes more anxiety among students and irritation among staff than any other feature of higher education. It occupies a great deal of time that might otherwise be devoted to teaching and learning, and it is the subject of considerable debate about whether it is fair, effective and worth spending so much effort on. Assessment is a topic about which people have strong opinions, though whether those opinions are backed up by a good understanding of what it is and how it works is less certain.

There is no doubt that many students and teachers would prefer assessment to be different to what they currently experience. However, in what ways should it be different? What should it take into account? Which directions should it pursue? And how can changes be implemented? Assessment seems such a fixed and given part of the educational scene that it might appear to be less susceptible to change than most other features of higher education.

But while this might once have been true, it is not the case now. We are probably seeing more substantial shifts in assessment policy and practice than have ever occurred before. These are being driven not just by the desires of participants for change in assessment – such desires have been present for many years without it making much difference – but by the external influences on higher education institutions for accountability, for responsiveness to changing employment conditions and by the increasing power of consumers. Governments are requiring universities to justify their practices as never before, employers and professional groups are placing expectations on institutions to deliver graduates who can more effectively cope with the world of work and students are starting to realise that they can have considerable influence when they are contributing a greater proportion of university budgets.

These pressures are being played out in complex ways and it will be some time before we can clearly discern what their overall effect will be. What is clear, however, is that they are leading to many innovations in higher education courses in general and in assessment in particular. These innovations are moving in a number of different directions. First, they are generating alternatives to traditional assessment practices that were once dominated by the unseen examination and the standard essay. These practices have proved unable to capture the range and nature of the diverse learning outcomes now sought from courses. Second, they are involving students more actively not only in teaching and learning activities, but in assessment itself. Society today demands more than passive graduates who have complied with a fixed assessment regime. It wants people who can plan and monitor their own learning and do so without continuous prompting from others. Third, they are generating new forms of portrayal of outcomes. A standard honours classification or a set of grades communicates little to employers or to those admitting students to further study. How can students present what they know and do so in ways that others will understand and which are validly recorded? Fourth, they are recognising that assessment itself has a powerful influence on learning and that changes to assessment may have a greater influence on students' learning than other changes to the curriculum. Assessment innovations are therefore needed to improve the quality of learning outcomes.

The contributors to this book are some of the leaders of change in assessment in higher education in the UK and elsewhere. They are pioneering new ways of thinking about assessment and new forms of assessment. They are responding to the changing environment and developing specific innovations to meet a variety of the needs identified above. They are doing so within a system that is not well funded and with colleagues that may not fully appreciate the need for many of these changes.

This collection points to new directions in assessment and provides illustrations of important initiatives. The entire area of assessment is in a state of flux and it is not clear how it will settle down from the current flurry of activity. The contributors to this volume show how they have been thinking about these issues and illustrate what they have put into practice. They also offer suggestions to stimulate further innovation in assessment practice. They do not provide recipes to follow, but new perspectives on problems. By engaging with them we can gain greater understanding of the issues we ourselves face.

Cordelia Bryan and Karen Clegg have done an excellent job in bringing together a stimulating range of chapters in an accessible form. A major strength of the collection is the work of Graham Gibbs and the accounts from various projects that have been stimulated by him and his colleagues in the Assessment Project Network. It is through the collaborative work of this network that the conceptual underpinning for the book evolved. In his two early chapters Gibbs takes a characteristically pragmatic and thoughtful approach to setting the scene and articulating how assessment frames learning. He regards the experience of students as central to what we should be doing in education and examines how assessment can aid learning and shape students' experience in positive ways. He places particular emphasis on the role of feedback and the need to improve the quality of information that students get about their work.

The editors and contributors share my own view that assessment advocates have ignored the consequences for student learning for too long. Assessment has been seen almost exclusively as an act of measurement that occurs after learning has been completed, not as a fundamental part of teaching and learning itself. In the past, by isolating assessment we failed to realise that it can have a very negative effect on student learning and can encourage students to do things that are counterproductive to their long-term interests. It also led to courses that did not utilise the positive influences that assessment can have on focusing students' attention on the most important concepts and practices they are studying. Righting the presently very skewed balance between assessment for measurement and certification and assessment for learning is an important and strong theme throughout this book.

In practice, innovating in assessment does not mean inventing assessment activities that no one has ever used before. Rather, activities need to be innovative in the context of the course and the experience of students so that students respond to the task in hand and not to their preconceptions of what a particular assessment method does. That is why books like this are important. They enable us to extend our repertoire of approaches and stimulate us to consider ways of designing assessment that addresses needs for which our present approaches are inadequate.

Finally, there is one important observation to make about how a reader should approach a set of new ideas in this area. In assessment practice the devil is always in the detail. Most innovative approaches fail not because they do not represent good ideas but because their implementation has been inadequately thought through. At the end of the day what makes a difference is exactly what a student does and how they experience what they do; it is not the intention of the teacher that counts. Students have been trained by many years of schooling to read tasks carefully and take them literally if they are to do well. This applies as much to innovative approaches as it does to the conventional essay question. If there are ambiguities in what is required by a task, if the boundaries are unclear, if the nature of what is to be produced is obscure, then the assessment activity is not likely to be effective. The implication of this is that when using approaches to assessment that students are likely to find unfamiliar, as is the case with many examples in this book, it is often worthwhile to err on the side of explicitness. The challenge in this is to construct an assessment task that is clear without trivialising a complex activity by turning it into a behavioural checklist.

Another level of detail should also be considered. It is common for a new approach to assessment initially to be less effective than anticipated. This is because it often requires several iterations before a new idea or new approach can work in one's own context. There are many factors to be taken into account and it is only through adjustment over time that really effective practices can be developed. It is in marrying the high-level concepts of assessment for learning with the micro-details of implementation that the art of good assessment practice lies.

In the end, a focus on assessment of all kinds is important because, as I have suggested elsewhere, students may well escape from poor teaching through their own endeavours, but they are trapped by the consequences of poor assessment as it is something they are required to endure if they want to graduate. The more we can engage students in assessment activities meaningful to them and which contribute to their learning, the more satisfying will be their experience of higher education.

David Boud, Professor of Adult Education,
University of Technology, Sydney

Acknowledgements

This book has been a genuine labour of love. It is underpinned by our shared values to enhance the learning experience and to recognise both the limitations and power of assessment to change lives. It has been a pleasure to work with some of the leading authors and practitioners in the UK and beyond, all of whom are committed to exposing traditional assessment methods to scrutiny and sharing their own ideas and practices in an attempt to improve assessment and learning. We would like to thank all the contributors for their hard work and diligence in keeping to deadlines: we couldn't have done it without you. Thanks also to Helen Pritt at Taylor and Francis for supporting us in our first collaborative endeavour.

Karen Clegg would also like to thank colleagues in Professional and Organisational Development at the University of York for their continued support throughout the time that it took to produce *Innovative Assessment in Higher Education*.

Last, but by no means least, thanks to Chris Clegg and Julian Mincham – for their love and support.

Introduction

Cordelia Bryan and Karen Clegg

> It serves no useful purpose to lower our educational aspirations because we cannot yet measure what we think is important to teach. Quite the contrary, measurement and assessment will have to rise to the challenge of our educational aspirations.
>
> (Cross in Crooks, 1988: 470)

Measuring achievement has become the obsession of higher education. We use terms such as 'deep' and 'surface' to describe approaches to learning but more precisely they are approaches to *assessment*. Research of the last twenty years provides evidence that students adopt strategic, cue-seeking tactics in relation to assessed work and we know that in the UK at least, academic staff pursue research funding and publications with promotion and the research assessment exercise (RAE) in mind. Whatever we may think, assessment has become the currency with which we trade; the better the grade, the bigger and better the reward.

Acknowledging the current obsession with measurement, *Innovative Assessment* provides a systematic attempt to redefine assessment as an instrument of liberation. It offers an antithesis to the old claims of objectivity and reliability in assessment and for some that will make uncomfortable reading. It makes the case that innovative assessments should *enhance* and *enable* self-regulated learning and judgements, rather than merely act as instruments of justification, measurement and limitation.

Innovative Assessment in Higher Education is a collaborative effort which enquires into how we innovate in assessment and what practices 'work' in different contexts and cultures. It provides a fundamental analysis of the role and purpose of assessment and how change can realistically be managed without compromising standards. Contributors reflect the active, organic nature of assessment and its relationship to student learning. *Innovative Assessment* is about continually reviewing and reflecting on current practices so as to enhance the learning experience. It sets out an agenda for innovation in assessment and explains why it is justified given the constraining nature of:

- existing assessment regulations;
- quality assurance procedures;

- concerns about standards and fairness, plagiarism and cheating;
- conservative student expectations;
- academic traditions;
- increased class sizes;
- reduced resources;
- diverse types of less well-prepared students.

A defining feature of this book which sets it apart from many other books on assessment is its conceptual framework which acknowledges that assessment frames learning, creates learning activity and orientates all aspects of learning behaviour. In Chapter 2 Gibbs outlines eleven conditions under which *assessment supports learning* based on the findings from the Assessment Experience Questionnaire (AEQ). The eleven assessment conditions proved to support learning are summarised here, clustered under the five headings used to structure the AEQ.

1   Quantity and distribution of student effort – assessed tasks need to capture sufficient study time and effort and distribute student effort evenly across topics and weeks.
2   Quality and level of student effort – assessed tasks need to engage students in productive learning activity and communicate clear and high expectations.
3   Quantity and timing of feedback – sufficient feedback needs to be provided both often enough and sufficiently quickly to be useful to students.
4   Quality of feedback – feedback should focus on learning rather than on marks, should be linked to the purpose of the assignment and to criteria and should be understandable to students.
5   Student response to feedback – feedback is pointless unless it is received by students and attended to. It needs to be acted upon in order to improve student work or learning.

Working within this conceptual framework, the book offers a comprehensive rationale for changing assessment and what such changes can and do achieve.

The authors of case-study chapters do not present assessments as a package of ready-made tactics to be pulled off the shelf, but instead provide rationales for their innovations which derive from relevant underlying principles (discussed in detail in the first part of the book). The innovations are problematic and set in complex contexts bounded by regulations, traditions, political pressures and beliefs. Despite these constraints, evidence of pedagogic impact is provided. Our intention is to expose current assessment practices to the scrutiny of peers, you the readers, and to invite you to make judgements about whether they can work.

Can you honestly claim that your assessments:

- enhance the student learning experience?
- provide useful and timely feedback?
- help students to understand and recognise quality?
- lead to improved performance?

If you have reservations about answering 'yes' to any of these questions, this book is for you. Good formative assessment *should* meet the above criteria. Yet too often we focus on the grades and quality assurance aspects of assessment and lose sight of the pedagogic role that assessment can and should play in improving learning. In this book, we have tried to redress this imbalance and move away from a 'one size fits all' approach to assessment and academic practice. We have set out to create for colleagues a model of critical examination of our own work in relation to the research and empirical data on student learning. The result is a collection of assessment interventions grounded within a unifying conceptual framework that has worked in practice and provides an evaluation of the conditions that enabled its success.

What unites us as editors is not just a commitment to enhancing assessment but a dogged determination to scrutinise what assessment can and can't do and to offer examples and evidence of the powerful impact it has on motivation, self-efficacy and the general experience of learning. Our common experiences include managing FDTL projects, supporting learning and teaching at subject level (LTSN), teaching and assessing at institutional level and evaluating assessment projects. As such we are active participants, recipients and stakeholders in the assessment game.

How and why is assessment changing?

Modern society is demanding and complex yet many of our assessments are magnificently basic in their nature. Despite work on educational taxonomies and more recently Biggs (1999) advocating a more sophisticated and aligned use of assessment to support high-level learning, much of our assessment still focuses on testing knowledge and comprehension and ignores the challenge of developing and assessing judgements. It is time we recognised the changing nature of society and acknowledged that quality is a more complex concept than traditional assessment criteria suggest – quality cannot be reduced to a set of easily quantified learning outcomes. The widespread use of the phrase 'anticipated learning outcomes' is in part a recognition of individualised, personal perceptions and reactions to learning situations. People learn what they want to learn and in different ways. The innovations described in this book show that assessment which supports learning is flexible and takes into account the need for individuals to make sense of feedback in the context of their own experience.

The book contextualises innovation in assessment within a range of academic disciplines and institutional settings. It provides both theoretical and empirical support, thus making a compelling case for why we need innovation to bring into alignment the processes of learning, teaching and assessment. The book brings together elements of assessment which bridge studies of innovative practice thereby contributing to the growing body of literature which is gradually beginning to impact on pedagogic practice.

How the book evolved through collaborative effort

The inspiration for this book came in 2003 when UK colleagues with a specific interest in the relationship between assessment and learning met to exchange experiences. Most participants were involved in funded projects (e.g. Higher Education Funding Council for England) so the group became known as the Assessment Project Network. Collaboration then extended to include colleagues from overseas who experienced similar problems to those of UK higher education.

On both sides of the Atlantic, calls were being made for assessment practices that enable students to do something with the feedback they are given; to experience the process of making judgements for themselves; and to become reflective, resilient learners who are able to progress to more sophisticated levels of understanding and application. In order to do this they need to be engaged in assessment processes, not simply feel the effects of someone else's assessment.

Structure of the book

The book is divided into four parts. Part I deals with the pedagogic context of assessment from different theoretical perspectives. Part II comprises case studies which illustrate the impact of appropriate and timely feedback in relation to the seven principles of good feedback. Case studies in Part III focus on how to stimulate learning through assessment. And case studies in Part IV illustrate how innovation in assessment encourages continuing professional development.

Assessment innovations are drawn from more than twenty UK higher education institutions (HEIs) with case studies covering a wide range of disciplines including medicine and allied caring professions; humanities; business studies; psychology; engineering; maths for science; geology; performing arts; and sport, leisure and tourism. The breadth and depth of the research make this book a valuable contribution to the scholarship of teaching and learning which should be of equal value when viewed from both theoretical and practitioner perspectives.

Graham Gibbs explains the pressures to change assessment and outlines the kinds of change taking place in the UK and elsewhere. He cites the collapse of some traditional modes of assessment due to increased class sizes reducing the level of personalised and prompt feedback. Reduced class contact time and the need for students to spend more time studying independently has necessitated different approaches to teaching which subsequently require new and more relevant ways of assessing learning.

In his second chapter Gibbs draws on extensive research and student experience to illustrate how assessment frames learning and in some courses has more impact on learning than does teaching. He then discusses the eleven conditions under which assessment supports learning, thereby providing a conceptual underpinning to the innovations in assessment described in the case study chapters.

Roger Murphy comments on the curious phenomenon that in the UK assessment debates which have occurred in HE have usually been quite distinct from those taking place in school-level education. The author explores some reasons why this has been the case, noting the marked disparity between professional training for teachers in schools (commonly four years) with that of HE lecturers (the majority of whom, until recently, required no formal teaching qualification). He welcomes the move towards professionalising the whole approach to the support for student learning within UK higher education.

Marcia Mentkowski invites readers to engage in reviewing the ideas and long-standing student assessment-as-learning practices at Alverno College, Milwaukee. She outlines the college-wide assessment process and articulates educational assumptions and learning principles that inform what students learn and connects them to elements of assessment substantiated by research evidence (e.g., public criteria, feedback, self-assessment) that lead to deep and sustainable learning.

David Nicol and Colin Milligan explore how formative assessment and feedback might be used to promote the development of self-regulated learning (SRL) in contexts in which face-to-face and online learning are integrated. Self-regulated learning refers to the active control by students of some aspects of their own learning; for example, the setting of learning goals and the monitoring and regulating of progress towards the attainment of these goals.

Evelyn Brown and Chris Glover describe how the analysis of feedback provided to students on their written assignments can shed light on the way in which they respond to that feedback. The Assessment Experience Questionnaire on which they base their findings has strong links with the conceptual framework for effective assessment and feedback discussed in this volume (Chapters 2 and 5).

Alan Robinson and Mark Udall offer a conceptual model which promotes the design of an aligned teaching, learning and assessment strategy. The focus is on increasing the quality and quantity of formative assessment activities, but within a manageable overall assessment workload for students and teachers.

Margaret Price and Berry O'Donovan offer a cost-effective approach to enhancing students' understanding of standards which goes beyond that conveyed by explicit description. The authors consider the application of a social constructivist approach to all aspects of the assessment cycle and how this might support improvement in student learning and performance.

Katherine Harrington *et al.* discuss the implementation of a programme of writing workshops designed around the concept of 'core' assessment criteria. The workshop approach aims to help undergraduates improve their essay writing and also to adopt a deep approach to their studies. It also aims to encourage strategically focused students to reach a more advanced conceptualisation and understanding of the discipline.

Shelagh Ross, Sally Jordan and Philip Butcher address the problem of providing rapid but detailed teaching feedback to large distance-education groups. Their case study researches online assessment of a 'maths for science' course in which meaningful feedback was given in response to student answers on formative and summative assessment exercises.

Sean Gammon and Lesley Lawrence analyse the effect of 'flow' theory (an experience of deep enjoyment, satisfaction and irresistible spontaneity) on the assessment experience of students. The authors tested whether the introduction of 'flow' might reduce student anxiety and ultimately engender some enjoyment of the whole assessment experience. Their findings suggest that 'flow' can positively affect the assessment experience of both lecturer and student.

Tony Gardner-Medwin's chapter looks at experience with confidence-based marking (CBM) at University College London over the last ten years. The CBM strategy was initially introduced to improve formative self-assessment and to encourage students to think more carefully about questions in objective tests. CBM is seen by the students as simple, fair, readily understood and beneficial. They are motivated to reflect and justify reasons either for confidence or reservation about each answer, and they gain by expressing true confidence, whether high or low.

Cordelia Bryan documents an innovative approach to assessment designed to encourage students to focus on the process of collaboration. It shifts student attention from focusing almost exclusively on performance and outcomes to attitudes which begin to value cooperation and group dynamics. Evidence is cited which shows how students' ultimate performance grade might be improved when collaborative skills were manifest, observed and an integral part of the learning and assessment process.

Kay Sambell, Liz McDowell and Alistair Sambell focus on assessment as a pedagogic tool to foster learner autonomy. The authors look at both procedural autonomy (managing learning) and critical autonomy (ways of thinking) to analyse students' views in two case studies. They address the philosophical paradox that to become autonomous, students need tutor help and direction. They recognise the need to structure activities and initially to direct students towards the means which will ultimately enable them to become autonomous learners. They advocate a developmental approach to build up both skills and concepts by scaffolding the student experience.

Sue Williams and Sheila Ryan report the findings of a study on personal development planning (PDP) for undergraduates. They highlight the need for targeted staff development based on a systematic evaluation of staff capabilities and readiness to act as both personal and academic tutors. Their findings clarify the responses required of institutions wishing to implement PDP, placing emphasis on staff training objectives being linked to defined organisational aims.

Christine Curle, Jim Wood, Catherine Haslam and Jacqui Stedmon address the needs of postgraduates in Clinical and Community Psychology by assessing learning outcomes using PBL exercises. The assessment episodes incorporate group outcomes and dynamics in a context where students must manage large amounts of knowledge while developing clinical and intrapersonal skills. The intention here is to make professional training mirror the nature and quality of work undertaken by qualified practitioners. The authors offer some evidence for the success of the approach and have subsequently developed it in other areas of the curriculum.

In their chapter Simon Cotterill, Philip Bradley and Geoff Hammond report on their experiences and lessons learned from developing and implementing electronic portfolios (ePortfolios) for Medicine. They address the challenges posed by students receiving educational input and assessment from numerous 'suppliers', with formal and informal learning often based in multiple locations and involving a range of different educational and IT infrastructures.

Sue Morison and Mairead Boohan examine the assessment methods developed and evaluated in interprofessional education (IPE) medical and nursing programmes. The clinical ward was selected as the most favourable learning environment and two studies were carried out. The first employed role-play to assess clinical, communication and teamwork skills and the second concerned history-taking, problem-solving and reflection.

Lewis Elton explores the extent to which the practice of academic staff may be considered 'professional', how this is currently assessed and how perhaps it should be. He makes a case that genuine professionalism requires a combination of training, education and acculturation and explores how the necessary systematic and personal changes required to achieve genuine 'professionalism' might be tackled.

Drawing on recurring themes from the book, Karen Clegg and Cordelia Bryan argue for a holistic approach to assessment which enhances students' skills, abilities and capabilities rather than one which attempts to measure such skills in the misguided notion that it is done so with 'scientific reliability'. The authors point to a need for further research into innovative assessments designed to enhance students' creative processes and develop their professional judgement. Such innovations, they argue, will be required if we are to equip the students of the future to cope with uncertainty and unpredictability inherent in our high-risk, super-complex society.

Part I
Pedagogic context

1 Why assessment is changing

Graham Gibbs

Introduction

There has been a proliferation of books about assessment in higher education containing case-study accounts of innovations or simply lists of ideas offered as if they were best practice. This proliferation reflects rapidly changing practice and this change is being brought about not only by the enthusiasm of expert teachers, but by a raft of changes in the context within which assessment operates. This chapter explores some of these contextual changes and the problems they bring, in order to provide a background in which innovations and their impacts are described. While some of the context described here may be specific to the UK, the phenomena are similar in higher education in many other countries.

Declining resources

Government funding per student has halved in real terms over the past fifteen years in England. An increasing proportion of the remaining available resource has been allocated to administration, meeting quality assurance requirements, to earmarked national initiatives (such as the Higher Education Funding Council for England's Human Resource Strategy and Widening Participation Strategy) and to ever more extensive uses of information technology. In addition, library costs have increased very much faster than inflation. As a consequence academic salaries make up a smaller proportion of institutional budgets than they used to, as in the USA. There is less academic time available per student and intense pressure on academics to increase research productivity. At the same time there is increased bureaucracy associated with meeting external requirements for quality assurance and requirements for accountability concerning use of funds. Even if student numbers had remained stable it would have been difficult to maintain the previous level of academic time invested in assessment.

And of course at the same time the total number of students has increased. An inevitable consequence has been that student–staff ratios have also increased. When I started writing about assessment in the early 1980s student–staff ratios at my institution were about 8:1 in the Sciences and 12:1 in Social Sciences. They are now commonly in the range 20:1 to 30:1, and where student recruitment cannot generate such high ratios the courses have been axed. Class sizes have increased considerably, accelerating first in the polytechnics in the 1980s (Gibbs *et al.*, 1996) and more recently in the research-led universities. When I joined Oxford Polytechnic in 1980 there were just over 400 academics to teach about 5,000 full-time students; when I left seventeen years later there were roughly the same number of academics but about 12,000 full-time students. In the period 1984 to 1994 the size of the largest class at Oxford Polytechnic increased from 196 to 462 students, and the number of courses with enrolments of over 70 had increased by 208 per cent. Class sizes have increased markedly in the decade since and the size of the smallest classes students experience has also increased. In 1994, 225 courses had enrolments of less than twenty, but since then twenty, has been considered the lower limit for a course to be considered viable (*ibid.*).

Students also now spend an increasing proportion of their total programme in large classes, rather than quickly moving on to small-enrolment specialist modules after their first year. The size of the largest class in most degree programmes has increased much faster than the decline in resources could explain. There has been 'rationalisation' of course provision, bringing courses together to increase student enrolments (for example, all first-year 'introduction to statistics' courses bundled together). The student fee income from large-enrolment first-year courses, in particular, has been used to cross-subsidise other courses with fewer enrolments (and with more expensive patterns of teaching and assessment), rather than allocating resources for teaching and assessment where they are earned. As a consequence the actual resource allocated per student in the largest classes may be much less, in real terms, than it was twenty years ago.

As class sizes have increased there have been some economies of scale in teaching (such as through larger lecture classes and 'tutorials' that may nowadays contain twenty-five students) but there have been few economies of scale in assessment. Assessment costs usually increase in direct proportion to the number of students. So as class sizes increase, assessment costs overtake teaching costs. In practical terms, lecturers can end up spending more time each week marking than they do in classrooms. If mechanisms to allocate academic staff time to assessment were proportional to the number of students involved this might not cause too many problems, but they are not. In many institutions the accountancy unit of 'duties' is the 'class contact hour' and this ignores class size. Assessment loads that are proportional to class sizes are often not taken into account. A lecturer may find that she has fifty hours allocated to give one lecture a week to a hundred students for ten weeks, and to lead four problem classes each of twenty-five students a week, but no time at all allocated to mark a hundred problem sheets a week or a hundred exam scripts at the end of the course. Lecturers then find themselves not only with large classes but with no more time to assess the many more students than they had when classes were much smaller. The phenomenon of assessment taking up more time than teaching does not last long as it is quickly followed by radical surgery to the volume of assessment and, in particular, the volume of feedback, in response to the lack of academic time available to do the job properly (given the duty allocation systems used). Even where the proportion of academic time allocated to assessment has increased, the time available per student to assess an individual student's work will often have declined to a small proportion of what it was twenty years ago. Not even library facilities or class contact has suffered, as resources have declined, to the extent that assessment has.

When I was an undergraduate in the late 1960s I wrote essays and submitted practical reports on my Psychology courses at regular intervals, and about once a week in the second half of each semester (spread across the four courses I took at a time). What I remember most about my studies are the essays I wrote (and the experiments I designed and carried out, and other assignments) and the comments of my lecturers on my work, which I often discussed by dropping into their offices. I have only the vaguest recollections of the content of lectures.

To help recognise the scale of change it is illuminating to contrast this picture with what has taken place at the Open University and at the University of Oxford, where assessment has not changed in this way. As a matter of Open University policy, '60 credit' courses (involving a nominal 600 hours of student learning effort) have 8 assignments; '30 credit' courses have 4 assignments. Tutors are allocated groups of up to twenty-four students on whose assignments they mark and comment. Even if overall student numbers are enormous, tutor-group size and tutor time per student to give feedback on assignments are not affected and have remained largely unchanged for thirty years. At the Open University today student enrolment on a single course can exceed 10,000. However, such extraordinary enrolments have had almost no impact on the volume of assessment or the volume of feedback that individual students experience. The Open University simply hires more tutors in direct proportion to the number of students. Each assignment receives extensive written tutor feedback, often consisting of several pages of overview comments in addition to detailed comments written on the scripts themselves. The quality of these tutor comments is carefully monitored to ensure they are of an appropriate nature and standard – the distance-learning equivalent of regularly observing teachers' classes to monitor their quality. There are creeping changes in the nature of assignments, including computer-based tests, and the use of automated feedback, but by and large students' experience of assessment will have changed little since the Open University was founded. Students' positive response to this protection of assignment writing and feedback is very evident in student feedback, compared with students' experience of assessment in conventional institutions, as we shall see in Chapter 2. This has been achieved by deliberately investing in assessment in a way that most institutions have not.

At the University of Oxford the main form of 'assignments' is the preparation students undertake for weekly tutorials in which they may read out or discuss the essay they have been assigned at the previous week's tutorial. Formative assessment consists of their tutor's oral feedback, sometimes accompanied by written feedback, on this essay. Usually no marks are involved. The frequency of essay writing and the volume of feedback are considerably larger than most other institutions manage (other than Cambridge, whose 'supervisions' are similar). Despite the considerable expense involved, the number of occasions on which 'essay writing plus individualised feedback' happens at Oxford has in some courses increased in recent years and some students may write as many as three essays a fortnight. As at the Open University, 'assignments plus feedback' is seen as central to students' overall experience of their learning environment, and so worth protecting.

These examples show up in stark relief what has happened to feedback in most higher education institutions. A generation after my own undergraduate experience my daughters have both studied in research-intensive universities in England in recent years, one studying Law and Sociology and the other Chemistry. They experienced courses with no assignment or no written feedback at all, courses with the one assignment returned only after the examination, laboratory reports returned a term later with marks but no comments, and so on. Where written feedback was provided and in reasonable time, it was often so brief as to be of little value. I calculated that an average Open University graduate would have received at least fifty times more written feedback than a graduate from my daughters' courses. If a university announced that it was going to cut back its teaching to 2 per cent of what another institution provided there might be something of an outcry. However, this is exactly what many institutions have done with regards to assessment and feedback, without announcing this, or even, I suspect, planning it. And they have done this not for educational reasons but for the kind of resource reasons identified above. Feedback has been easy to cut back on by individual teachers (where other changes in teaching may require approval and debate) and has saved a great deal of time. Importantly, it has been difficult for external quality assurance inspections even to notice this decline in feedback.

Assignments and study time

As class contact time has been cut back, students ought to compensate by spending more time studying independently out of class in order to maintain a reasonably hard-working learning week. This is what happens in a 'steady state' system where an increase in teaching time results in a reduction in study time, and vice versa (Vos, 1991). An undergraduate working year is defined in the UK as 1,200 hours, and a '10 credit' course as 100 hours. This means 100 hours of student effort of whatever kind, including class contact and independent study. If a 100-hour course experiences a reduction in class contact time from 50 hours to 40 hours (the kind of change I remember in science courses at Oxford Polytechnic in the mid-1980s) then independent study ought to increase from 50 hours to 60 hours to compensate and to make the total back up to 100 hours. This represents a shift in the ratio of class contact to study time from 1:1 to 1:1.5. Losing 20 per cent of the class contact has increased the amount of studying required to be generated by each class contact hour by 50 per cent. If, as is more common today, class contact is reduced from 30 hours to 20 hours then studying has to increase from 70 hours to 80 hours to compensate. This represents a shift in the ratio from 1:2.3 to 1:4. This involves a 74 per cent increase in the number of hours of study each hour in class has to support. Today it is common for each hour in class to have to support three to four times as many hours out of class as in the early 1980s. I have not seen a sufficient change in how class contact is used to convince me that the nature of teaching is capable of achieving such a dramatic change in student learning behaviour.

So how is this additional study time to be generated? In many contexts social pressures generate study effort. If you are in a small seminar group or problem class and you have not done the reading or preparation then it can be embarrassingly obvious. One reason why students at the University of Oxford work so hard despite very low class contact time is that in one-to-one tutorials there is no place to hide. Each tutorial hour is known to generate eleven to fourteen hours of independent study (Trigwell and Ashwin, 2003), a ratio of between 1:10 and 1:14. As seminars, problem classes (and even tutorials) increase in size, and social coherence declines, the social pressure to prepare properly decreases. Students avoid eye contact and use other cunning strategies to get away with superficial preparation, and they simply study for fewer hours. What leverage to capture study effort is left derives almost entirely from the demands of the formal assessment system.

Students have always been strategic, as studies at the end of the 1960s in both the USA and UK vividly illustrated (Snyder, 1971; Miller and Parlett, 1974). Students largely study what is assessed, or, more accurately, what they perceive the assessment system to require. The Open University has maintained the volume of assignments because it is hard to see what else would maintain the volume and quality of distance students' studying if they were taken away. But conventional higher education institutions have cut back on assessment as well as on class contact, due to the costs involved. For a student today, being strategic would involve focusing effort more narrowly and less frequently and simply doing less.

At the same time students' working lives have changed in a way that puts pressure on their time. First, students undertake part-time paid work to a much greater extent than in the past. Students' financial difficulties, exacerbated by fees and loans, have accelerated this trend. Studies have shown how this affects grades (presumably as a consequence of spending less time on assignments) (Paton-Saltzberg and Lindsay, 1993). In the USA a considerable proportion of students 'work their way through college' and take fewer courses at a time than a full-time student would, or take time out in some terms or years to earn before returning to study. In the UK, by contrast, students seem to expect to be able to register as full-time students even when they are working twenty hours a week to earn income, and expect to complete their degree programmes in three years regardless. An increasing proportion of students are actually studying part time but enrolled full time, and the assessment arrangements allow them to do this.

If students were to progress through their degrees at a rate commensurate with their current study hours, as institutions are funded in relation to the volume of student progression quite a few institutions would find themselves in severe financial difficulties. Departments are increasingly aware of such financial consequences and so courses are under intense pressure to collude to reduce demands on students in order to maintain fee income. Despite reduced class contact, assessment demands have been reduced as well and students' study hours per week have declined. The main threat to quality and standards I perceive is the shrinking total volume of studying which results directly from reduced assessment demands.

'Modularisation' and assessment

In 1980 in the UK a proportion of Oxford Polytechnic was 'modular', in the sense that course units were of identifiable (and mainly equal) size and that students could construct their own programmes by combining 'modules', taking credits until an undergraduate degree was accumulated. In some subject areas the rules governing module choice (such as prerequisite rules and compulsory modules) made these modular programmes not different in many respects from conventional three-year programmes comprising course units. Nevertheless, over the next twenty years almost all of UK higher education 'modularised' its programmes. Most of North American higher education was of course already 'modular' (though it did not call itself this).

One of the purposes of this enormous curriculum redesign exercise was to allow students to move flexibly between institutions as a consequence of a common 'tariff' of course credits: the 'Credit Accumulation and Transfer System' (CATS). Student demand for mobility between institutions did not materialise to anything like the same extent as in North America, though the Bologna Agreement may well lead to increased volumes of transfer of students between institutions within Europe.

Modularisation has had some profound (and largely unintended) side-effects on assessment systems. Modules tended to be small – as little as 10 credits or 100 hours of student effort. A traditional linear degree programme might have involved four courses each lasting three terms and these would have translated into 30-credit or 300-hour courses. At one time at Oxford Polytechnic 10-credit modules lasted one term and students normally took four at a time for three terms. At one time some institutions offered 10-credit modules which lasted one semester and students took six at a time.

A consequence of small study units is that summative assessment has to take place more frequently. The total volume of summative assessment may have doubled as a direct consequence of modularisation, without any increase in staffing, and this has put pressure on finding more cost-effective assessment methods or simply cheaper methods regardless of their effectiveness. Tests of memory under examination conditions and objective tests and multiple choice question tests, on- or off-line, are much more common as a result.

Another consequence of the shorter length of study units has been that there is little time for students to gain familiarity or practice with material or skills before they are assessed. Turning feedback round in time to be useful to students before the module is finished can be difficult. 'Early' formative assessment may mean halfway through the module.

As each examination or assignment tends to assess a smaller quantity of content area it is less common to see integrative assessment that pulls together a wide range of material. Usually regulations prevent any assessment that is not associated with an individual module and so integrative assessment at the end of a degree programme cannot take place unless there is an integrative module. A consequence has been a narrowing of the focus of assessment to more discrete units of content, and less coherent progression.

Because all assessment has to take place within modules, and modules are short (as short as ten weeks), examinations may take place only a week after teaching is finished. The opportunity for students to use extended revision periods to pull material together into a meaningful whole (Entwistle and Entwistle, 2003) is lost.

It is harder to plan sequences of linked assignments where each feeds in to the next, when timescales are short and resources allow only one or two assignments in a module. It may be difficult to make any kind of arrangement that would make feedback flow forwards effectively.

Where modules are larger (as at the Open University, where the standard size is 60 credits or 600 hours spread over nine months, with students taking one course at a time) it is more common for there to be more assignments per course and for each assignment to be larger in size and scope. Where small, short modules, at conventional institutions, have tried to retain a reasonable number of assignments they have each tended to be rather narrow in scope and undemanding in nature, simply because of the limitations on both students' and teachers' time within such small, short courses.

As a consequence of these problems there has been a recent trend to move back to a smaller number of larger and longer modules, including two-semester modules. But regulations often prevent this, and where this happens draconian and educationally unsound solutions have been imposed, such as forbidding summative assessment in the first semester.

Plagiarism

Judging from the press coverage, the number of publications and advertisements for national conferences on the topic, and the scale of investment in electronic tools designed to identify it in students' work, plagiarism is a rapidly growing phenomenon in the UK, as evidenced by the establishment of the JISC Plagiarism Advisory Service. It has been exacerbated by:

- the use of short, easy-to-mark assignments, designed to cope with resource problems, that are easier to plagiarise;
- the difficulty of producing unique assignments for each student, due to large student numbers;
- increased use of the internet to locate learning resources, and electronic submission of assignments, which makes it easy to 'cut and paste' assignments together;
- increased use of peer learning and group-based learning that encourages collaboration while learning (for sound pedagogic reasons), and even during assessment in some circumstances;
- 'delinquency' and a lack of regard for socially binding but informal rules about cheating, resulting from the alienation which impersonal large classes can foster;
- an increasing proportion of students coming from educational backgrounds where reproduction of content and of the teachers' own words is perceived to be the purpose of education;

- the general increase of 'coursework' of all kinds, not under invigilated examination conditions, that is marked, and where the marks contribute to overall student grades. In the past these may have been 'formative only' assignments but today's students are rarely prepared to undertake tasks unless they are marked.

One of the main consequences of the increase in worries about plagiarism has been a reversion to invigilated examinations and a reduction in 'take home' coursework. This inevitably reduces students' study effort during courses and probably lowers the cognitive level of student engagement with study material.

Computer-aided assessment

Using computer-based multiple-choice question testing is hardly a new phenomenon, but compared with the USA it has been adopted rather slowly and to a limited range of subjects and contexts in the UK. The implementation of institution-wide 'virtual learning environments' has made it much easier to use simple forms of computer-based assessment and there has been ever more funding, projects, dissemination and staff development to support those who would like to use such methods. Unlike the USA, much use of computer-aided assessment is largely formative in nature: to give students practice and feedback and to highlight where more studying might be appropriate before the 'real' assessment at a later point. Evidence from the comparison of assessment methods, including computer-based assessment, is, however, fairly consistent in its findings. Students tend to adopt a surface approach to their studies to a greater extent (attempting to reproduce) rather than a deep approach (trying to make sense) if computer-based assessment is used or is even included as one component of assessment (Scouler and Prosser, 1994).

There has been plenty of development of software that enables the construction of more sophisticated and demanding question types and plenty of literature and guidance about how to construct more demanding computer-based assessment. However, lecturers still tend to ask questions that make low-level demands, mainly because it is easier, and students still assume that only low levels of demand will be made, even when this turns out not to be the case. There is very little evidence (notwithstanding the benefits for feedback as discussed in Chapter 5 of this volume) that the increase in the use of computer-based assessment has had beneficial impacts on the quality of student learning, though there is some evidence that it has increased its quantity.

Declining student retention

The types of student now entering higher education are more diverse, with less predictable educational backgrounds and prerequisite knowledge than in the past. They require more support in the form of feedback on progress and guidance about how to improve, but are instead experiencing reduced support from assessment and more hurdles (in the form of tests) that trip them out of courses. Retention is declining. Institutions are losing substantial funds because their students do not complete their courses. This can be caused by inappropriate (but cheap) assessment. In order to identify 'at risk' students early enough to intervene, some courses are introducing early formative assignments that are graded in difficulty (so as to develop students' self-efficacy, or belief that they are able to study effectively in higher education) and which provide positive feedback but no marks (so as to encourage and guide students). The use of conventional tests, with marks, early on may have a detrimental impact on students, even if the teacher is able to identify which students need help (Yorke, 2001).

The specification and assessment of new kinds of learning outcomes

In the UK, as in many countries, there has been a shift over the last twenty years in terms of what higher education is perceived to be for, and especially a shift towards a utilitarian view of higher education as preparation for employment. In the UK the Quality Assessment Agency specification of subject benchmarks for all disciplines, and the move to specifying curricula in terms of learning outcomes, has required new kinds of assessment designed to assess 'key skills', 'transferable skills', 'generic skills' or 'graduate attributes' rather than assessing solely the acquisition of knowledge. These types of assessment place even more emphasis on feedback (as skills are learned through cycles of practice and feedback) and are inherently more expensive and time consuming than conventional written exams. Inexperience at specifying these skills has often resulted in specifying far too many for each individual course, resulting in an increase in the number of occasions on which students are assessed, and more complex and multifaceted assignments and tests. The resource implications have often led to more superficial, rather than more sophisticated, assessment.

While the reliability and consistency of standards involved in assessing conventional subject knowledge are not very impressive, standards are even less well articulated and implemented when assessing 'generic skills'. Lecturers tend to have at least some shared understanding of what a 'first-class' essay looks like in their discipline, but there is as yet no such consensus about what 'first-class' group skills look like.

At best, this movement has resulted in a reconceptualisation of curricula in which generic skills are conceived of as an inherent part of scholarly study of a specific discipline, rather than as unrelated vocational extras (Barrie, 2004). This can lead to profound changes in the nature of the kinds of 'performances of understanding' students are expected to display, and then to parallel changes in the kinds of criteria used to assess these performances. This can even lead to a reduction in volume and increase in sophistication of assessment; for example, concentrating on a small number of large, complex assignments, such as a final-year project, in which there is sufficient scope for a range of high-level skills to be exemplified and observed in a single, complex performance.

Problems of innovation

All of the above pressures have led to an unprecedented amount of innovation in assessment as teachers attempt to cope with contending pressures – but this has proved highly problematic for a range of reasons. Resources are still declining and academic staff time (either to redesign assessment or to conduct more, or more time-consuming assessment) is at a premium, especially in the context of acute pressures to increase research output.

Worries about declining standards have resulted in institutions being cautious about approving changes to assessment, and extremely cautious about innovating in assessment in ways with which external examiners might be unfamiliar, of which they might not approve or to which students might object. The dominant culture is conservative and defensive rather than bold. It is often more difficult and more time consuming to gain approval for changes in assessment than for changes to any other aspect of courses.

Students are also often conservative. Pressed for time, they are instinctively wary of approaches with which they are not familiar or that might be more demanding. Paying fees, in debt, and aware of the financial consequences of failure, or even of not obtaining a good class of degree, they are unhappy about assessment methods where the outcomes might be less predictable. They are also increasingly litigious and may challenge assessment grades where criteria and standards are not explicit or where they feel they have not adequately been prepared to tackle the assignment or test. The starting position in many contexts is one of fairly uniform patterns and methods of assessment across entire degree programmes. Students may expect that each successive course they take will be assessed in much the same way. When they discover major variations they may be quite unhappy. Students' unfamiliarity with new assessment methods may also make it harder for the teacher to make the innovation work well.

There are also some contexts, especially in recently developed subject areas without disciplinary histories, where there is no consensus or tradition about assessment, and no agreed approaches or standards. Criteria may be different on every course. Ways of allocating marks to individuals who have tackled a group project may be different for every course that uses a group project. Rules about plagiarism, collaboration, deadlines, penalties for late submission, or word limits and penalties for exceeding them, opportunities to resit tests or resubmit assignments, all may differ widely between courses within a single degree programme. In such contexts students can be so confused that it can be difficult to succeed with any innovation.

Students are increasingly strategic in the way they allocate their time and effort (MacFarlane, 1992) and may study only what is assessed (Innis, 1996). While in the past it may have been possible to be experimental and to take risks with assessment where grades did not contribute to course marks and degree results, now students may be unwilling to tackle unassessed, or only formatively assessed, assignments in a serious way, or to tackle them at all. Teachers' response to such instrumentalism has been summatively to assess all assignments, no matter how small. Once an assignment's marks contribute to course grades the full panoply of external examination regulations comes into force, such as blind double marking, student anonymity and not informing students of their grades until after the examination board has met, usually after a course has finished. As a consequence assessment costs increase. To cope with these increased costs, the assignments and tests then have to be made quick and easy to mark. This has changed the nature of the assignments and tests, making them less open-ended and less likely to foster a deep and thoughtful approach to studying. Instead of being imaginative and innovative, assessment reverts to simple and crude basics. It can be a vicious and downwards spiral.

Conclusion

The case studies in this volume should be read in the light of the problematic contexts in which they are set, as discussed above. These are not innovations for innovation's sake, but changes designed to improve student learning after traditional approaches to assessment have become problematic in some way given the changed context. In some cases the nature of these problems has been clearly identified and the specific educational goals of the innovation have been clearly specified in relation to these problems. In some cases the extent to which these problems have been successfully addressed is clear from the evaluation evidence provided. In other cases the context and associated problems are implicit and the evidence is less narrowly focused.

Part of the difficulty of the context of assessment described in this chapter is how hard it can be to make changes to assessments that are based on different rationales and purposes than those of the methods they replace. Some of the case studies illuminate how change was brought about and there is a focus on what innovation in assessment comprises, as well as a focus on the assessment methods themselves.

References

Barrie, S. C. (2004) A research-based approach to generic graduate attributes policy. *Higher Education Research and Development*, 23, 3, pp. 261–75.

Entwistle, N. and Entwistle, D. (2003) Preparing for examinations: the interplay of memorising and understanding, and the development of knowledge objects. *Higher Education Research and Development*, 22, 1, pp. 19–41.

Gibbs, G., Lucas, L. and Simonite, V. (1996) Class size and student performance: 1984–94. *Studies in Higher Education*, 21, 3, pp. 261–73.

Innis, K. (1996) *Diary Survey: how undergraduate full-time students spend their time*. Leeds: Leeds Metropolitan University.

MacFarlane, B. (1992) The 'Thatcherite' generation of university degree results. *Journal of Further and Higher Education*, 16, pp. 60–70.

Miller, C. M. I. and Parlett, M. (1974) *Up to the mark: a study of the examination game*. Guildford: Society for Research into Higher Education.

Paton-Saltzberg, R. and Lindsay, R. (1993) *The effects of paid employment on the academic performance of full-time students in higher education*. Oxford: Oxford Polytechnic.

Scouler, K. M. and Prosser, M. (1994) Students' experience of studying for multiple choice question examinations. *Studies in Higher Education*, 19, 3, pp. 267–79.

Snyder, B. R. (1971) *The hidden curriculum*. Cambridge, MA: MIT Press.

Trigwell, K. and Ashwin, P. (2003) *Undergraduate students' experience of learning at the University of Oxford*. Oxford: Institute for the Advancement of University Learning.

Vos, P. (1991) *Curriculum control of learning processes in higher education*. Edinburgh: 13th International Forum on Higher Education of the European Association for Institutional Research.

Yorke, M. (2001) Formative assessment and its relevance to retention. *Higher Education Research and Development*, 20, 2, pp. 115–26.

2 How assessment frames student learning

Graham Gibbs

Introduction

Students are strategic as never before, and they allocate their time and focus their attention on what they believe will be assessed and what they believe will gain good grades. Assessment frames learning, creates learning activity and orients all aspects of learning behaviour. In many courses it has more impact on learning than does teaching. Testing can be reliable, and even valid, and yet measure only the trivial and distorted learning which is an inevitable consequence of the nature of the testing. This chapter is not about testing but about how assessment leads to effective study activity and worthwhile learning outcomes. It starts by quoting students describing how they respond to perceived assessment demands. It then outlines eleven 'conditions under which assessment supports learning'. These conditions are based on a review of theoretical literature on formative assessment and on a review of published accounts of successful innovations in assessment, across all discipline areas, undertaken in order to identify why they were successful. Economical assessment methods are described that meet these conditions, each based on published evidence of worthwhile impact on learning and student performance. Associated diagnostic tools have been developed to help faculty to identify how their students respond to their assessment regime, and some uses of these tools will be described. The chapter is intended to provide a conceptual underpinning to the innovations in assessment described elsewhere in this volume.

Students' experience of assessment

The two most influential books I read at the start of my teaching career were from parallel studies of a very similar nature on opposite sides of the Atlantic, focusing on similar phenomena. In the US Benson Snyder was undertaking an ethnographic study of the experience of students at MIT. He had not intended to focus on assessment but he discovered that it completely dominated student experience and so that is what he wrote about most. *The hidden curriculum* (Snyder, 1971: 50 and 62–3) described the way students strategically negotiated their way through impossibly large curricula, trying to work out what faculty were really after and what they could safely ignore.

I just don't bother doing the homework now. I approach the courses so I can get an 'A' in the easiest manner, and it's amazing how little work you have to do if you really don't like the course.

From the beginning I found the whole thing to be a kind of exercise in time budgeting. . . . You had to filter out what was really important in each course . . . you couldn't physically do it all. I found out that if you did a good job of filtering out what was important you could do well enough to do well in every course.

The central idea in Snyder's work was the gap between the course as presented publicly in course documentation and by faculty and the narrower and rather different course students experienced and actually studied. The shape and size of this narrower curriculum was determined by students' perceptions of assessment demands. Studying was an exercise in selective negligence.

In Sweden, Fransson (1977) reported how students who were unable to understand or work out what to study, and so attempted to study everything, quickly became depressed by the impossibility of the task. After initially working diligently, the number of hours they studied each week declined and they eventually performed badly or dropped out. There are few rewards for students who are not strategic.

At the same time as Benson Snyder was being astonished by students at MIT, studies at the University of Edinburgh, an ancient, research-intensive university in Scotland, found exactly the same phenomenon, when they interviewed students:

I am positive there is an examination game. You don't learn certain facts, for instance, you don't take the whole course, you go and look at the examination papers and you say, 'looks as though there have been four questions on a certain theme this year, last year the professor said that the examination would be much the same as before', so you excise a good bit of the course immediately.

(Miller and Parlett, 1974: 60)

This study, *Up to the mark: a study of the examination game*, described some students as 'cue conscious'. These students were aware of cues about what to study and what to neglect. Others were described as 'cue seekers' and took their professors for a beer in the hope of finding out what questions would be on the exam paper. The remainder were described as 'cue deaf' and no matter how often they were advised what to focus on, this information passed over their heads. It proved easy to predict students' grades simply by categorising the extent to which they were tuned in to cues about assessment, and neglected the right things.

Subsequently, in my own research I have often glimpsed the world of the student in relation to perceived assessment demands. The following student on a masters course in Oceanography was only too aware of the gap between his learning and what gained him good grades:

If you are under a lot of pressure then you will just concentrate on passing the course. I know that from bitter experience. One subject I wasn't very good at I tried to understand the subject and I failed the exam. When I re-took the exam I just concentrated on passing the exam. I got 96% and the guy couldn't understand why I failed the first time. I told him this time I just concentrated on passing the exam rather than understanding the subject. I still don't understand the subject so it defeated the object, in a way.

(Gibbs, 1992a: 101)

At Oxford University assessment for grades is almost entirely separated from learning, and from 'assessment for learning'. Most assessment for learning takes place orally in tutorials, which are often weekly one-to-one (or two or three) meetings between a tutor (an academic or a graduate student) and an undergraduate student. The work the student has been doing (on average ten to fourteen hours of reading and writing to produce an essay) is discussed. Metaphorically, or in some cases actually, the tutor and student sit on the same side of the table and explore the subject matter presented in the essay together as a joint scholarly exercise. They 'do anthropology' or 'do history' together. Assessment here is all 'formative' and is designed to support learning. Students may even complain after a tutorial that they still do not know how they are getting on, as essays are not usually graded. Exams happen mainly at the end of three years. The tutor has little or no input into the design of the exam questions and is not supposed to be preparing the student for exams. This gives students considerable freedom to explore what confounds them in the subject matter and tutors considerable freedom to explore students' misconceptions.

I am not trying to sell the tutorial method: in any case tutorials are cripplingly expensive even for Oxford! But there is a phenomenon that occurs often in other universities but which happens less commonly at Oxford: that of 'faking good'. This is an attempt by students to present themselves and their work as if they know and understand more than they actually do, for the purpose of maximising grades. Students in most institutions normally choose those essay questions that they know most about and that they will need to do the least learning for, not those that will result in most learning. I remember, to my shame, that in my undergraduate essays I sometimes cited more references than I had read.

In the example below an engineering student (not from Oxford!) describes how he presents his 'problem sheets' to his tutor for marking, not in a way which reveals his difficulties of understanding or the blind alleys he went down as he tackled the problems, but in a way which is designed to trick the tutor into giving him a good grade. Here assessment is a hurdle to be negotiated, a game to be played, at the expense of learning.

The average lecturer likes to see the right result squared in red at the bottom of the test sheet, if possible with as few lines of calculation as possible – above all else don't put any comments. He hates that. He thinks that you are trying to fill the page with words to make the work look bigger. Don't leave your mistakes, either, even corrected. If you've done it wrong, bin the lot. He likes to believe that you've found the right solution at the first time. If you're still making mistakes, that means you didn't study enough. There's no way you can re-do an exercise a few months after because you've only got the plain results without comments. If you have a go, you may well make the same mistakes you've done before because you've got no record of your previous errors.

(Gibbs, 1992a)

This is the opposite of an Oxford student choosing to spend most time on what they do not yet understand or a tutor deliberately choosing to discuss what the student does not yet understand fully. Faking good is a direct consequence of the form of assessment.

Students' experience of feedback

It is a truism that learning requires feedback. The importance of feedback is enshrined in the 'Seven principles of good practice in undergraduate education' (Chickering and Gamson, 1991) and is developed by Nicol and Milligan (Chapter 5, this volume). But how do students experience feedback? A number of studies have found that they can find feedback incomprehensible, that they glance at the mark and then throw their work away, or even that they do not bother to collect their work from the departmental office (e.g., Higgins *et al.* 2000; Hounsell, 1987). In interviews I encountered the following statement that was representative of common student perceptions. It concerns another of the 'seven principles': that feedback has to be provided promptly if it is to be attended to and be useful. 'The feedback on my assignments comes back so slowly that we are already on the topic after next and I've already submitted the next assignment. It's water under the bridge, really. I just look at the mark and bin it.'

The crucial variable appears not to be the quality of the feedback (which is what teachers tend to focus on) but the quality of student engagement with that feedback. For example, Forbes and Spence (1991) report a study of innovation in assessment in an engineering course where peer feedback and marks, of very mixed quality and uncertain marking standards, provided instantly during lecture classes, produced a truly dramatic increase in student performance (in subsequent exams) compared with the previously high-quality teacher feedback and reliable marking which came back slowly and which students as a consequence had not attended to.

This second example of a student statement concerns a general problem with feedback associated with objective testing – including computer-based multiple-choice question testing and open entry forms of computerised feedback. The following student was studying a 'maths for science' course where the assessment was online. Students could tackle maths assignments in their own time and then type in their maths solutions. A very sophisticated computer program then generated instant and appropriate qualitative feedback.

I do not like the online assessment method . . . it was too easy to only study to answer the questions and still get a good mark . . . the wrong reasoning can still result in the right answer so the student can be misled into thinking she understands something . . . I think there should have been a tutor-marked assessment part way through the course so someone could comment on methods of working, layout, etc.

This problem with a focus of assessment on outcome rather than process is echoed in reviews of the impact of different kinds of feedback on pupil behaviour in schools (Black and Wiliam, 1998). It is now clear that feedback without marks leads to better learning than marks only, or even than marks with feedback. Any feedback that focuses on an individual's overall performance (in the form of a mark or grade), rather than on their learning, detracts from learning.

Who makes the judgements?

Thirty years ago I was struck by Carl Rogers' principles that stated that learning is maximised when judgements by the learner (in the form of self-assessment) are emphasised and judgements by the teacher are minimised (Rogers, 1969). At the time it seemed a noble but hopelessly idealistic and impractical notion. I now know better. Much research on self- and peer assessment appears to be obsessed with the reliability of student marking in the hope that student-generated grades can substitute for teachers' grades and save the teacher a great deal of work. If you go to enough trouble, students are indeed capable of reliable marking (or, rather, as reliable as the rather low-level teachers usually achieve). But this completely misses the point. What is required is not more grades but more learning. The value of self- and peer assessment is that students internalise academic standards and are subsequently able to supervise themselves as they study and write and solve problems, in relation to these standards. It is the act of students making judgement against standards that brings educational benefits, not the act of receiving a grade from a peer. This issue is explored in much greater depth in Chapter 5 of this volume.

There are now many studies of the positive impact of self- and peer assessment on student performance. In the US this has been associated with the 'Classroom Assessment' initiative. In Europe and Australia it has been associated with less organised, but no less voluminous attempts by teachers to support better learning through changing assessment. My favourite example comes from a psychology department where the teachers were exhausted by spending every weekend marking experimental and laboratory reports. They would provide feedback such as 'You have not labelled the axes of your graphs', week in, week out, despite abundant guidance to students on lab report writing and repeated feedback of an identical kind. The teachers suspected that their diligence in providing feedback was to little purpose. They devised a feedback sheet which contained about fifty of the most frequent comments they wrote on students' reports (such as 'Have not labelled axes of graphs'). Next to each was a 'tick box' and they provided feedback in the form of ticks next to comments. While this saved their wrist from repetitive strain injury from writing the same feedback endlessly it did not improve students' lab reports. They then had a brainwave and gave the students the feedback sheet and required them to attach a copy to the front of each laboratory report they submitted, but with a tick next to all the things they had done wrong. Students were then able to submit technically perfect lab reports because they could undertake useful self-assessment before submission, and the teachers had to develop new, tougher criteria in order to avoid everyone achieving perfect grades. It is not until students apply criteria and standards to judge their own work as part of self-supervision while working (just as I am doing while writing this chapter) that their work will improve. And this is at no cost to the teacher (or in my case the book's editors).

Conditions under which assessment supports learning

I have written a number of books over the years about assessment methods, with the intention of increasing teachers' repertoire of alternatives to suit different contexts, and because variety is the spice of life (see Gibbs, 1992b and 1995; Habeshaw *et al.*, 1993). I had not provided a coherent rationale for deciding which kind of method suited which kind of context or educational problem. I have recently set out to turn observations such as those in the previous sections into a coherent rationale (Gibbs, 1999). This involved reading theoretical literature (mostly schools-based) about formative assessment, but most importantly I read large numbers of case-study accounts of changed assessment set in higher education where claims were made about improved student performance, but where there was usually no explanation of what had prompted this improvement. For example, in Forbes and Spence (1991) there is a full description of the assessment innovation and full data about the improvement in grades but no articulation of the underlying pedagogic principles involved. I was interested in what 'pedagogic work' was being done by various assessment tactics that resulted in them being effective. In the case studies it was also rare to find a rationale for selecting the particular innovation the authors chose to implement. I was interested in how you could diagnose a problem so as to guide the choice of an appropriate assessment solution.

This literature review led to the articulation of eleven 'conditions under which assessment supports students' learning' (Gibbs and Simpson, 2004). A student questionnaire was then developed, the Assessment Experience Questionnaire (AEQ) (Gibbs and Simpson, 2003; available for free use at <http://www.open.ac.uk/science/fdtl/tools.htm>) which has been used widely to diagnose which of these conditions are being met and which are not. In the UK, South Africa and Hong Kong there is currently quite widespread use of the AEQ as part of action research projects undertaken by the science faculty in order to find ways to support student learning better through innovation in assessment. Scores from the AEQ help to diagnose problems and select appropriate assessment solutions, and then the AEQ is being administered again after the innovation has been implemented, to monitor changes in student learning behaviour. A national project is documenting some of these projects (<http://www.open.ac.uk/science/fdtl/>). These eleven conditions are summarised here, clustered under the headings used to structure the questionnaire.

Quantity and distribution of student effort

1. Assessed tasks capture sufficient study time and effort

This condition concerns whether your students study sufficiently out of class or whether the assessment system allows them to get away with not studying very much at all. This is the 'time on task' principle (Chickering and Gamson, 1991) linked to the insight that it is assessment, not teaching, that captures student effort.

2. These tasks distribute student effort evenly across topics and weeks

This condition is concerned with whether students can 'question spot' and avoid much of the curriculum, or stop turning up to class after the last assignment is due. It is about evenness of effort week by week across a course and also across topics. I once saw data on the distribution of students' answers for an examination in which they had to answer three of fifteen questions. Almost everyone answered the same three questions. The topics addressed by the other twelve questions were presumably hardly studied at all.

Quality and level of student effort

3. These tasks engage students in productive learning activity

This condition is partly about whether the assessment results in students taking a deep approach (attempting to make sense) or a surface approach (trying to reproduce) (Marton, 1997) and also about quality of engagement in general. Do the things students have to do in order to meet assessment requirements engender appropriate, engaged and productive learning activity? Examinations may induce integration of previously unconnected knowledge, during revision, or memorisation of unprocessed information. Which approach to revision will be induced depends not so much on the examination demands as on students' perceptions of these demands.

4. Assessment communicates clear and high expectations to students

This condition is again drawn from Chickering and Gamson (1991): 'Good practice communicated high expectations'. This is partly about articulating explicit goals that students understand and can orient themselves towards, and partly about the level of perceived challenge. Can students spot, within ten minutes of the first class of a course or within the first thirty seconds reading a course description, that this is going to be an easy course and that they will be able to meet assessment demands without much effort or difficulty? From where do students pick up these clues? Without internalising the standards of a course, students cannot monitor their own level of performance or know when they have not yet done enough to be able safely to move on to the next task or topic or to reallocate their scarce time to another course they are studying in parallel. On the Course Experience Questionnaire, scores on the 'Clear Goals and Standards' scale correlate with the extent to which students take a deep approach to learning (Ramsden, 1991).

The remaining conditions concern feedback. They are not elaborated here as feedback is addressed in depth in Chapter 5 of this volume.

Quantity and timing of feedback

5. Sufficient feedback is provided, both often enough and in enough detail

6. The feedback is provided quickly enough to be useful to students

Quality of feedback

7. Feedback focuses on learning rather than on marks or students themselves

8. Feedback is linked to the purpose of the assignment and to criteria

9. Feedback is understandable to students, given their sophistication

Student response to feedback

10. Feedback is received by students and attended to

11. Feedback is acted upon by students to improve their work or their learning

Outline ideas for meeting these conditions are summarised later in this chapter and addressed in more detail in subsequent case studies.

Use of the AEQ to diagnose where to innovate

Evidence from the use of the AEQ (Gibbs *et al.*, 2003) is cited here to illustrate the way in which it can be used to diagnose problems with the way assessment supports students' learning and in particular the extent to which the eleven conditions outlined above are met. This data comes from 776 students on fifteen science courses at two UK universities. The students at the two universities were revealed to have very different perceptions of their assessment systems. In fact, there was more variation between the universities than between courses, suggesting that there are institutional assessment system cultures or norms. In response to data such as that in Table 2.1, Institution B has focused its efforts on improving feedback to students. Institution A has, in contrast, focused its efforts on students making more use of the high volume of feedback that they are given. This data comes from a national scale project ('Formative Assessment in Science Teaching', <http://www.open.ac.uk/science/fdtl/>) that is supporting action research into the way assessment supports learning. The 'scale scores' in Table 2.1 are out of a maximum score of 30 and are derived from five-point rating scales on each of six questionnaire items making up each scale. The differences between these institutions in terms of the 'quantity and timing of feedback' are very marked.

The data also showed marked differences between different courses in the extent to which, for example, students found feedback helpful, or acted upon feedback. Table 2.2 examines differences between courses within Institution A and displays a selection of data from the 'best' and 'worst' course (in terms of scores

Table 2.1 Comparison of fifteen science courses at two universities in terms of the reported volume and distribution of student effort, and students' perception of the quality and promptness of feedback

Scale	University A	University B	t	p*
	Scale Score			
Time demands and distribution of student effort	20.3 (s.d. 3.16)	18.6 (s.d. 2.91)	7.387 (d.f. 772)	p < 0.001
Quantity and timing of feedback	22.0 (s.d. 4.40)	15.6 (s.d. 4.48)	19.28 (d.f. 766)	p < 0.001
Sample items	**% agree or strongly agree**			
I only study things that are going to be covered in the assignments	8%	27%		
	% disagree or strongly disagree			
On this course it is possible to do quite well without studying much	64%	33%		
Sample items	**% agree**			
On this course I get plenty of feedback on how I am doing	68%	26%		
Whatever feedback I get comes too late to be useful	11%	42%		

Key: *two-tailed t-test

Table 2.2 Comparison of science courses within University A in terms of students' use of feedback

AEQ items	'Best' course	'Worst' course
	% strongly agree	
The feedback helps me to understand things better	36%	6%
The feedback shows me how to do better next time	31%	4%
The feedback prompts me to go back over material covered earlier in the course	13%	1%

on the AEQ) in the sample. The data show that the AEQ is capable of distinguishing between courses even within a single institution within a single subject. Note just how unlikely it is for students to be prompted by feedback to go back over material. What is clear from such data is that there are major differences in how effectively assessment systems work to support student learning and to foster student behaviour that is likely to lead to learning. There is clearly plenty of scope for using methods that improve matters.

Assessment tactics that solve learning problems

This section summarises assessment tactics that, from accounts in the literature, have the capacity to address particular conditions well. There is obviously no one-to-one relationship between their use and changed student learning behaviour – that will depend on an interaction of many variables in each unique context.

Addressing problems with the quantity and distribution of student effort

It is possible to capture student time and effort simply by using more assignments or assignments distributed more evenly across the course and across topics. The Open University, for example, traditionally employs eight evenly spaced assignments on each 'full credit' course, to ensure that distance-learning students work steadily throughout the year and on all course units.

To cope with the consequent marking load, it is possible to make the completion of assignments a course requirement, or a condition to be met before a summative assessment is tackled at a later date, without marking any of these assignments. It is also possible to sample assignments for marking (e.g., from a portfolio) such that students have to pay serious attention to every assignment in case they are selected for marking. Mechanised and computer-based assessment can obviously achieve similar ends (of high levels of assessment without tutor marking), though often without meeting the other conditions fully and sometimes at the cost of quality of learning and mis-orienting of learning effort. The use of self- and/or peer assessment (provided that it is required) can also generate student time on task without generating teacher time on marking. It is also possible to design examinations that make demands that are unpredictable, or which sample almost everything, so that students have to study everything just in case, though this too can result in other conditions not being met, such as failing to generate high quality and level of learning effort through students taking a surface approach as a result of anxiety and excessive workload.

Problems with the quality and level of student effort

Assignments that are larger, more complex and open-ended, requiring 'performances of understanding', are more likely to induce a deep approach to study than are short-answer tests or multiple-choice questions. Assignments involving interaction and collaboration with other students, in or out of class, are usually more engaging. Social pressures to deliver, for example through making the products of learning public (in posters, or through peer assessment) may induce more care and pride in work than 'secretly' submitted assignments to the teacher. Clear specification of goals, criteria and standards, and especially the 'modelling' of the desired products, for example through discussion of exemplars, will make it less likely that students will set themselves low or inappropriate standards. If students internalise these goals, criteria and standards, for example through student marking exercises and public critique of work, they are likely to be able to use these standards to supervise their own study in future.

Problems with the quantity and timing of feedback

Regular feedback requires regular assignments, ideally starting early in a course so that students are oriented to the standard required as early as possible. Some institutions or departments have quality standards for the volume and turnaround time of tutor feedback and also have the means to monitor the achievement of these standards. Mechanised feedback can be used to increase its volume at low cost and much contemporary innovation in assessment is concerned with computer-generated marking and feedback, where mechanised tests are used. The challenge then is to meet other conditions at the same time. The quality of feedback can be traded off against speed of return: for example, using peer feedback or model answers, or the tutor sampling students' assignments to produce generic feedback based on the first five assignments assessed, but not reading the rest. The balance of gains and losses from such practices are matters for empirical study to explore. Ultimately the fastest and most frequent feedback available is that provided by students to themselves from moment to moment as they study or write assignments. Investing effort in developing such self-supervision may be much the most cost-effective use of tutors' time.

Problems with the quality of feedback

If students receive feedback without marks or grades, they are more likely to read the feedback as the only indication they have of how they are progressing. This has been demonstrated to have a significant positive impact on learning outcomes (Black and Wiliam, 1998). If feedback is structured around the goals of the assignment, and relates clearly to criteria and standards, this is more likely to result in clarity and impact than unstructured arbitrary feedback that focuses on student characteristics.

The quality and impact of feedback can be improved through clear briefing to teachers. The Open University in the UK trains all its tutors in how to give thorough and motivating feedback, and also periodically monitors the quality of this feedback (rather than monitoring the quality of their teaching) and provides individualised coaching where there are perceived to be quality problems. Students' ability to make sense of and use feedback can be improved through classroom discussion of what specific examples of feedback mean and through discussion of improvements students intend to make to subsequent assignments in response to the feedback.

Problems with students' response to feedback

If feedback is provided faster, there is more likelihood that students will read and respond to it. If students tell the teacher what they would like feedback on, they are more likely to pay attention to this feedback when they receive it (Habeshaw *et al.*, 1993). If students discuss feedback on their assignments, in class, they are more likely to think about it and take it seriously (Rust *et al.*, 2003). If students receive feedback on a draft of an assignment they are likely to use this feedback to improve the assignment. If the assignment allows drafting, with feedback on the draft, students are likely to make good use of this feedback. Students are usually capable of giving each other useful feedback on drafts. Tutors can also ask students to submit a cover sheet to their assignment explaining how the peer feedback (or the feedback from the tutor on the previous assignment) was used to improve this assignment. If testing is 'two-stage' with an opportunity between a mock test and the real test to undertake more studying on those aspects which were not tackled well in the mock test, then they are likely to use this opportunity (Cooper, 2000). If assignments are 'multi-stage', with each stage building towards a larger and more complete final assignment, then students will almost inevitably use feedback as they put together the whole thing. If assignments have multiple components, tackled in sequence (e.g., stages of a project, elements of a portfolio of evidence) in which each assignment contributes to a larger whole, feedback on early sections is very likely to be used by students to improve the whole. If students are asked to demonstrate how the current assignment benefits from feedback on the previous assignment, and are allocated marks for how well they have done this, they are likely to take feedback seriously. If at least some of the feedback is generic in nature there is more likelihood that it will also apply to subsequent assignments on different topics.

Conclusions

This chapter has provided a conceptual framework for diagnosing the extent to which assessment regimes are likely to create effective learning environments. The conditions under which assessment supports student learning are based on educational theory and empirical evidence concerning either weak student performance where these conditions are not met or improved student performance where innovations in assessment have been introduced specifically to address one or more of these conditions. It is clear both that student learning can be poor largely because the assessment system does not work well, and that changes solely to the assessment, leaving the teaching unchanged, can bring marked improvements. The chapter has provided a glimpse of the wide variations that exist between courses and between institutions, even within the same discipline area, in terms of how well assessment regimes support learning. Finally, the chapter has outlined some of the ways in which these assessment conditions can be met – the tactics that can be adopted to address specific weaknesses. Later sections of this book contain case studies that illustrate some of these tactics in action.

References

Black, P. and Wiliam, D. (1998) Assessment and classroom learning. *Assessment in Education: Principles, Policy and Practice*, 5, 1, pp. 7–74.

Brown, E., Gibbs, G. and Glover, C. (2003) Evaluation tools for investigating the impact of assessment regimes on student learning. *Bioscience Education e-Journal*, 2, <http://www.bioscience.heacademy.ac.uk/journal/vol2/beej-2-5.htm>.

Chickering, Z. F. and Gamson, A. W. (1991) *Applying the seven principles for good practice in undergraduate education*. San Francisco: Jossey-Bass.

Cooper, N. J. (2000) Facilitating learning from formative feedback in Level 3 assessment. *Assessment and Evaluation in Higher Education*, 25, 3, pp. 279–91.

Forbes, D. and Spence, J. (1991) An experiment in assessment for a large class, in R. Smith (ed.) *Innovations in engineering education*. London: Ellis Horwood.

Fransson, A. (1977) On qualitative differences in learning, IV – effects of motivation and test anxiety on process and outcome. *British Journal of Educational Psychology*, 47, pp. 244–57.

Gibbs, G. (1992a) *Improving the quality of student learning*. Bristol: Technical and Educational Services.

—— (1992b) *Assessing more students*. Oxford: Oxford Centre for Staff Development.

—— (1995) *Assessing student-centred courses*. Oxford: Oxford Centre for Staff Development.

—— (1999) Using assessment strategically to change the way students learn, in S. Brown and A. Glasner (eds) *Assessment matters in higher education*. Buckingham: Society for Research into Higher Education and Open University Press.

Gibbs, G. and Simpson, C. (2003) *Measuring the response of students to assessment: the Assessment Experience Questionnaire*. 11th International Improving Student Learning Symposium, Hinckley.

—— (2004) Conditions under which assessment supports students' learning. *Learning and Teaching in Higher Education*, 1, pp. 3–31.

Gibbs, G., Simpson, C. and Macdonald, R. (2003) *Improving student learning through changing assessment – a conceptual and practical framework*. Padova: European Association for Research into Learning and Instruction.

Habeshaw, S., Gibbs, G. and Habeshaw, T. (1993) *53 interesting ways to assess your students*, 3rd edn. Bristol: Technical and Educational Services.

Higgins, R., Hartley, P. and Skelton, A. (2001) Getting the message across: the problem of communicating assessment feedback. *Teaching in Higher Education*, 6, 2, pp. 269–74.

Hounsell, D. (1987) Essay-writing and the quality of feedback, in J. T. E. Richardson *et al.* (eds) *Student learning: research in education and cognitive psychology*. Milton Keynes: SRHE and Open University Press.

Marton, F. (1997) Approaches to learning, in F. Marton, D. Hounsell and N. Entwistle (eds) *The experience of learning*, Edinburgh: Scottish Academic Press.

Miller, C. M. I. and Parlett, M. (1974) *Up to the mark: a study of the examination game*. Guildford: Society for Research into Higher Education.

Ramsden, P. (1991) A performance indicator of teaching quality in higher education: the course experience questionnaire. *Studies in Higher Education*, 16, pp. 129–50.

Rogers, C. (1969) *Freedom to learn*. Columbus: Merrill.

Rust, C., Price, M. and O'Donovan, B. (2003) Improving students' learning by developing their understanding of assessment criteria and processes. *Assessment and Evaluation in Higher Education*, 28, 2, pp. 147–64.

Scouler, K. M. and Prosser, M. (1994) Students' experience of studying for multiple choice question examinations. *Studies in Higher Education*, 19, 3, pp. 267–79.

Snyder, B. R. (1971) *The hidden curriculum*. Cambridge, MA: MIT Press.

3 Evaluating new priorities for assessment in higher education

Roger Murphy

Recent years have seen a welcome move towards professionalising the whole approach to the support for student learning within higher education in the UK. Staff taking up academic posts in more or less any university are now expected to undertake some initial educational training in their first year or two in the job. Hopefully this will help them to develop some appropriate skills and knowledge in relation to the complicated challenges that they will face in providing support for student learning within the rapidly changing world of higher education. Gone therefore are the days when it was assumed that anyone clever enough to gain a university post through their demonstrated scholarship and research would without doubt be able to pass on their wisdom to students without thinking too much about how to do it effectively. Even so, the amount of educational training provided for staff in universities is still fairly slight, compared for example to that expected of those preparing to teach in schools. Also requirements to engage in initial preparation are in most institutions still unlikely to be followed up by any definite expectation of ongoing training and development throughout the rest of an academic career. Thus most university lecturers at best have experienced a short taster course to support their approach to providing university-level education, and many appointed more than ten years or so ago won't even have benefited from that. This marked disparity between school and higher education is hopefully slowly beginning to be diminished. Nevertheless, it will take a long time and a marked change in attitudes for university staff to be expected to be as professional in their approach to educational provision, as is expected of them in relation to their own particular area of scholarship.

Recent initiatives such as the Centres for Excellence in Teaching and Learning (CETLs), the Fund for the Development of Teaching and Learning (FDTL) projects and all the Higher Education Academy developments (including the twenty-four subject centres) signal a gradual move towards professionalising the educational side of the work of higher education institutions. Ever so slowly the support for student learning is coming to be properly recognised as a substantial and difficult challenge. Many factors have contributed to this change, including the move towards widening participation, which is undoubtedly presenting university lecturers with new challenges. Technological change is another factor in increasing the range of techniques and approaches for supporting student learning and reconceptualising the educational approaches being used. Even experienced university teachers are facing challenges in terms of reconceptualising their approaches to teaching both individual modules and indeed entire courses. Although I wouldn't want to overstate the movement that has occurred so far, some academics at least are beginning to see the value of educational theory and research, and training that draws upon such a body of scholarship. Others also recognise the need for experimentation, reflection, the adoption of new approaches, and the value of spending time observing colleagues teaching students in radically different ways. In some subject areas e-learning, problem-based learning and off-campus work-based learning have become parts of a move away from traditional lecture-theatre-based approaches to the organisation of higher education. Even where lectures still have a big role to play, they may now be supported by e-learning materials, either used within the lecture theatre or available for students to access to assist with their own independent learning.

Amid all of this, one area across standard university courses was very slow to change and innovate: the way in which students in higher education are assessed. Unlike school education, where the reform of assessment systems has been seen as a key factor in bringing about improvements in student learning, much of higher education has tended to plod along, seeming to take traditional forms of assess-ment as a given (with some notable exceptions, some of which are reported in this volume). While school teachers have consistently regarded student assessment as something that needs to be reviewed, updated and reconfigured at regular intervals, many universities have continued with very similar systems of assessment decade after decade. Viewed from the outside, this contrast between two areas of education operating alongside each other in the same geographical and educational context is rather puzzling, and is something that I want to examine. In doing this I am mindful of a quote from Boud, who puts his finger on what I regard as one of higher education's most exposed shortcomings: 'Students can, with difficulty, escape from the effects of poor teaching, they cannot (by definition, if they want to graduate) escape the effects of poor assessment' (Boud, 1995: 35).

Few would debate the fact that the role of assessment in education is fairly fundamental, and that reform of old-fashioned assessment approaches within higher education has been rather slow. Student assessment is for many educators one of the hardest things to resolve satisfactorily and in many settings leads to some of the fiercest debates. Some educational courses deliberately exclude any assess-ments of student learning as a matter of principle. Such courses can be regarded both by students and other interested parties as less important than those that do include such assessment. Clearly this depends a great deal upon the context of the course, and the motivations of the students for undertaking them. However, where unassessed courses exist alongside courses that are assessed, then it is widely acknowledged that they are frequently perceived as being of less importance (Murphy and Torrance, 1988). In some settings this has led those involved in so-called 'minority subjects' to campaign to have their courses assessed in the same way as other, more mainstream subjects. The paradox here is that the teachers of those subjects which are subjected to rigorous assessment regimes are often highly envious of teachers in other subjects, where there is less of an emphasis on student assessment. Such a scenario is most common in school-level education, where subject status within an overall curriculum can often reflect the assessment emphasis accorded to different subjects/parts of the curriculum. In higher education, optional unassessed modules may suffer in the same way. Equally, parts of assessed courses, if they are known to fall outside the likely assessment emphases, may be given lower priority by students, and in some cases be completely disregarded; or students may focus very instrumentally on what they need to do to get good assessment results by the end of the course (*ibid.*).

In the paragraph above I have identified what I regard as two crucial aspects of the role of assessment in education. Assessment arrangements can, first, have a considerable impact upon the way in which educational courses are perceived. Second, and closely related to the first point, assessment requirements can have a strong back-wash effect on students' learning approaches and motivation. Thus assessment has the potential to make or break good educational learning opportunities. In the case-study chapters that come later on in this volume, we will be looking at a number of higher education assessment innovations which have been introduced in an attempt to enhance student learning. In the remainder of this chapter I shall look at some major trends in educational assessment theories and principles over the last twenty years to provide a broader conceptual framework against which those case studies can be evaluated.

As already noted, it is a curious phenomenon that in the United Kingdom the assessment debates that have occurred in higher education have usually been quite distinct from those that have occurred in school-level education. Indeed, the crossover between research, theory, policy and practice in these two sectors has been so low that there has been a marked divergence both in assessment practices and in the assumptions which tend to drive them. Why has this been the case? What is it about higher education that has led it to stand outside both the debates and the developments that have characterised school education in the UK over the last fifty years or so? A partial answer to such questions must relate to the different status of universal publicly provided state-school education and the elite status of our older universities. Elite systems of education, whether private schools or universities with high status, tend to stick with traditional approaches to education and have been slow to change their approaches to support student learning. One factor such institutions have in common is that they select the students who enter them, and can therefore expect to work largely with students who have already demonstrated an advanced capacity for organising their own learning. But on its own that difference hardly explains such a marked disparity between such different approaches to going about the business of assessing student learning. There is a fine line that can be drawn between elite educators maintaining tried and tested methods because of years of successful experience and the same people being seen to be arrogantly ignoring new knowledge and experience because of a lack of respect for modern ideas and evidence of success arising from different settings. Another issue is the respect held by society for educators in these two different worlds. University teachers, it can be argued, are held in higher regard than schoolteachers, and because of that their assessment judgements seem to have been more readily accepted than those of teachers working in the school sector. Whether that is in any way a rational basis for approaching assessment so differently in these two sectors is highly debatable.

In higher education, in the vast majority of cases, students are assessed by staff members teaching the course that they are following. In many institutions there is still a strong reliance on formal end of course/module/year examinations, and the general approach to marking such examinations is relatively straightforward with little formal use of things such as detailed marking schemes, or elaborate mechanisms for standardising the marking of the different staff members involved. There is, of course, a long-established external examiner system, but this is widely recognised as being a fairly 'light touch' nod in the direction of attempting to maintain some degree of equivalence between different institutions. With a vastly expanded system of higher education it is now generally acknowledged that the standards required by different universities are, to say the least, variable. Only the most naïve users of degree outcomes would assume that a degree classification received by a student graduating from one university (Oxford, say) represents exactly the same type of educational achievement as the same degree classification received by a student graduating from another university (Bournemouth, say).

All of that contrasts markedly with the highly regulated system of assessment which has been developed in the school sector. High-stakes assessments (such as GCSE and A-level examinations) virtually exclude any involvement in the conduct of assessments by the teachers who are teaching the students. Examinations are set, administered, marked and graded by public examination boards (awarding bodies) and there is great emphasis on the standardisation of marking through examiner training, detailed marking schemes, cross checks, examiner mark monitoring and mark adjustments. The assessment industry in the school sector has grown into a gigantic, billion-pound enterprise with ever more layers of assessment being introduced through the national curriculum and other initiatives. It is also characterised by increasing levels of sophistication in the assessment techniques used, technological interventions including an increase in on-screen assessments, and the application of expert research to attempt to make assessments more accurate, more efficient, fairer, and, as far as possible, comparable across subjects, awarding bodies and year groups.

So we have two systems with very little in common. It is rare to find people working in one who know much about the other and it is very difficult to point to ways in which insights from one have been transferred to be used in the other. From my experience, the assessment system in higher education is generally regarded with some amazement by assessment experts working in the school sector. How can academics, who are supposed to be committed to knowledge creation and the development and use of the latest research, continue to operate a student assessment system that looks so unimaginative and dated?

In the sections that follow I want to take a deeper look at some of those major trends that have emerged in assessment approaches outside higher education and examine their relevance for the innovations being evaluated within this book.

The dependability of assessment results

One of the biggest areas of concern in the wider educational assessment literature over the years relates to the dependability of assessment results (Murphy, 2004). If the assessment results are to be taken seriously, then those who use them need to be reassured that they can trust them. Such an emphasis has been linked to an acknowledgement that there are 'high-stakes assessments', upon which crucial decisions depend, and other kinds of assessments, which in a real sense do not lead to quite such crucial outcomes.

In situations where high-stakes assessments are being conducted, judgements by those who have been teaching the students are generally regarded as less robust and dependable than assessment results relating to more sophisticated tests and examinations set and marked by individuals who are not at all involved in teaching the individual students. In this context it is interesting that in United Kingdom higher education the reliability (or dependability) of assessments appears to have been much less of a concern than it has been in other places of education. Most assessments are carried out by the same individuals who teach students, albeit with some checks through double marking procedures, and external examiner light-touch oversight. Only with Ph.D.s does the assessment of students depend strongly on the judgement of staff from outside the institution, and even in that case such examiners receive no training, appear to be chosen in something of a haphazard way, and are able to operate personal assessment standards rather than following anything that could be described as a detailed assessment framework. It is a little disappointing that no case studies relating to innovative approaches to assessing Ph.D.s could be found to include in this volume.

Nevertheless, concerns about the fairness of student assessments have surfaced within the sector, and some particular issues have been foci for much research and innovation. Anonymous marking to try to mitigate against unfair uses or prior knowledge and expectations is now widely used and has been shown effectively to counteract certain kinds of bias that can occur when markers know things relating to the identity of the students whose work they are marking. Also, counter-acting plagiarism by students has become a major preoccupation, especially with the rise in opportunities to borrow and buy ready-completed essays, project reports and dissertations on the internet. In addition some universities have developed assessment guidelines that require assessment criteria to be made available and which also require departments to organise systems of double marking of student work or other approaches to minimise the grossest manifestations of marker bias or unreliability.

Increasingly there has been much speculation about the comparability of assessment standards across the greatly expanded higher education sector in the United Kingdom. While it is hard to imagine how, for example, a first-class honours degree in History from the University of Oxford is equivalent to the same award from a post-1992 institution such as Bournemouth University, there has been a great deal of reluctance to discuss such matters fully in an open way (Murphy, 1996). Employers are known to exercise their own judgements in interpreting the value of degrees from different universities, whereas the government has been keen to stress the overall quality of degree-level education and standards in the United Kingdom. Compared to the level of attention to comparability of awarding standards between the GCSE and A-Level awarding bodies in England, Wales and Northern Ireland (Forrest and Shoesmith, 1985), there is a strange reluctance to address such matters in higher education.

In the current turbulent world of higher education it seems unlikely that the present fairly underdeveloped approach to student assessment will be allowed to continue. An increasing emphasis on quality assurance and quality control has already started to make an impact. Increased competition between institutions will, I am sure, lead to many wishing to take a more professional approach to assessing student learning outcomes, and that in turn will inevitably lead to a greater public awareness of the somewhat uncertain basis that underpins most student assessments in higher education today. Universities need to become more professional in their use of assessment techniques. That will involve all university staff who are going to play a part in the important and highly skilled task of assessing students being given more training and support in relation to their assessment practices. Quite simply, higher education can no longer hide behind its elite status in this respect, and in my view urgently needs to become much more professional in its approach to the assessment of students. Hopefully, this volume, with its open critique of many common assessment practices linked to a fresh look at alternative approaches, can play a significant part in that process.

Assessment for learning

One of the strongest emerging themes in the literature on educational assessment, outside higher education, has been the increasing emphasis on exploring, understanding and exploiting the strong influences that particular assessment approaches have on student learning (Black *et al.*, 2003). Undesirable back-wash effects on the curriculum have long been recognised and have highlighted reasons for developing better alignment between course aims and assessment methods. In addition, the powerful motivating effect that good formative assessments can have on student learning (Black and Wiliam, 1998; Torrance and Prior, 1998) has hastened a big drift towards an 'assessment for learning' culture in school education in the United Kingdom. Here the prime interest is in developing classroom assessment approaches that support and enhance student learning, and this has led to quite different discussions both about the types of assessment that are most desirable and new considerations about this use by classroom teachers within the context of their normal classroom work.

'Assessment for learning' is a neat catchphrase that needs defining (Assessment Reform Group, 1999; Sutton, 1995). It is a concept that can be undermined if we are not careful to clarify what it means. First, it relates to debates about matching learning goals and priorities to assessment goals and priorities. Unless these goals are matched, learning which occurs may be primarily assessment-driven and therefore quite different to the intended learning priorities. Biggs' (2003) notion of 'constructive alignment' is helpful here in providing a model around which learning goals and assessment goals can be aligned in a way that makes the most of the impact of one upon the other (and several case studies in this volume use this concept as a guiding principle). A second major priority relates to the use of assessment to give learners constructive feedback on how their learning is progressing. The power of Black and Wiliam's (1998) work is in identifying the positive benefits that can accrue to learners, when formative assessment processes are used effectively to give the frequent feedback on how they are getting on in relation to their developing learning. It is clear that learning processes can be enhanced by the appropriate application of good formative assessment procedures. There is a growing body of knowledge about how to do that in school classrooms, but in higher education we are still at an earlier stage of understanding how effectively this approach to assessment can be developed within different higher education institutions and in different areas of the curriculum (although Bond (1995), Knight (1995) and Hinett (1997) have all made useful contributions to thinking about how such a development could progress).

The movement of many higher education assessment practices towards a greater use of coursework and continuous assessment, and less reliance on end of course/module examinations, opens greater possibilities for assessment for learning, but this movement on its own does not guarantee a positive impact on student learning. Coursework and other forms of continuous assessment can still focus on summative assessment goals such as 'assessment for grading', unless genuine attempts are made to use such processes as the basis for feeding back constructive information to students in a way that can influence their future learning.

In later chapters of this book, many examples of innovative approaches to assessment will be presented. Quite a few of them will be based upon a motivation to improve student assessment by matching it more closely to overall course aims and objectives. In several cases the assessment innovations will also be motivated by a desire to make student assessment in higher education a better and more educational experience for students. It is clear that higher education has moved away from a model where several years of learning were followed by a major concentration on 'finals' (final-year end of degree course examinations), and the only feedback that students received was a final degree classification on a short four- or five-point scale. Having said that, the movement away from finals and/or a concentration on summative end of course assessments, the purpose of which is largely to determine degree classifications, does not guarantee a move fully into the realm of assessment for learning. We will need to evaluate each assessment innovation separately to see the benefits it offers in relation to this important new way of conceptualising assessment benefits.

An old-fashioned approach to evaluating assessment innovations was to explore solely the extent to which the assessments used were 'reliable' and 'valid'. Such concepts were imported into education from psychometric traditions in psychology, and are now seen to have limited usefulness because of the way that they assume that all assessments are unidimensional, and that they are steps towards producing a single 'true score' to summarise the educational achievement level of a student

(Gipps, 1994). Our more modern stance is now to recognise that assessment procedures can and should contribute to student learning as well as measure it, and to acknowledge that student learning across the higher education curriculum is complex, multifaceted and may need to be assessed in a wide variety of ways, and indeed be reported in ways that recognise the diversity rather than mask it.

Authentic assessment

Another important theme in the literature on educational assessment in schools concerns the extent to which the assessment of educational courses matches the key aims and intended outcomes of such courses. This has been encapsulated by some through the concept of 'authentic assessment' (Torrance, 1995). On first sight this might appear to be a rather obvious requirement for educational assessment ('inauthentic assessment' might appear a rather strange alternative). However, it has long been recognised that the design of educational assessments is often influenced by considerations other than the extent to which they match the core learning objectives of the educational course to which they apply. Pragmatic considerations, such as the amount of time available for staff and students to engage in assessment activities, can dictate that certain types of assessment are chosen in preference to others. To take an extreme example, multiple-choice tests are still sometimes favoured in some areas of higher education, not necessarily because they produce the most revealing and authentic assessment information, but because they can provide a quick and easy way to produce assessment results with a minimum of time input from students and staff. At worst, assessments can be designed on the basis of choosing something easy to assess, which will perform the function of producing student results or grades with no real regard to whether the things being assessed adequately reflect the major learning goals for the course or module. It is just this tendency that has led to many unfortunate situations where an inappropriate assessment tail has wagged a curriculum dog. In contrast authentic assessment is about a drive to look first to the curriculum in order to seek guidance about the shape and priorities for an assessment system to fit to it. Knowledge about how they are going to be assessed we know has a powerful influence on how students learn. The challenge for all educators is therefore to seek ways to marry curriculum and assessment in such a way as to maximise student learning in relation to priority goals. Enhancing student learning in this way is of course the key goal of educators, and a good assessment system will simply reinforce this goal rather than subvert it.

There are ways in which this theme interacts with some of the issues covered in the previous section of this chapter. If the designers of an educational course are working on the basis of an assessment for learning philosophy rather than, say, an assessment for grading philosophy, then their interest in choosing assessments that are 'authentic' and can be built into the course structure in an integrated way, which is likely to enhance the learning objectives, is likely to be higher. This can be seen as contrasting with the opposite type of instrumental and pragmatic approach which might work along the lines of recognising that there needed to be an assessed element associated with the course and seeking the most straightforward way of fulfilling that requirement. Many of the innovations that are presented in this book will be based upon assessment for learning and authentic assessment philosophies, and need to be judged largely in terms of their ability to foster appropriate student learning as well as their ability to report it.

A further dimension of the 'authentic assessment' philosophy relates to the range and type of different learning objectives, which are deemed to be appropriate within the context of a particular higher education course. Increasingly, following guidelines which have been developed as a result of quality assurance and quality assessment procedures, the extent of different learning objectives associated with individual courses have been specified in some detail in 'programme specifications' or similar statements about specific intended learning outcomes. Such objectives can cover knowledge and skills that are highly specific to the discipline(s) to which the course relates, and in many cases some other types of knowledge and skills that are more generic and may correspond to knowledge and skills covered in other courses. The further one goes towards specifying discrete and identifiably different learning goals associated with a course, the more one may be making the case for authentic assessments that can adequately assess such different aspects of learning in that subject. In some cases this may justify the use of quite different assessment techniques to assess different learning outcomes.

To illustrate this point, one could refer to the increased emphasis on core, generic or key skills in higher education (Murphy, 2001). Such skills have been widely recognised as forming a valid part of student learning across the higher education curriculum (CVCP, 1998). Furthermore, some universities have encouraged processes for assessing such skills within specific discipline-based courses in such a way that students' progress in developing such 'generic skills' can be observed and in some instances reported alongside, but separate from, their learning achievements that are more specific to the subject that they are studying in higher education. This type of approach does not necessarily mean that generic skills have to be assessed through different assessment procedures to 'subject-related skills', and in some areas innovative approaches have been developed to derive both generic and subject-related information from common assessment tasks. For example, students may, in an engineering course, engage in a group project which is both written up and presented to other students. The assessment of such a project may reveal highly specific engineering-related knowledge and skills, while also allowing some generic skills, such as working with others, problem solving, communication, information and communication technology (ICT), numeracy and managing own learning, to be assessed as well. This is a very good example of an innovation that has in a more coherent way addressed more than one assessment need within an HE context.

This discussion of assessing discrete elements within higher education courses also raises the question of how such elements are reported. Here we have an increasing interest in reporting mechanisms, which allow more information to be given than has traditionally been the case with a single scale of degree classifications. Records of achievement, progress files, e-portfolios and student transcripts all open up the possibility of reporting the results of student assessments in relation to a wider range of learning outcomes than has been the tradition in the United Kingdom in the past. The distinctiveness of such approaches lies in the way in which they do not try to condense diverse assessment information into a single grade or degree classification and open up the likelihood that more complex accounts of student learning can emerge from related assessment procedures.

So authentic assessment is a concept, which has much to offer higher education, and is one which matches the philosophy of many HE assessment innovations. It has, however, also led us into a consideration of more meaningful ways of reporting student achievements in situations where distinct learning goals are identified for particular courses.

A discussion such as this also takes us back to the 'dependability of assessments' section, as any attempt to report assessment outcomes across a wider range of learning objectives will inevitably raise questions about precision, reliability and dependability of assessment outcomes in relation to each area which is to be reported.

References

Assessment Reform Group (1999) *Assessment for learning: beyond the black box.* Cambridge: University of Cambridge School of Education.

Biggs, J. (2003) *Teaching for quality learning at university.* Buckingham: SRHE/Open University Press.

Black, P. and Wiliam, D. (1998) Assessment and classroom learning. *Assessment in Education*, 5(1), pp. 7–71.

Black, P., Harrison, C., Lee, C., Marshall, B. and Wiliam, D. (2003) *Assessment for learning.* Maidenhead: Open University Press.

Bond, D. (1995) *Enhancing learning through self-assessment.* London: Kogan Page.

Boud, D. (1995) Assessment and learning: contradictory or complementary? in P. Knight (ed.) *Assessment for learning in higher education.* London: Kogan Page.

CVCP (1998) *Elitism to inclusion.* London: CVCP.

Forrest, G. and Shoesmith, D. J. (1985) *A second review of GCE Comparability Studies.* Manchester: JMB.

Gipps, C. (1994) *Beyond testing: towards a theory of educational assessment.* London: Falmer Press.

Gipps, C. and Stobart, G. (1993) *Assessment: a teachers' guide to the issues.* London: Hodder and Stoughton.

Hinett, K. (1997) *Towards meaningful learning: a theory for improved assessment in higher education.* Unpublished Ph.D. thesis, University of Central Lancashire.

Knight, P. (1995) Assessment for Learning in higher education. London: Kogan Page.

Murphy, R. (1996) Firsts among equals: the case of British university degrees, in B. Boyle and T. Christie (eds) *Issues in setting standards: establishing comparabilities.* London: Falmer Press.

—— (2001) *A briefing on key skills in higher education.* York: LTSN Generic Centre.

—— (2004) *Grades of uncertainty: reviewing the uses and misuses of examination results.* London: Association of Teachers and Lecturers.

Murphy, R. and Torrance, H. (1988) *The changing face of educational assessment.* Buckingham: Open University Press.

Sutton, R. (1995) *Assessment for learning*. Manchester: R. S. Publications.

Torrance, H. (1995) *Evaluating authentic assessment*. Buckingham: Open University Press.

Torrance, H. and Prior, J. (1998) *Investigating formative assessment: teaching, learning, and assessment in the classroom*. Buckingham: Open University Press.

4 Accessible and adaptable elements of Alverno student assessment-as-learning

Strategies and challenges for peer review

Marcia Mentkowski

The initial chapters of this book identify common issues for innovators in assessment who seek better to engage students in learning and to foster learning that lasts beyond college. A common challenge for us as authors or readers is to learn from each other despite enormous diversity in our contexts, conceptual frameworks and students. We differ in how we configure curricula or experience the educational policies that differentiate institutions of higher education. Yet a common goal is to probe alternative models for enhancing curricular coherence between what and how students learn and how they are assessed.

The challenge to Alverno in this chapter is to engage you, our peers, in reviewing our ideas and practices so you may judge for yourself what might be learned from the Alverno experience that is relevant to your own unique praxis. Our task is to serve readers who themselves seek to clarify, debate and discuss their own unique approaches. As you proceed with your review of our practice in relation to your own, we hope you may discern the more applicable from the more contextual elements of student assessment-as-learning, based on evidence for why and how those elements foster knowledgeable, competent, reflective and committed learners. To aid you, this chapter a) briefly overviews the Alverno faculty experience; b) considers strategies that peers may use for judging the accessibility and adaptability of elements of student assessment-as-learning, including some challenges in doing so; and c) sets forth adaptable elements of assessment-as-learning from collaborative analyses of practice across institutions.

Overview of the Alverno faculty experience

Alverno College Faculty (1979/1994 and 2000) define student assessment-as-learning as a process in operation at Alverno College, integral to learning, that involves observation, analysis/interpretation, and judgment of each student's performance on the basis of explicit, public criteria, with self assessment and resulting feedback to the student. It serves to confirm student achievement and provide feedback to the student for the improvement of learning and to the instructor for the improvement of teaching.[1]

In some ways, the Alverno faculty is unique in that it deliberately evolved assessment-as-learning as a necessary response to its efforts in the early 1970s to redefine the meaning of the baccalaureate degree through an outcome or ability-based curriculum. From the start, student and program assessment were situated as key curricular components in a learning-centered college culture. The College's ability-based curriculum focused on student learning outcomes and experiences organized for developing not only knowledge in the disciplines and expertise in the professions, but also maturity, leadership and service. The Alverno faculty gradually redefined the meaning of the baccalaureate to make explicit eight abilities taught within the context of an integrated liberal arts and professions curriculum (communication, analysis, problem solving, valuing in decision-making, social interaction, developing a global perspective, effective citizenship, and aesthetic engagement). Each of the abilities has been continually redefined through a series of sequential levels to clarify pathways to student success (Alverno College Faculty, 1976/2005).

Most faculty members assumed that once they had reshaped what students should learn, then existing assessment techniques such as multiple-choice tests, essays and internships could probably be adapted to assess these capabilities. When they found they could not be adapted successfully – nor did alternative assessments exist elsewhere – they began to design and develop an assessment process that was coherent with their emerging definition of the baccalaureate. Faculty members began to implement and refine assessment so that it was consistent with what they had now articulated: education goes beyond knowing to being able to do what one knows. Making explicit this expectation to understand and use learning was integral to the goal of better preparing students for what contemporary life requires; for example, learning to conceptualize the big picture, thinking critically in interaction with others from different backgrounds, doing science when assumptions change continually, or creating art across cultures.

The faculty gradually evolved the required ability-based curriculum by reflecting on their practice to see what could be taught across the curriculum and by carefully studying student performance on assignments and assessments to see what students could learn. Over the years, faculty members have provided rich descriptions of how they have changed their practices within and across the curriculum (Riordan and Roth, 2005) and developed its educational theory, research and policy base (Mentkowski and Associates, 2000). Throughout, student assessment-as-learning has remained a central element of the curriculum.

As Alverno instructors made their practices accessible to each other across the disciplines, they could better discuss potentially usable elements across the entire curriculum. In the act of doing so, what and how faculty members practiced assessment-as-learning became more interesting to other faculties. Being clear about the Alverno curriculum and culture, we quickly learned, strongly influenced whether it could be reviewed by peers both on and off campus. The *accessibility* of Alverno practice is reflected in how well faculties from diverse colleges can understand it. Alverno's assessment elements, such as making learning outcomes explicit through criteria or rubrics, giving appropriate feedback, and building in instructor, peer and self assessment, may seem directly adaptable at first. Yet the *adaptability* of Alverno's integration of these conceptual frameworks shapes whether and how any one institution's faculty can apply or elaborate – *not adopt or replicate* – elements of a curriculum developed by another faculty.

Strategies for peer review of student assessment-as-learning

As faculties from a range of institutions began to design and implement their own student assessment systems, we have learned that they engage in several strategies ior reviewing other systems. They seek to evaluate the adaptability of elements of any other assessment system and often seek evidence for the long-term coherence, efficacy and feasibility of assessment practices across a curriculum. Other faculties have consistently asked the following questions of Alverno practices. What is assessment-as-learning? Is it sustainable even though new faculty members join in shaping the curriculum and students' individual differences become increasingly characterized by more diverse backgrounds? To what degree is assessment-as-learning shaped by each of the disciplinary/professional departments? How is it influenced by the college's commitment to each individual's learning and its ethos of professional service? What is its theory and research base? What other faculties have studied this approach and what have they learned? Perhaps the more persistent and stubborn question has been: may we visit and see for ourselves?

Opening practice to observation and dialogue

As a first step in their review strategy, many educators began to visit the college to probe the Alverno history of transformation, to study how the eight abilities are integrated within the content of the liberal arts and professions as learning outcomes,[2] to see assessment in action, to hear first hand from current students how they experience assessment, and to question different students on what they learn from the process.[3] Many visitors have since worked with their own colleagues in intensive Alverno workshops to determine and break open the meaning of their own expected learning outcomes, to define them through developmental performance criteria for assessment, and to get and give peer review and feedback with Alverno faculty members. Through these interactions, Alverno practice became more accessible and accountable to peer institutions. While Alverno faculty members' definitions of learning outcomes have constantly changed over the years, collaborative efforts to make explicit what students need to know and be able to do have enabled them better to discuss and debate, with students and through mutual peer review with others, what should be assessed across the curriculum.

Opening a learning community and culture to educational policy analysis

Campus visitors have long probed their own educational policies and cultural characteristics, stimulated by shared values for maximizing student learning, but also by facing their own unique challenges. Alverno faculty members acknowledge that campus conditions and culture matter, and strive to clarify infrastructures and policies so peers may make clear comparisons. Faculties and administrators at institutions larger in scale and programs have sometimes worked at the level of subunits that create their own policies and infrastructures to articulate and support desired outcomes for their students. For example, professional schools of pharmacy have determined and defined explicit outcomes and assessment with support from their national associations. Others have found broader support systems. For example, technical and community colleges that are part of a system, such as Washington State community colleges, have had support for innovation in assessment at the state level.

Alverno is a culture with a heritage of educational values, though we also continually analyze and debate their implications as day-to-day conditions change. More observable characteristics include its smallness, single gender and the community orientation of its Franciscan traditions. Alverno's private college status has supported a mission of continually creating opportunities for diverse, first-generation undergraduate women. This mission requires persuading potential funders to supplement Alverno as a tuition-based institution where most students receive financial aid from grants and loans and then graduate with considerable debt. Alverno studies show that those deeper cultural qualities account for alumnae perspectives: the curriculum is a source of both individual challenge and support to their development of both autonomy and orientation to interdependence in professional and community service (Mentkowski and Associates, 2000).

Across types of institutions, student success in college is a result of creating conditions that matter (Kuh *et al.*, 2005). Kuh *et al.*'s study of twenty institutions (including Alverno), where student bodies consistently gave their institutions high marks for engagement in learning, points to several common educational policies that enabled these institutions to outperform peers: 'Assessment serves many important institutional purposes, only one of which is measuring student performance. . . . Curricular improvements that enhance student learning are typically grounded in a contemporary fusion of the liberal and practical arts' (pp. 279, 286). At the same time, both small liberal arts colleges and large universities continue to struggle to balance teaching and research even as faculty reported that 'expectations for scholarship were as high as they've ever been, even increasing' (p. 288).

Debating conceptual frameworks for what to learn

At any one point in time, Alverno faculty members are having free and frank discussions about particular issues and potential revisions. Over the years, peers have also enjoined debates about Alverno's conceptual frameworks, especially when they have experienced its educational values and learning culture during a campus visit. This peer review strategy means clarifying frameworks from multiple disciplinary perspectives so both we and our peers can continually probe implications.

One educational assumption that leads to questioning the accessibility and adaptability of Alverno's conceptual frameworks concerns the ways that faculty members determine what students should learn. What does it mean that required learning outcomes are articulated as abilities integrated in the disciplines? Alverno gradually evolved this definition of student learning outcomes as abilities:

> *Abilities* are complex combinations of motivations, dispositions, attitudes, values, strategies, behaviors, self-perceptions, and knowledge of concepts and of procedures: 'These combinations are dynamic and interactive, and they can be acquired and developed both through education and experience. Abilities become a cause of effective performance when these components are integrated. A complex ability cannot be observed directly; it must be inferred from performances . . . "Ability" is a *concept* that communicates, because it is also *experienced*. One can conceptualize abilities and also experience having or using one's abilities in situations' . . . Abilities are connected to multiple intelligences that, to some degree, may be both inherent in the person and strong dispositions by the time students reach college. Situated learning perspectives further emphasize how context is inseparable from the person and developed abilities . . . That means assisting learners in integrating their abilities with their unique qualities – an often untapped reservoir of human potential – and to integrate their developing abilities with the domains of knowledge in their field of study.
>
> (Mentkowski and Associates, 2000: 10)

This complex meaning of abilities is central to Alverno's mission but may contrast sharply with that of other colleges. It stems from a philosophy that education should develop the whole person – mind, heart and spirit – as well as intellectual capability. Abilities are holistic in that they are gradually integrated in the developing identity and maturity of the person. This assumption is often particular to liberal arts colleges – and yet it also reflects why Alverno evolved an integrated liberal arts and professions curriculum. Thus, student learning of specialized disciplinary content and practicing the expertise of a profession is maximized, faculty members found, when abilities and disciplines are integrated frameworks for learning (Riordan and Roth, 2005).

Alverno faculty members across the professions such as nursing, teaching and management have concluded that broad abilities, which may look easily transferable on the surface (e.g., communication, problem solving, analysis), are best learned in depth in a discipline and within a coherent curriculum that scaffolds increasing levels of complexity, so students can experience and master integrative and transferable learning outcomes (Doherty *et al.*, 1997). Thus, instructors assist students to experience learning outcomes situated in a course, but also situated within the broad content of arts, humanities, sciences and a major field of specialized study. As instructors determine and define learning outcomes explicitly and interactively with students, they also make outcomes open to debate with peers across other departments and learned societies.

Debating conceptual frameworks for what to assess

Another educational assumption that challenges accessibility and adaptability of any student assessment process involves the kind of student work that faculty members, external assessors and students themselves use to demonstrate achievement. For Alverno, complex abilities are made visible, and so observable, in multidimensional performance assessment. Thus, an example of student work is a sample of performance that instructors, peers, external assessors and even the student will assess. The following definition of performance may distinguish Alverno assessment, and contrast with definitions at other colleges.

> By performance we denote an individual's discretionary and dynamic action in an ambiguous situation that effectively meets some contextually conditioned standard of excellence. Such multidimensional performance goes beyond technical or narrowly specified task performance. Performance entails the whole dynamic nexus of the individual's intentions, thoughts, feelings, and construals in a dynamic line of action and his or her entanglement in an evolving situation and its broader context. Such a context may be within or across work, family, civic, or other settings.
>
> (Rogers *et al.*, in press)

The Alverno faculty deals with the complex nature of performance in student assessment just as it has dealt with the complex nature of knowledge. For ability-based learning outcomes, instructors specify performance criteria for observation, analysis/interpretation and judgment of samples of student work. The faculty further specifies criteria or rubrics developmentally, at beginning, intermediate or advanced levels. For students at the intermediate level of valuing, for example, students will be asked to explain how core values of a specific discipline contribute to the development of principles and policies in the broader community, then how their own commitments and decisions contribute to the development of principles and policies in broader communities, and ultimately constructively critique decisions and policies emerging from various value frameworks. In doing so, an individual instructor in a course gradually opens up complex pictures of what effective performance looks like for his or her students.

Instructors at most colleges also use examples of expert performance in a discipline (e.g., this Booker prize-winning novel; that new method for understanding the structure of genetic material) for students to critique in essays or model in lab experiments. Alverno faculty members, in particular, directly assist students to infer what disciplinary standards may have been met by, for example, explicitly assessing for analysis in literature (show using metaphor to evoke emotion) and problem solving in science (make statistical comparisons across samples).

There is increasing evidence for the accessibility and adaptability of the Alverno conceptual frameworks for what to learn and assess. Many other faculties now have student learning outcomes identified across their curricula (e.g., communication, critical thinking) and expect students to perform them for assessment in situations from essays to internships. Still, how these outcomes are specifically defined and assessed sets departments and institutions apart from each other. Thus, there is no substitute in any setting, Alverno faculty members believe, for collaborative faculty judgment in deciding what to teach, what students should learn, and what to assess. Is this an impossible barrier for other colleges who are learning from each other? It can be, but it is also an affirmation of the essential role of a faculty in any college: a faculty takes collective responsibility for student learning and the meaning of the baccalaureate degree.

Connecting learning principles to elements of assessment

Given the historic challenges of any faculty member's role in assessment, it has become all the more important to ground any assessment approach in learning principles that also ground teaching. Assessment, like teaching, maximizes faculty investment when it is also a source of student learning. Coherence of ideas across settings (e.g., learning principles) and elements of systems (e.g., feedback and self assessment) is a better ground for evaluating replication of practice than the particular construction of practices found in any one setting (National Research Council, Committee on Scientific Principles for Education Research, 2002). These learning principles have shaped the elements of Alverno assessment-as-learning:

- If learning that lasts is active and independent, integrative and experiential, *assessment must judge performance in contexts related to life roles.*
- If learning that lasts is self-aware, reflective, self assessed and self-regarding, *assessment must include explicitness of expected outcomes, public criteria and student self assessment.*
- If learning that lasts is developmental and individual, *assessment must include multiplicity and be cumulative and expansive.*
- If learning that lasts is interactive and collaborative, *assessment must include feedback and external perspectives as well as performance.*
- If learning that lasts is situated and transferable, *assessment must be multiple in mode and context.* (See Alverno College Faculty, 1979/1994; Mentkowski and Associates, 2000.)

Learning principles can more readily ground the role of assessment as an evolving system in continual transformation when a college culture and curriculum are learning centered.

Studying evidence for how assessment-as-learning benefits student achievement

A further way of judging adaptability is for peers to examine the evidence for *immediate benefits for learners* as a guide to how much time and effort to invest in designing assessment. For example, we found that as learning outcomes became more accessible, students began to focus their informal conversation with their instructors on more than strategies for meeting deadlines or externally motivated goals (Mentkowski and Associates, 2000). By requiring student peer assessment along with collaborative learning (social interaction and teamwork), instructors jump-started learning relationships among students that assisted them to respect what each person brought to the class rather than to categorize a peer as more or less smart. By refocusing the comparison away from ranking to performance by the self, faculty members guided students to rely on each other's expertise, as well as to challenge it. Classmates began to hold each other to expectations for completing joint work more characteristic of authentic teamwork situations.

A useful strategy Alverno faculty members developed showed students how to use broad abilities (e.g., social interaction, effective citizenship) and more particular assessment criteria to analyze and interpret their own performances and shape their learning plans. We found some key ways that developmental performance criteria supported learning. These criteria made faculty standards accessible through a common language so students and faculty members could discuss student work without artificially limiting student creativity and unique expression. As a result, effective feedback became grounded in observations of performance, and made differences more visible in student and faculty constructions of what students had learned. Further, assessors could substantiate their judgments in order to come to a broad consensus with other assessors, as in 'ready for student teaching'.

Alverno research showed that students who analyzed their performance in relation to criteria for judgment could readily retrieve and apply criteria to a particular performance, and so became able to improve or innovate in a situation quite different from the typical setting of a college-administered examination. These standards, distinguishable by experts, had usually not been well articulated to the student. As the ability-based curriculum evolved, we found that students learned to identify strategies for analyzing and improving performance in a new situation as they also became better able to distinguish between levels in their own performances. Faculty members took on more responsibility for developing this kind of independent learner and saw themselves as accountable to students for how their preparation in one course contributed to their performance in another. Thus, faculty members became more likely to attribute learning to perseverance and practice rather than general intelligence: 'Yes, the course of study worked for her' rather than 'She has been a star from the beginning; it has been interesting watching her unfold.'

Two elements of assessment, we found, flow from this visibility of performance: *feedback* and *self assessment*. Feedback requires interactive and collaborative learning, and maximizes learning from one of its most powerful elements – student and faculty interaction. Thus, assessment began to focus face-to-face interactions between teachers and students on expectations and improvements, and provided more opportunities for intervening in students' misconceptions about concepts, ideas and theories as expressed in classes, essays, projects or internships.

Self assessment is the ability of a student to observe, analyze and judge her/his performance on the basis of explicit, public criteria and determine how s/he can improve it (Alverno College Faculty, 2000). Once students learned to self assess with more confidence, they became much more able to open themselves up to considering different points of view on their work, from an external assessor, internship mentor or faculty member in another discipline who was requiring mastery of a quite different set of theoretical frameworks (physics rather than biology) or writing style (APA publication standards rather than the *Chicago Manual of Style*). Self assessment has become increasingly central to the faculty's understanding of learning. Further, a group of faculty and researchers are currently studying the benefits of the Diagnostic Digital Portfolio, Alverno's patented, web-based process of self assessment and reflection over time. It appears to be a more tangible tool for students to plan for their future learning and performing in college and across future settings and roles.

Review by colleagues from other institutions of the adaptability of our curricular approach to student assessment-as-learning also has meant probing for *long-term benefits for learners*. Can students, as a result of the assessment process, transfer their learning to settings outside the classroom and the college, and to various roles they choose after college? Is their learning deep, durable, responsible and usable? Presumably, based on evidence for this kind of impact on learning, colleagues at other colleges could make their own independent judgments about the likelihood that an assessment process might be worth the investment for their own students. Yet how might any educator know?

As Alverno faculty members continually improved their practice, they began to recognize that ongoing educational research on curriculum, its causes and long-term results were critical to improving practice. Sustained research by Alverno's educational research and evaluation department confirmed that the set of learning principles and related elements of the assessment process were transferable, with the caveat that techniques or strategies needed to be appropriately situated in courses.

Research on what kind of learning lasts opened up how students became able to integrate and transfer their learning across a wide variety of situations and roles. For example, complex abilities become theories of knowledge and performance. Learners cycle through using abilities as metacognitive strategies to recognize patterns, to think while they are performing, to think about frameworks, and to engage in knowledge restructuring as they demonstrate their learning in performance assessments. Through cycles of self assessment, reflective learning and envisioning and monitoring their own role performance, students gain a sense of self-confidence rooted in their capacities. The student develops an identity as a learner and a professional. Engaging diverse approaches, views and activities fosters independent learning that becomes self-directed and leads to further development as a whole person, appreciation of multiple perspectives and mutuality, and breadth of learning. More specifically, studies showed that students develop the self assessment ability through practice with assessment-as-learning and that this accounts in part for effective performance after college. Alumnae continued to become even more articulate about and able to master new learning in complex situations than was the case at the completion of their degree. This kind of mastery is evident in alumna performance samples five years after college (Mentkowski and Associates, 2000; Rogers and Mentkowski, 2004).

Anticipating challenges to adaptability

A faculty invested in designing and implementing assessment-as-learning needs to anticipate inherent challenges that flow from both internally authored and externally authored studies of innovation at Alverno. Collaborative scholarship among groups of assessment leaders from various disciplines has illuminated the challenges (Mentkowski and Loacker, 2002). Scholars outside the college have independently researched transferable elements of effective curricula at Alverno, and many of these studies involve comparisons with other higher learning institutions (e.g., Colby *et al.*, 2003; Darling-Hammond, 2000; Dean and Lauer, 2003; Ewens, 1979; Hinett, 1995; Kuh *et al.*, 2005; Winter *et al.*, 1981). Four challenges follow.

One challenge is continually adjusting an assessment system to maximize learning and debating inherent models of motivation. Alverno students, we have found, benefit by unlearning their relationship to marks and grades, but many other institutions are locked into educational policies that require them. Rather than motivating students through competing with peers for scarce rewards, the Alverno faculty's strategy was to remove the GPA – the grade point average – as the target. The faculty replaced it with evidence-based judgments about whether students had met developmental performance criteria for publicly defined ability levels required for graduation, as they were specified by the various departments in the disciplinary and professional fields. Thus, students who had usually judged themselves both more and less successful by the GPA indicator faced ambiguity in self-definition. They had to learn to concentrate their energy on analyzing samples of their own performance in order to meet faculty members' expectations. Observing classmates' performances called for learning about many ways to demonstrate criteria, rather than managing competitive stress. And instructors found they had to guide a student to sit beside her own performance and to critique it interactively along with the faculty member. The latter, in turn, had to open up broad abilities with explicit criteria that made his or her own expertise more available to the student for comparison with her own beginning efforts.

The power of this approach became visible when students found they could leave their test anxiety aside, and use their emotional energy for meeting standards they once thought were either beyond their individual talents or that had merely confirmed their usual place toward the top of the class. And faculty members were gradually able to rely on students to transfer their learning to increasingly ambiguous and complex assignments without eliciting a flurry of inappropriate memorization. Rather, students became more likely to do a focused review of concepts that might apply across a number of challenging situations (e.g., define the new paradigm, articulate assumptions, synthesize information and judge potential impact).

A second challenge that follows is to master the continual analysis of current student performances for criteria that were not met, were matched or were exceeded.

Standing aside in this way has helped faculty members figure out where to target redesign of assessment for alignment with teaching and learning. The particular structures a faculty uses to fit together various program components are often specific to one college, making examples of efforts to align teaching, learning and assessment usually institution-specific. Nonetheless, making particular practices accessible to another faculty can lead to identifying issues that no one faculty can easily solve alone: creating assessment processes that are coherent within the context of practice but also reflect the diversity of voices, sources of ideas and evidence; or assessing unique learning outcomes that respect individual differences but also certify for common disciplinary expectations and societal and professional standards.

A third challenge for a faculty is integrating theories of measurement and judgment in designing assessment systems. This implies acknowledging a need for an emerging theory of measurement more common to the sciences that can more readily stand beside a theory of judgment more common to the arts and humanities. The educational sciences were challenged, for the sake of student learning, to move away from norm-referenced assessments that measure individual differences for the purpose of selection and sorting to assessments that probe the multiple ways that learning happens across multiple modes of performance. In that way, many more learners could figure out how to meet expected criteria – a necessary step to becoming licensed as a competent professional (e.g., health sciences, teaching). The arts and humanities were challenged, for the sake of student learning, to become more explicit about their expectations and to make the criteria applied in judging student work more public and accessible to students so that students could gradually use these to evaluate their own progress and use this new learning to engage faculty members more fully in a discussion of how to maximize their unique talents as apprentices in a discipline.

A fourth challenge is understanding the role that student assessment-as-learning plays in learning that lasts – an educational theory of human growth and potential and its set of learning principles. This educational theory of learning that lasts has gradually evolved over the last decades (Mentkowski and Associates, 2000). The theory combines formal research, collaborative inquiry on campus and with consortia of institutions, reviews of literature and practice on how people learn (Bransford *et al.*, 2000; Marton and Booth, 1997; Pellegrino *et al.*, 2001), and shifts in psychometric theory (Mentkowski and Rogers, 1988; Moss, 1992). These diverse sources of ideas and evidence were integrated with continual learning about assessment that emerged from educating an increasingly diverse student population. Over the years, these research findings have illuminated the long-term, deep and durable results for student and alumna learning from Alverno's curriculum. Such systematic research studies have distilled the more transportable and adaptable practices, such as assessment-as-learning, from those that are more situated and context specific. Other researchers have acknowledged Alverno's rigorous educational research base (Baxter Magolda, 2002; Hakel, 2001; Brabeck, 2001; Svinicki, 2002).

Adaptable elements of assessment-as-learning across institutions

Elements of assessment that bridge studies of innovative practices are gradually being articulated and embedded in a range of educational contexts (Banta and Associates, 2002). Many of these result from conducting collaborative analyses of practice. A recent example of deliberative inquiry is the Student Learning Initiative, where a group of twenty-six institutions joined a consortium formed on this premise: a goal of an undergraduate institution is student learning.[4] Each institution sent representatives to Alverno to collaborate over two years to author a framework for student learning (Student Learning Initiative, 2002). In characterizing the process, they noted: 'The institutional representatives shared related but different experiences to shape the framework and to assist one another in addressing common challenges across diverse institutional types and sizes' (p. iv). The following are adaptable elements arrived at by this collaboration.

Student assessment-as-learning:

- Is integral to teaching and learning
- Is designed by faculty to determine each student's degree of success in course or program
- Provides opportunity for students to apply their knowledge and ability in integrated performances in varied settings
- Involves expert observation and judgment in relation to explicit criteria/rubrics
- Involves diagnostic and prescriptive feedback combined with a student's own self assessment to strengthen future performance

(Student Learning Initiative, 2002: 14)

The Student Learning Initiative also defined program, curriculum and institution-wide assessment that builds on student assessment and that supports curricular transformation. While discussion of these other levels of practice is beyond the scope of this chapter, it is notable that these extensions of assessment-as-learning build on similar learning principles.

Program, Curriculum, and Institution-Wide Assessment:

- Is integral to learning about student learning
- Creates processes that assist faculty, staff, and administrators to improve student learning
- Involves inquiry to judge program value and effectiveness for fostering student learning
- Generates multiple sources of feedback to faculty, staff, and administrators about patterns of student and alumni performance in relation to learning outcomes that are linked to curriculum

- Makes comparisons of student and alumni performance to standards, criteria, or indicators (faculty, disciplinary, professional, accrediting, certifying, legislative) to create public dialogue
- Yields evidence-based judgments of how students and alumni benefit from the curriculum, co-curriculum, and other learning contexts
- Guides curricular, co-curricular, institution-wide improvements

(Student Learning Initiative, 2002: 22)

The experiences and deliberative inquiries from working with still other multi-institution consortia (ten consortia made up of a hundred institutions) identify converging guidelines for institutional transformation toward learning-centered education (Mentkowski and Associates, 2000: 459–64). In Alverno's experience, and that of its partners, curricular transformation does not begin with assessment. Rather, it extends from continual reframing of what a faculty decides should be taught, what and how its students learn, and how students experience a curriculum as learning centered.

Summary

The higher education literature is studded with references to best practices and to the institutions that use them. What is not clear is how to support mutual peer review such that learning about innovations happens, or how to know what difference it makes for student learning over a longer time frame (Eckel *et al.*, 1997). One support for innovating in assessment is that faculties in quite different institutions can learn from each other, even though one system, in practice, cannot be adopted or replicated by another. This chapter serves educators who are continuously improving their student assessment designs by studying elements of other assessment systems. Seven strategies enable educators to review and learn from diverse curricula and assessment systems. These open assessment theory, research, practice and policy to broader communities of judgment and learning. Toward this goal, Alverno College faculty members have worked to make their emerging educational theory, research, practice and policy more open to critique and comparison. They have benefited from peer review, common insights and other faculties' experiences that together help higher education continuously to improve and establish the variety and validity of assessment systems. The chapter sets forth adaptable elements of student assessment identified through collaborative analyses of practice across institutions. In sum, innovations that are grounded in conceptual frameworks, evidence for student learning, interactive peer review and collaborative scholarship may have implications across departments and colleges and the potential to clarify pathways to institutional change and organizational learning.

Notes

1   The author acknowledges the contributions of the other members of the Alverno College Council for Student Assessment (Dr Jeana Abromeit and Dr Robert O'Brien Hokanson, co-chairs; Zita Allen; Dr Mary Diez; Linda Ehley; Dr Lauralee Guilbault; Dr Daniel

Leister; Dr Dena Lieberman; Dr Georgine Loacker; Dr Kathleen O'Brien; Dr William Rickards; Dr John Savagian; Dr Judeen Schulte; Kelly Talley; and Dr Kate Weishaar). Dr Jeana Abromeit, Dr Kathleen O'Brien and Dr Glen Rogers reviewed the manuscript.
2   Illustrations of ability-based learning and assessment in a major field of study include Biology, Business and Management, Chemistry, English, Environmental Science, History, Management Accounting, Mathematics, Nursing Education, Philosophy, Professional Communication, Psychology, Religious Studies, Social Science and Teacher Education. Each statement reviews learning outcomes of the major field, as well as examples of beginning, intermediate and advanced outcomes in courses. Examples of assessment criteria and strategies include both course and integrative assessments that require students to draw on their expertise across courses. Order from Alverno College Institute at <http://www.alverno.edu/for_educators/publications. html#tab> (see Other Publications) or Alverno College Institute, 3400 S. 43rd Street, PO Box 343922, Milwaukee, WI 53234–3922; phone (414) 382–6087; fax (414) 382–6354; email institute@alverno.edu. The Alverno College Institute offers a one-day seminar each semester and a weeklong summer workshop for educators from all levels, K–12 through professional schools. See <http://www.alverno.edu/for_educators/ institute.html> or <http://depts.alverno.edu/ere/>.
3   Alverno College's Fall 2004 enrollment was 2241 students, including weekday and weekend College undergraduates and 188 students in the Weekend College co-ed Master of Arts in Education program. Sixty-one percent of Alverno students come from the Milwaukee metropolitan area. Nearly 37 per cent are students of color and over 70 per cent are first-generation college students. Alverno has 102 full-time and 116 part-time members of the faculty.
4   The twenty-six participating institutions of higher education included: Alverno College; Avila College; Birmingham-Southern College; Bowling Green State University; California State University, Fullerton; California State University, Monterey Bay; Central Missouri State University; Clayton College and State University; DePaul University School for New Learning; Fort Valley State University; Huston-Tillotson College; Indiana University of Pennsylvania; Indiana University Purdue University Indianapolis; James Madison University; Niagara University; North Carolina State University; Olivet College; Rivier College; Rose-Hulman Institute of Technology; Samford University; Seton Hill College; State University of New York College at Fredonia; Truman State University; University of Alaska Southeast; University of Washington; and University of Wisconsin-La Crosse.

References

Alverno College Faculty (1976/2005) *Ability-based learning outcomes: teaching and assessment at Alverno College*. Milwaukee, WI: Alverno College Institute. (Original work published 1976, revised 1981, 1985, 1989, 1992 and 2005.)
—— (1979/1994) *Student assessment-as-learning at Alverno College*. Milwaukee, WI: Alverno College Institute. (Original work published 1979, revised 1985 and 1994.)
—— (2000) *Self assessment at Alverno College*, in G. Loacker (ed.). Milwaukee, WI: Alverno College Institute.
Banta, T. W., and Associates (2002) *Building a scholarship of assessment*. San Francisco: Jossey-Bass.
Baxter Magolda, M. B. (2002) Review of *Learning that lasts: integrating learning, development, and performance in college and beyond*, *Journal of Higher Education*, 73(5), 660–6.
Brabeck, M. M. (2001) Review of *Learning that lasts: integrating learning, development, and performance in college and beyond*, *Journal of Moral Education*, 30(4), 404–7.

Bransford, J. D., Brown, A. L. and Cocking, R. R. (eds) (2000) *How people learn: brain, mind, experience, and school* (expanded edn). Washington, DC: National Academy Press.

Colby, A., Ehrlich, T., Beaumont, E. and Stephens, J. (2003) *Educating citizens: preparing America's undergraduates for lives of moral and civic responsibility*. San Francisco: Jossey-Bass.

Darling-Hammond, L. (ed.) (2000) *Studies of excellence in teacher education: preparation in the undergraduate years*. Washington, DC: American Association of Colleges for Teacher Education.

Dean, C. B. and Lauer, P. A. (2003) *Systematic evaluation for continuous improvement of teacher preparation. Volume 1: Cross-case analysis*. Washington, DC: Mid-continent Research for Education and Learning.

Doherty, A., Chenevert, J., Miller, R. R., Roth, J. L. and Truchan, L. C. (1997) Developing intellectual skills, in J. G. Gaff, J. L. Ratcliff and Associates (eds), *Handbook of the undergraduate curriculum: a comprehensive guide to purposes, structures, practices, and change* (pp. 170–89). San Francisco: Jossey-Bass.

Eckel, P., Green, M. and Hill, B. (1997) *Transformational change: defining a journey*. Washington, DC: American Council on Education.

Ewens, T. (1979) Transforming a liberal arts curriculum: Alverno College, in G. Grant and Associates (eds), *On competence: a critical analysis of competence-based reforms in higher education* (pp. 259–98). San Francisco: Jossey-Bass.

Hakel, M. D. (2001) Learning that lasts [review of *Learning that lasts: integrating learning, development, and performance in college and beyond*], *Psychological Science*, 12, 433–4.

Hinett, K. (1995) Fighting the assessment war: the idea of assessment-in-learning, *Quality in Higher Education*, 1(3), 211–22.

Kuh, G. D., Kinzie, J., Schuh, J. H., Whitt, E. J. and Associates (2005) *Student success in college: creating conditions that matter*. San Francisco: Jossey-Bass.

Marton, F. and Booth, S. (1997) *Learning and awareness*. Mahwah, NJ: Erlbaum.

Mentkowski, M. and Associates (2000) *Learning that lasts: integrating learning, development, and performance in college and beyond*. San Francisco: Jossey-Bass.

Mentkowski, M. and Loacker, G. (2002) Enacting a collaborative scholarship of assessment, in T. W. Banta and Associates (eds), *Building a scholarship of assessment* (pp. 82–99). San Francisco: Jossey-Bass.

Mentkowski, M. and Rogers, G. (1988) *Establishing the validity of measures of college student outcomes*. Milwaukee, WI: Alverno College Institute.

Moss, P. A. (1992) Shifting conceptions of validity in educational measurement: implications for performance assessment, *Review of Educational Research*, 62(3), 229–58.

National Research Council, Committee on Scientific Principles for Education Research (2002) *Scientific research in education*, R. J. Shavelson and L. Towne (eds). Washington, DC: National Academy Press.

Pellegrino, J. W., Chudowsky, N. and Glaser, R. (eds) (2001) *Knowing what students know: the science and design of educational assessment*. Washington, DC: National Academy Press.

Riordan, T. and Roth, J. (eds) (2005) *Disciplines as frameworks for student learning: teaching the practice of the disciplines*. Sterling, VA: Stylus Publishing.

Rogers, G. and Mentkowski, M. (2004) Abilities that distinguish the effectiveness of five-year alumna performance across work, family, and civic roles: a higher education validation, *Higher Education Research and Development*, 23(3), 347–74.

Rogers, G., Mentkowski, M. and Reisetter Hart, J. (in press) Adult holistic development and multidimensional performance, in C. H. Hoare (ed.), *Handbook of adult development and learning*. New York: Oxford University Press.

Student Learning Initiative (2002) *Student learning: a central focus for institutions of higher education*, A. Doherty, in T. Riordan and J. Roth (eds). Milwaukee, WI: Alverno College Institute.

Svinicki, M. (2002) Book review: the Alverno College experience: a case with many levels of interpretation [review of *Learning that lasts: integrating learning, development, and performance in college and beyond*], *Contemporary Psychology*, 47(3), 272–4.

Winter, D. G., McClelland, D. C. and Stewart, A. J. (1981) *A new case for the liberal arts: assessing institutional goals and student development*. San Francisco: Jossey-Bass.

5 Rethinking technology-supported assessment practices in relation to the seven principles of good feedback practice

David Nicol and Colin Milligan

Introduction

This chapter explores how formative assessment and feedback might be used to promote the development of self-regulated learning in contexts in which face-to-face and online learning are integrated. Self-regulated learning (SRL) refers to the active control by students of some aspects of their own learning; for example, the setting of learning goals, and the monitoring and regulating of progress towards the attainment of these goals (Zimmerman and Schunk, 2001; Pintrich, 1995). Empowering students to self-regulate their learning is a key goal of higher education and of lifelong learning. In this chapter, formative assessment is defined as 'assessment that is specifically intended to provide feedback on performance to improve and accelerate learning' (Sadler, 1998: 77). In this context, feedback is information about how a student has performed in relation to some standard or goal (knowledge of results).

Nicol and Macfarlane-Dick (2004; in press) have argued that both internal and external feedback are important for the development of SRL. All students generate internal feedback as they monitor engagement with learning activities and tasks. This feedback derives from an assessment of how they are performing in the light of what they are attempting (defined by internally set goals). Strengthening this capacity to self-assess and to generate internal feedback is indispensable to the development of self-regulated learning (Boud, 2000; Yorke, 2003). Feedback is also provided externally by others; for example, by teachers and peers. It is assumed here that such external feedback should also focus on scaffolding students towards greater self-regulation in learning.

The seven principles of good feedback practice

Nicol and Macfarlane-Dick (2004; in press) identified from the research literature seven principles of good feedback practice that might help support learner self-regulation. Good feedback practice:

- helps clarify what good performance is (goals, criteria, expected standards);
- facilitates the development of reflection and self-assessment in learning;
- delivers high-quality information to students about their learning;

- encourages teacher and peer dialogue around learning;
- encourages positive motivational beliefs and self-esteem;
- provides opportunities to close the gap between current and desired performance;
- provides information to teachers that can be used to help shape the teaching.

The following sections provide a rationale for each principle in relation to the development of self-regulation and to the research on formative assessment and feedback. These sections also demonstrate how each principle might be implemented in blended learning contexts. In this chapter, technology-supported assessment refers to assessments that are wholly online and to those that involve online–offline interactions. The latter might include an online test of in-class or out-of-class learning (e.g., a series of multiple-choice questions to test knowledge or understanding) or an offline assessment of an online activity (e.g., a student's contribution to a discussion forum).

Principle 1: Good feedback practice 'helps clarify what good performance is (goals, criteria, expected standards)'

Students can only regulate and self-correct their progress towards learning goals if they have a clear understanding of the goals and of the standards and criteria that define goal attainment (Sadler, 1989; Black and Wiliam, 1998). In academic settings, understanding goals means that there must be a reasonable degree of overlap between the task goals in the mind of the student and the goals originally set by the teacher. This is logically essential given that it is the student's goals, not the teacher's, that serve as the criteria for self-regulation. Nonetheless, there is considerable research evidence showing mismatches between teachers' and students' conceptions of goals and of assessment criteria and standards.

Hounsell (1997) has shown that tutors and students often have quite different conceptions about the goals and criteria for essays in undergraduate courses in history and in psychology and that poor essay performance is correlated with the degree of mismatch. In a similar vein, Norton (1990) has shown that when students were asked to rank specific assessment criteria for an essay task they produced quite different rankings from those of their teachers. Weak and incorrect conceptions of goals not only influence what students do but limit the value of feedback information. If students do not share (at least in part) their tutor's conceptions of assessment goals (criteria/standards) then the feedback information they receive is unlikely to 'connect' (Hounsell, 1997). In this case, it will be difficult for students to assess gaps between required and actual performance.

One commonplace way of clarifying task requirements (goals/criteria/standards) in e-learning contexts is to publish (e.g., within a virtual learning environment, VLE) descriptions of assessment criteria and/or standards for different levels of achievement. However, many studies have shown that it is difficult to make assessment criteria and standards explicit through such written documentation (Rust *et al.*, 2003). Most criteria for complex tasks are difficult to articulate and are often 'tacit' and unarticulated even in the mind of the teacher (Yorke, 2003). Hence there is a need for strategies that complement online criteria. One strategy is to create an online discussion space where students feel free to ask questions about assessment tasks and their criteria, or are even prompted to do so (Palloff and Pratt, 2005).

Another approach that has proved particularly powerful in clarifying goals and assessment requirements has been to provide students with 'exemplars' of performance (Orsmond *et al.*, 2002). Exemplars are effective because they define an objective standard against which students can compare their work. In an online or blended learning context, exemplars are easily made available to students for consultation, for example, within a virtual learning environment. However, it might be more effective to supplement this strategy with additional activities that encourage students to interact with, and externalise, criteria and standards. For instance, groups of students might be required, before carrying out an assignment, to examine two exemplars of a completed task (e.g., a good and a poor essay) and to post within an online discussion board their reasons why one is better than the other, including the criteria they had used to make this judgement. The teacher might then clarify any areas of misunderstanding (mismatches in conceptions) and publish online a criterion sheet that draws on this student-generated discussion.

Principle 2: Good feedback practice 'facilitates the development of reflection and self-assessment in learning'

One of the most effective ways to develop self-regulation in students is to provide them with opportunities to practise regulating aspects of their own learning (Pintrich, 1995). Students are (at some level) already engaged in monitoring gaps between their learning intentions and the effects that they are producing. This monitoring of performance is a by-product of purposeful engagement in learning tasks. However, in order to build on this, and to develop systematically the learner's capacity for self-regulation, teachers need to create more structured opportunities for self-monitoring and the judging of progression to goals. Self-assessment tasks are a good way of doing this, as are activities that encourage reflection on progress in learning.

Over the last decade there has been an increasing interest in self-assessment in higher education (Boud, 1995; Falchikov, 2005). For example, Boud (2000: 151) maintains that the development of lifelong learning skills requires that assessment must 'move from the exclusive domain of the assessors [teachers] into the hands of learners' while Sadler (1998) argues that the intention of formative assessment should be to equip students gradually with the same evaluative skills that their teachers possess. These writers are concerned that an overemphasis on teacher assessment might increase students' dependency on others rather than develop their ability to self-assess and self-correct.

A key principle behind self-assessment and self-regulation is that students are involved both in identifying the standards/criteria that apply to their work and in making judgements about how their work relates to these standards (Boud, 1986 and 2000). Hence Principle 1 above (clarify goals, criteria and standards) might be seen as a prerequisite for the effective implementation of Principle 2 (self-assessment).

In the online context, there are many ways of organising for self-assessment and many tools to support these processes. The most common practice, however, is to create and administer online objective tests and quizzes that can be used by students to assess their understanding of a topic or area of study (Bull and McKenna, 2004). Students taking online tests normally get some feedback about their level of understanding either as an overall test score or as automatically delivered feedback comments. While such tests do provide for a degree of self-regulation there are important limitations with these methods. First, and importantly, students usually have no role in setting goals or standards for online tests and are therefore not able to clarify the test question or its purpose (which might violate Principle 1). Second, the feedback provided is generally limited and predetermined during test construction. Hence there is limited scope for individualisation of feedback comments. Third, many researchers maintain that multiple-choice-type questions, the most common format for online objective tests, are not good at testing for high-level cognitive learning, although some would argue that this is dependent on how the tests are constructed (Cox, 1976; Johnstone and Ambusaidi, 2000).

Despite these difficulties, there is a role for online objective tests in the development of self-regulation. Research shows that students find such tests useful as a way of checking their level of understanding and that they will often make repeated attempts at such tests in order to enhance their knowledge and skill acquisition. Also, there are ways to make online objective tests more learner-focused and empowering. For example, students could submit their own test questions for inclusion in the test bank. As well as benefiting learning and motivation, student-generated questions would help the teacher build up a bank of questions that could be reusable across new student cohorts.

Another format for online assessment involves students interacting with a simulation (e.g., of an engineering or business process). This can be a more effective form of self-assessment in that it aligns more closely than objective tests with the notion of self-regulation. Wiggins (2001: 46) describes effective feedback as 'information about how a person performs in the light of what was attempted – intent versus effect, actual versus ideal performance'. In a simulation the student gets direct, immediate and dynamic feedback about the effects of their actions (Thomas and Milligan, 2004). Feedback within simulations is also likely to be clearer to the performer, and its links to specific targets and standards more transparent.

A third approach to self-assessment is to provide students with opportunities to assess their own work as part of an assignment submission. Online environments make this easy to manage (see Davies, 2003). A related approach is to provide opportunities for students to assess and provide feedback on each other's work. Peer processes help develop the skills needed to make objective judgements against standards, skills which are often transferred when students turn to regulating their own work (Gibbs, 1999). Software now exists which supports peer feedback processes (Bhalerao and Ward, 2001; Davies, 2003). For example, Bhalero and

Ward (2001) created a peer assessment system that can be delivered from within a VLE. In this system, written work (scripts) submitted by students is duplicated, anonymised and distributed to other students for feedback comments and marks. The scripts are then returned to the student who submitted them. Hence, the student has the opportunity both to comment on the work of other students and to receive feedback comments from a number of peers on their own work. Such document management software can significantly alleviate the workload burden of managing peer assessment.

Another way to involve students directly in monitoring and regulating their own learning is through portfolios. The construction of a portfolio often requires that students reflect on their achievements and select work that meets defined standards. In addition, students might be asked to write a reflective essay or keep a reflective journal in relation to their learning. Portfolios help increase students' sense of ownership over their work and help them to integrate learning across different subject domains. Many educationalists have been experimenting with electronic portfolios (e-portfolios) because they add new dimensions to this form of assessment (see Chapter 17). For example, students can combine various media (print, graphics, sound, animations, video, etc.) in e-portfolios and they can also integrate and interrelate selections of their work (e.g., through hyper-linking) in ways that depict their understanding of the subject matter (Nicol *et al.*, in press). E-portfolios are also generally easier to maintain and share than traditional paper-based portfolios and they can allow students more control over how they select and present coursework for assessment.

Principle 3: Good feedback practice 'delivers high-quality information to students about their learning'

While research shows that teachers have an important role in developing their students' capacity to self-assess and self-correct, they also have a key role in providing external feedback. Feedback from teachers is a source against which students can check their internal constructions of goals, criteria and standards. It also helps students become more aware of their strengths and weaknesses, thereby enabling them to take steps to address deficiencies in their own learning (Pintrich, 1995). In effect, feedback from teachers can help substantiate student self-regulation.

In online contexts some significant work has been carried out to assist teachers in giving feedback on written work to large groups of students. Denton (2001) has developed an electronic feedback system that enables teachers to construct feedback reports to students. These reports contain general comments, standard comments (about specific elements of the work) and personal comments (to the individual). Standard feedback comments represent a time-saving feature of this system; they can be selected by number or from a drop-down list and attached to student work. Another advantage of this system is that feedback comments are typed and hence more readable than handwritten responses. Denton reports that teachers claim they can give higher-quality feedback and that the system saves time. However, one problem with the work of Denton and others is that hardly any research has been carried out to identify what types of feedback comments are most effective. This is as true for traditional written feedback using proformas as it is for online systems (Nicol and Macfarlane-Dick, in press). Most research is concerned that feedback is timely, is focused on high-level learning and that the tone is not judgemental.

Nicol and Macfarlane-Dick, in addressing this issue in traditional assessment contexts, offered the following definition for good-quality external feedback based on the notion of learner self-regulation: '[It] is information that helps students trouble-shoot their own performance and self-correct; that is, it helps the students take action to reduce the discrepancy between their intentions and the resulting effects' (Nicol and Macfarlane-Dick, in press). This definition implies that feedback comments from teachers should in some way help scaffold the development of learner self-regulation. But how is this to be achieved in blended or online learning contexts? Wiggins (2001) maintains that quality feedback is descriptive rather than evaluative; it provides information about the gap between current student performance (effect) and the goals, standards and criteria that define academic competence. Comments that provide non-specific advice such as praise/blame or exhortations (e.g., 'try harder') or unclear statements ('this essay is poorly structured') do not help develop self-regulation. Descriptive information about performance in relation to stated assessment criteria is more effective and more likely to be acted upon by students. While linking comment banks to assessment criteria is easily accomplished with online forms, the challenge for the future is to enhance the application of Denton's system by providing guidance to teachers on how to build up data banks of feedback comments grounded in educational principles such as those provided by Wiggins.

In the literature on essay assessment, some researchers have tried to formulate guidelines for feedback comments that show a correspondence with the principle underlying the definition of feedback quality given above. Lunsford (1997) examined the feedback comments given by writing experts on students' essays. From his analysis he made a key proposal – that quality feedback comments should indicate to the student how the reader (the teacher) experienced the essay as it was read (i.e., playing back to the students how the essay worked). Such reflective comments (e.g., 'When I read this it made me think . . .') help the student grasp the difference between his or her intentions (goals) and the effects of the writing. Lunsford also advises that the comments should, where possible, offer corrective advice (about the writing process as well as the content) instead of just information about strengths and weaknesses. In relation to self-regulation, Lunsford's 'reader-response' strategy supports the transition from feedback provided by the teacher to students' evaluation of their own writing. However, while it would be easy to provide hyper-links to resources that would help students correct the writing process, it is more difficult to envisage how one might develop a bank of teacher comments to support the kinds of reflective processes suggested by Lunsford. This suggests a degree of individualisation that is better dealt with through dialogic feedback as described in the next section.

An online environment can, however, increase the flexibility and range of feedback delivery. For example, teachers can easily provide feedback to a group of students or to an individual student. And if, as happens in project-based learning, students use online workspace tools to manage the project and to store developing outputs (e.g., reports, diagrams) the teacher can easily monitor progress and give timely feedback both on the processes of learning and on the products.

Principle 4: Good feedback practice 'encourages teacher and peer dialogue around learning'

If external feedback is to help scaffold the development of student self-regulation, it must be understood, internalised and ultimately used by the student to make evaluative judgements about their own learning outcomes. Otherwise it is difficult to see how such feedback could form the basis of corrective action. Yet in the research literature (Chanock, 2000; Hyland, 2000) there is a great deal of evidence that students do not understand the feedback they are given (e.g., 'This essay is not sufficiently analytical') and therefore are not able to use feedback to reduce the gap between their intentions (goals) and the effects they would like to produce (i.e., the student may not know what to do to make the essay 'more analytical'). External feedback as a transmission process involving 'telling' ignores the active role the student must play in constructing meaning from feedback messages and of using this to regulate performance.

One way of increasing the effectiveness of external feedback and the likelihood that the information provided is understood is to conceptualise feedback more as a *dialogue* rather than as information transmission. However, with the current growth in class sizes it can be difficult for the teacher to engage students in dialogue. This is an area where technology can play a crucial role.

Nicol and Boyle (2003) describe the use of a technology called a classroom communication system (CCS) that can be used to enhance feedback dialogue. With a CCS, students make responses to multiple-choice questions (MCQs) presented in class using handsets that send signals to wall-mounted sensors. Responses are collated in real time (through software located on an attached computer) and then displayed by digital projection to the student cohort as a bar chart. This bar chart provides almost immediate quantitative feedback on class responses.

Nicol and Boyle (2003) and Boyle and Nicol (2003) have shown how this simple feedback system can be used to support classroom dialogue. One approach is teacher-facilitated 'class-wide discussion'. After the MCQ responses are collated and presented back to the students, the teacher asks different groups of students to explain the reasoning behind their answers and facilitates discussion across these groups. A second approach is where collated responses are used to trigger 'peer discussion'. Here, students in groups might be asked to convince their neighbour that they have the right answer before they are retested on the same questions. This computer-supported methodology results in students receiving three different levels of feedback – computerised quantitative feedback (bar chart), dialogic feedback from peers (in the peer discussion scenario) and/or class-wide feedback provided by the teacher during facilitated discussion.

In a similar way, dialogue can also be used to make objective tests more effective when delivered in online contexts. For example, Russell and Bullen (2003) in teaching mechanical engineering used a VLE to provide unique weekly assessed tutorial sheets (WATS) to students. These sheets comprised objective tests that were intended to reinforce the delivered lecture materials. Uniqueness was achieved by randomising the data embedded in the tutorial questions. The students tackled the tutorial sheets at a time that suited them and delivered their answers electronically. A key benefit of this procedure was that it prevented students just sharing problem solutions (since they each had a different test) while at the same time it encouraged students to work collaboratively in study groups and to discuss the thinking and reasoning underpinning the tutorial problems. The introduction of this peer feedback around objective online testing was shown to result in higher examination averages and passes.

As well as supporting traditional feedback processes, online and blended learning courses make new kinds of dialogue and assessments possible (MacDonald, 2003). Using online conferencing environments or bulletin boards, it is easy for teachers to organise discussions around different themes or topics. Two unique features of this asynchronous online discussion are that it takes place in writing and there is a delay between contributions. This provides students with opportunities to reflect before making a response in a way that is not possible in classroom discussions (Lea, 2001). Also these discussions are permanently recorded, making them a useful reusable resource. For example, samples of discussions can be archived by the teacher to serve as a form of feedback or as model answers with subsequent student cohorts. Alternatively students can revisit the discussion and reflect on how it progressed. Online conferences are empowering; they enable students not only to reflect but to benefit from the learning of their peers.

Principle 5: Good feedback practice 'encourages positive motivational beliefs and self-esteem'

Motivation, self-esteem and self-regulation are inextricably linked. Garcia (1995: 29) maintains that self-regulated learning is 'a fusion of *skill* and *will*'. Current research suggests that students 'construct their motivation' based on their appraisal of the teaching, learning and assessment context (Paris and Turner, 1994). This construction influences the goals that students set (personal and academic) as well as their commitment to these goals. Feedback can have a positive or a negative effect on motivation and on self-esteem; it influences how students feel about themselves, which in turn affects what and how they learn (Black and Wiliam, 1998).

Online assessment can help increase student motivation (Grebenik and Rust, 2002; Bostock, 2004). First, where objective tests are used students are able to assess their understanding in private and make comparisons with their own learning goals rather than with the performance of other students. This is consistent with research which shows that motivation is higher if students focus effort on making improvements in their own learning rather than just on competing and comparing themselves with their peers (e.g., Elliot and Dweck, 1988). Raising awareness about the learning goals is also essential to the development of self-regulation (Pintrich, 1995). Online simulations and business games are also motivational because students can see the progress they are making towards goals in a dynamic way while receiving immediate feedback.

Another benefit of online objective tests is that students can retake the same test many times. Studies have shown that this can be highly motivational: students will repeat the test many times in an effort to improve their performance (Grebenik and Rust, 2002; Bostock, 2004). This fits well with the argument that teachers should increase the number and frequency of low-stakes assessments (where students get feedback on performance) and correspondingly decrease the number of high-stakes assessments (where marks are given). For example, Gibbs and Simpson (2004) have made this one of their ten conditions of good assessment and feedback practice.

Dweck (1999) has widened the context of motivational research to include considerations of self-theories. She has proposed a developmental model that differentiates students into those who believe that ability is fixed and that there is a limit to what they can achieve (the 'entity view') and those who believe that their ability is malleable and depends on the effort that is input into a task (the 'incremental view'). These views affect how students respond to learning diffi- culties. Those with an entity view (fixed) interpret failure as a reflection of their low ability and are likely to give up whereas those with an incremental view (malleable) interpret this as a challenge or an obstacle to be overcome.

Grant and Dweck (2003) and Yorke and Knight (2004) have confirmed the validity of this model in higher education, with Yorke and Knight showing that one-third of a sample of 2269 undergraduates in first and final years held beliefs in fixed ability. A solution to this issue, and to the issue of learning versus perfor- mance goals, is to focus much more effort on developing our students' ability to manage their own learning. Online learning contexts offer some benefits in this regard. Unlike traditional learning contexts, there is a more detailed record of learning processes and outcomes (e.g., online discussions, records of test performance, draft outputs produced during learning, records of test performance and feedback). Hence it is possible for teachers to set tasks in which students revisit and reanalyse past learning experiences and develop new learning strategies. In this way students can learn to become more effective at self-regulation.

Principle 6: Good feedback practice 'provides opportunities to close the gap between current and desired performance'

According to Yorke (2003), two questions might be asked regarding external feedback. Is the feedback of the best quality? And does it lead to changes in student behaviour? Many researchers have focused on the first question but the second is equally important. External feedback provides an opportunity to close the gap in the learning process between the current learning achievements of the student and the goals set by the teacher. As Boud (2000: 158) notes:

The only way to tell if learning results from feedback is for students to make some kind of response to complete the feedback loop (Sadler, 1989). This is one of the most often forgotten aspects of formative assessment. Unless students are able to use the feedback to produce improved work, through for example, re-doing the same assignment, neither they nor those giving the feedback will know that it has been effective.

Boud's arguments about closing the gap can be viewed in two ways. First, closing the gap is about supporting students while engaged in the act of production of a piece of work. Second, it is about providing opportunities to repeat the same 'task–performance–feedback cycle' by, for example, allowing resubmission. External feedback should support both processes: it should help students to recognise the next steps in learning and how to take them both during production and for the next assignment.

Supporting the act of production requires the generation of concurrent or intrinsic feedback with which students can interact while engaged in an assessment task. This feedback would normally be built into the task (e.g., a group task with peer interaction) or the task might be broken down into components each associated with its own feedback. Many forms of electronic feedback can be automatically generated to support such task engagement (multiple-choice tests, FAQs), with simulations being a particularly good example.

In higher education most students have little opportunity to use directly the feedback they receive to close the gap and make performance improvements, especially in the case of planned assignments. Invariably they move on to the next assessment task soon after feedback is received. While not all work can be re-submitted, many writers argue that resubmissions should play a more prominent role in learning (Boud, 2000). Also, greater emphasis needs to be given to providing feedback on work in progress (e.g., essay structures, plans for reports, sketches, etc.) and to engage students in planning strategies for improvement. Virtual learning environments facilitate this by making tutor–student communication and assignment submissions more efficient. Workflow management tools in VLEs also allow students and staff to keep records of work at different stages.

Principle 7: Good feedback practice 'provides information to teachers that can be used to help shape the teaching'

Good feedback practice is not only about providing good information to the students about learning but about providing good information to teachers. As Yorke (2003: 482) notes: 'The act of assessing has an effect on the assessor as well as the student. Assessors learn about the extent to which they [students] have developed expertise and can tailor their teaching accordingly.' In order to produce feedback that is relevant and informative, teachers themselves need good data about how students are progressing. They also need to be involved in reviewing and reflecting on this data and in taking action to help students close the learning gap.

Frequent assessment tasks, especially diagnostic tests, can help teachers generate cumulative information about students' levels of understanding and skill so that they can adapt their teaching accordingly. This is one of the key ideas behind the use of classroom communication systems (Nicol and Boyle, 2003; Boyle and Nicol, 2003). These researchers have shown how teachers can gain regular feedback information about student learning within large classes by using short test-feedback cycles (see Principle 4). The teacher receives feedback on areas of student difficulty signalled by the spread of responses to multiple-choice tests and through listening to students' explanations of concepts during the class-wide discussions. It is also possible with classroom communication systems to analyse the data kept on the computer about students' responses to tests to identify specific areas of conceptual difficulty that recur from year to year. All this information can be used to shape subsequent teaching.

Online assessment tools can also provide invaluable quantitative and qualitative information to the teacher about student learning. These tools normally have inbuilt reporting functionality. Two types of information are common to online assessment systems – class reporting and individual reporting. At class level, the teacher can identify questions that posed problems across a large cohort of students. From an analysis of student responses, areas of conceptual difficulty in the subject matter or poor questions can be identified and corrective action taken. At the individual level, the strategies used by specific students to problems being tackled can be unpacked and feedback targeted to that individual (Ashton *et al.*, 2004).

Online discussions can also be designed to provide similar information about student learning. By analysing discussions teachers can identify areas of difficulty and teachers and students can share, on a regular basis, their conceptions about both the goals and processes of learning (Stefani and Nicol, 1997).

Conclusion

The use of technology to support assessment practices has a long history. Yet the focus to date has largely been on developing online objective tests rather than on using technologies to address fundamental educational issues. In this chapter we have argued that e-tools are effective when they are allied to assessment approaches that enhance the students' ability to generate internal feedback against standards and to self-regulate their learning. Current technologies can support these processes. Tools to support self-assessment are available, as are tools to support the delivery of teacher and peer feedback, although more research is required to determine the effectiveness of different types of teacher feedback. It is also easy to support dialogic feedback through web-based systems (e.g., VLEs). Overall, new technologies are not only leading to new ways of enhancing current assessment practices and offering new possibilities (e.g., assessing online discussion) but are leading to deeper thinking about how we conceptualise assessment in higher education.

References

Ashton, H. S., Beevers, C. E., Schofield, D. K. and Youngson, M. A. (2004) Informative reports – experiences from the Pass-IT project. Paper presented at the 8th International Computer Assisted Assessment Conference, Loughborough University, UK. Available at <http://sd.lboro.ac.uk/caanew/pastConferences/2004/proceedings/ashton.pdf> (accessed 6 April 2005).

Bhalero, A. and Ward, A. (2001) Towards electronically assisted peer assessment: a case study, *Association for Learning Technology Journal*, 9(1) 26–37.

Black, P. and Wiliam, D. (1998) Assessment and classroom learning, *Assessment in Education*, 5(1), 7–74.

Bostock, S. J. (2004) Motivation and electronic assessment, in S. Alexander and A. Irons (eds), *Effective learning and teaching in computing*. London: RoutledgeFalmer.

Boud, D. (1986) *Implementing student self-assessment*. Sydney: Higher Education Research and Development Society of Australia.

—— (1995) *Enhancing learning through self-assessment*. London: Kogan Page.

—— (2000) Sustainable assessment: rethinking assessment for the learning society, *Studies in Continuing Education*, 22(2), 151–67.

Boyle, J. T. and Nicol, D. J. (2003) Using classroom communication systems to support interaction and discussion in large class settings, *Association for Learning Technology Journal*, 11(3), 43–57.

Bull, J. and McKenna, C. (2004) *Blueprint for computer-assisted assessment*. London: RoutledgeFalmer.

Chanock, K. (2000) Comments on essays: do students understand what tutors write? *Teaching in Higher Education*, 5(1), 95–105.

Cox, K. R. (1976) How did you guess? Or what do multiple choice questions measure? *Medical Journal of Australia*, 1, 884–6.

Davies, P. (2003) Closing the communication loop on computerised peer-assessment of essays, *Association for Learning Technology Journal*, 11(1), 41–54.

Denton, P. (2001) Generating coursework feedback for large groups of students using MS Excel and MS Word, *University Chemistry Education*, 5, 1–8.

Dweck, C. S. (1999) *Self-theories: their role in motivation, personality and development*. Philadelphia: Psychology Press.

Elliot, E. S. and Dweck, C. S. (1988) Goals: an approach to motivation and achievement, *Journal of Personality and Social Psychology*, 54, 5–12.

Falchikov, N. (2005) *Improving assessment through student involvement*. Abingdon: RoutledgeFalmer.

Garcia, T. (1995) The role of motivational strategies in self-regulated learning, in P. R. Pintrich (ed.), *Understanding self-regulated learning*. San Francisco: Jossey-Bass.

Gibbs, G. (1999) Using assessment strategically to change the way students learn, in S. Brown and A. Glasner (eds), *Assessment matters in higher education: choosing and using diverse approaches*. Buckingham: SRHE/Open University Press.

Gibbs, G. and Simpson, C. (2004) Conditions under which assessment supports students' learning, *Learning and Teaching in Higher Education*, 1, 3–31. Available at <http://www.glos.ac.uk/adu/clt/lathe/issue1/index.cfm> (accessed 6 April 2005).

Grant, H. and Dweck, C. S. (2003) Clarifying achievement goals and their impact, *Journal of Personality and Social Psychology*, 85(3), 541–53.

Grebenik, P. and Rust, C. (2002) IT to the rescue, in P. Schwartz and G. Webb (eds), *Assessment: case studies, experience and practice in higher education*. London: Kogan Page.

Hounsell, D. (1997) Contrasting conceptions of essay-writing, in: F. Marton, D. Hounsell and N. Entwistle (eds), *The experience of learning*. Edinburgh: Scottish Academic Press.

Hyland, P. (2000) Learning from feedback on assessment, in A. Booth and P. Hyland (eds), *The practice of university history teaching*. Manchester: Manchester University Press.

Johnstone, A. H. and Ambusaidi, A. (2000) Fixed response: what are we testing?, *Chemistry Education: Research and Practice in Europe*, 1(3), 323–8.

Lea, M. (2001) Computer conferencing and assessment: new ways of writing in higher education, *Studies in Higher Education*, 26(2), 163–81.

Lunsford, R. (1997) When less is more: principles for responding in the disciplines, in M. D. Sorcinelli and P. Elbow (eds), *Writing to learn: strategies for assigning and responding to writing across the disciplines*. San Francisco: Jossey-Bass.

MacDonald, J. (2003) Assessing online collaborative learning: process and product, *Computers and Education*, 40, 377–91.

Nicol, D. J. and Boyle, J. T. (2003) Peer instruction versus class-wide discussion in large classes: a comparison of two interaction methods in the wired classroom, *Studies in Higher Education*, 28(4), 457–73.

Nicol, D. J. and Macfarlane-Dick, D. (2004) Rethinking formative assessment in HE: a theoretical model and seven principles of good feedback practice. Higher Education Academy. Available at <http://www.heacademy.ac.uk/assessment/ASS051D_ SEN LEF_ model.doc> and <http://www.enhancementthemes.ac.uk/uploads/documents/ NicolMacfarlane-Dickpaper-revised.pdf> (both accessed 4 April 2005).

—— (in press) Formative assessment and self-regulated learning: a model and seven principles of good feedback practice, *Studies in Higher Education*.

Nicol, D. J., Littlejohn, A. and Grierson, H. (2005) The importance of structuring information and resources within shared workspaces during collaborative design learning, *Open Learning*, 20(1), 31–49.

Norton, L. S. (1990) Essay writing: what really counts?, *Higher Education*, 20(4), 411–42.

Orsmond, P., Merry, S. and Reiling, K. (2002) The use of formative feedback when using student derived marking criteria in peer and self-assessment, *Assessment and Evaluation in Higher Education*, 27(4), 309–23.

Palloff, R. M. and Pratt, K. (2005) *Collaborating online: learning together in community*. San Francisco: Jossey-Bass.

Paris, S. G. and Turner, J. C. (1994) Situated Motivation, in P. R. Pintrich, D. R. Brown and C. E. Weinstein (eds), *Student motivation, cognition and learning*. Hillsdale, NJ: Lawrence Erlbaum Associates.

Pintrich, P. R. (1995) *Understanding self-regulated learning*. San Francisco: Jossey-Bass.

Russell, M. B. and Bullen, P. R. (2003) Improving student success through the implementation of weekly, student unique tutorial sheets. Paper presented at the 7th International Computer Assisted Assessment Conference, Loughborough University, UK. Available at <http://sd.lboro.ac.uk/caanew/pastConferences/2003/procedings/russell.pdf> (accessed 6 April 2005).

Rust, C., Price, M. and O'Donovan, B. (2003) Improving students' learning by developing their understanding of assessment criteria and processes, *Assessment and Evaluation in Higher Education*, 28(2), 147–64.

Sadler, D. R. (1989) Formative assessment and the design of instructional systems, *Instructional Science*, 18(2), 119–44.

—— (1998) Formative assessment: revisiting the territory, *Assessment in Education*, 5(1), 77–84.

Stefani, L. and Nicol, D. (1997) From teacher to facilitator of collaborative enquiry, in S. Armstrong, G. Thompson and S. Brown (eds), *Facing up to radical changes in universities and colleges*. London: Kogan Page.

Thomas, R. C. and Milligan, C. D. (2004) Putting teachers in the loop: tools for creating and customising simulations, *Journal of Interactive Media in Education (Designing and Developing for the Disciplines Special Issue)*. Available at <http://www-jime.open.ac.uk/2004/15/thomas-2004-15.pdf> (accessed 6 April 2005).

Wiggins, G. (2001) *Educative assessment*, San Francisco: Jossey-Bass.

Yorke, M. (2003) Formative assessment in higher education: moves towards theory and the enhancement of pedagogic practice, *Higher Education*, 45(4), 477–501.

Yorke, M. and Knight, P. (2004) Self-theories: some implications for teaching and learning in higher education, *Studies in Higher Education*, 29(1), 25–37.

Zimmerman, B. J. and Schunk, D. H. (2001) *Self-regulated learning and academic achievement: theoretical perspectives*. Hillsdale, NJ: Lawrence Erlbaum Associates.

Part II
Implementing feedback

6 Evaluating written feedback

Evelyn Brown and Chris Glover

Introduction

There has been a proliferation of studies over the past two decades looking at aspects of feedback to students and identifying how feedback can best encourage students' learning. Based on an extensive literature search, Gibbs and Simpson (2004) identified seven conditions under which feedback is believed to influence students' learning. These have been used to form part of a conceptual framework for improving students' learning through changing assessment (Gibbs *et al.*, 2003). These conditions concern the quantity, timing and quality of the feedback and the students' response to it. Nicol and Macfarlane-Dick (2004) identified seven broad principles of good feedback practice from the literature, discussed by David Nicol and Colin Milligan in Chapter 5 of this volume in the context of technology-supported assessment practices. Six of these are to do with the learning process, students' understanding of good performance or the effects of feedback on students' motivation and self-esteem. The feedback conditions and principles of good feedback practice are stated in Table 6.1.

Important outcomes of feedback identified in both studies are that students should act upon it and be able to use it to close the gap between their current performance and the desired performance in order to improve future work. These outcomes define the formative nature of feedback.

Students receive tutor-authored feedback, generic or individualised, in a variety of forms, as marks/grades, orally, written and computer-generated. This chapter focuses on the written feedback that students receive on assignments and shows how tutors can evaluate its strengths and weaknesses empirically within the conceptual frameworks described above.

Which sort of feedback do students find most useful and helpful?

A study involving 147 students at Sheffield Hallam University (SHU) (Glover, 2004) showed that although the students perceived marks or grades to be the primary vehicle for measuring their progress, they perceived written feedback as the most useful form of feedback. Feedback that helped them to understand where they had

Table 6.1 The seven conditions under which feedback is believed to influence students' learning and the seven principles of good feedback practice

Feedback conditions	Principles of good feedback practice
• Sufficient feedback is provided often enough and in enough detail • The feedback is provided quickly enough to be useful to students • Feedback focuses on learning rather than on marks or students • Feedback is linked to the purpose of the assignment and to criteria • Feedback is understandable to students, given their sophistication • Feedback is received by students and attended to • Feedback is acted upon by students to improve their work or their learning	• Helps clarify what good performance is (goals, criteria, expected standards) • Facilitates the development of self-assessment (reflection) in learning • Delivers high-quality information to students about their learning • Encourages teacher and peer dialogue around learning • Encourages positive motivational beliefs and self-esteem • Provides opportunities to close the gap between current and desired performance • Provides information to teachers that can be used to help shape teaching

Sources: Gibbs *et al.*, 2003; Nicol and Macfarlane-Dick, in press

gone wrong was the most helpful, presumably in part because it aided their understanding of their marks (see, e.g., Jackson, 1995, cited in Cooper, 2000).

Questionnaire responses from twenty-two Open University (OU) distance-learning geology students (Roberts, 1996) suggested that they viewed 'good feedback' as that which was encouraging and positive. They valued tutor comments that clearly indicated where they were incorrect, and the provision of specimen answers that included how or why these were the desired answers. They also valued highly the individualised attention that the written feedback provided and having their problems and difficulties explained in detail. A more recent study involving telephone interviews with 112 OU science students, to probe responses to a much wider survey using an Assessment Experience Questionnaire (AEQ) (Brown *et al.*, 2004), confirmed these findings. The students also valued feedback on the science content of their assignments more highly than feedback on skills.

Classifying written feedback

Given the high value that students place on individualised written feedback, the role that good-quality feedback may play in aiding student learning (Black and Wiliam, 1998) and the significant time costs to teachers in its delivery, it is surprising that few attempts have been made to classify systematically the different types of teacher comments that constitute feedback so that the quality of feedback can be analysed.

Bales (1950) devised a set of categories for the analysis of face-to-face small group interactions that distinguishes between task-oriented contributions and socio-emotional contributions, both positive and negative. The feedback categories of Hyland (2001) were designed specifically for language distance learners. The two broad categories are feedback that focuses on the product, i.e., the student's work (content, organisation, accuracy and presentation), and feedback that focuses on the learning process (praise and encouragement, and the strategies and actions students should take to improve their learning).

Whitelock *et al.* (2004) explored the applicability of Bales's framework to the analysis of tutor comments on OU students' assignments. They felt that all comments could be included within Bales's categories and concluded that his system could therefore form the basis for a model of tutor written feedback. Our view is that neither Bales's nor Hyland's system is universally applicable because they do not distinguish sufficiently between the different facets of content and skills-oriented feedback that help to guide students' learning. Nor do they shed light on the extent to which closure of the performance–feedback–reflection–performance feedback loop is enabled.

We have devised a feedback classification system which both addresses these criticisms and allows written feedback to be analysed within the conceptual frameworks of Gibbs *et al.* (2003) and Nicol and Macfarlane-Dick (2004). Although our system of classification codes has been constructed primarily for feedback on science assignments, it can be adapted easily to suit the needs of other disciplines. Five main categories of feedback comments are recognised based on current feedback practice on science assignments at the OU:

- Comments about the *content* of a student's response: i.e., the student's knowledge and understanding of the topics being assessed (coded 'C').
- Comments that help a student to develop appropriate *skills* (coded 'S').
- Comments that actively encourage *further learning* (coded 'F').
- Comments providing a qualitative assessment of a student's performance that are *motivational* (coded 'M').
- Comments providing a qualitative assessment of a student's performance that may *de-motivate* (coded 'DM').

The first four of these have the potential to help students improve their work or learning. The fifth includes what Rorty (1989) termed 'final vocabulary': i.e., value-laden, judgemental words that may inhibit further learning by damaging students' self-esteem. Each category is subdivided to enable a finer analysis of the types of feedback within each category (Table 6.2). The lower-case letter codes ascribed to each have been chosen to reflect directly the type of feedback comment that has been made by adopting the same first letter (shown in bold in the second column of Table 6.2).

The extents to which feedback comments may help students to improve their performance or learning are determined by analysing their depth. Different levels of feedback are assigned number codes to reflect the depth, with the exception of the 'de-motivational' feedback. With respect to content and skills a tutor may:

- *Acknowledge* a weakness: i.e., acknowledge a performance gap exists (level 1).

Table 6.2 The coding system used for the analysis of written feedback to students

Code	Type of comment	Relation to feedback conditions (Gibbs et al., 2003)	Relation to principles of good feedback practice (Nicol and Macfarlane-Dick, 2004)
Comments on content of student's response (coded 'C')			
Ce	error/misconception	Feedback is linked to the purpose of the assignment and may be acted upon by students to improve their work or learning.	Helps clarify what good performance is (expected standards), provides opportunities to close the gap between current and desired performance, delivers high-quality information to students about their learning.
Co	omission of relevant material		
Ci	irrelevant material included		
Ctc	tutor clarification of a point		
Csc	student's clarification of a point requested by tutor		
Comments designed to develop student's skills (coded 'S')			
Sc	communication	Feedback may be acted upon by students to improve their work.	Helps clarify what good performance is (expected standards), provides opportunities to close the gap between current and desired performance.
Se	English usage		
Sd	diagrams or graphs		
Sm	mathematical		
Sp	presentation		
Comments that encourage further learning (coded 'F')			
Fd	dialogue with student encouraged	Feedback is acted upon by students to improve their learning.	Encourages teacher dialogue around learning, facilitates development of reflection in learning.
Ff	future study/assessment tasks referred to		
Fr	resource materials referred to		
Qualitative assessment of student's performance – motivational comments (coded 'M')			
Mp	praise for achievement	Feedback is acted upon by students to improve their work or learning.	Encourages positive motivational beliefs and self-esteem.
Me	encouragement about performance		
Qualitative assessment of student's performance – de-motivational comments (coded 'DM')			
DMn	negative words/phrases (e.g. 'you should not/ never') used	Feedback focuses on student rather than student's work.	Discourages positive motivational beliefs and self-esteem.
DMj	judgement of student's performance is personal and negative, (e.g. 'careless')		

Source: modified from Brown *et al.*, 2003

- Provide *correction*: i.e., give the student the information needed to close the gap (level 2).
- *Explain why* the student's response is inappropriate/*why* the correction is a preferred response: i.e., enable the student to use the information to close the gap (level 3) by making connections between the feedback and the student's work (Sadler, 1998). The action taken by the student to close the gap is the core activity of formative assessment, the closure of the feedback loop (Sadler, 1989).

Praise and encouragement are often basic: e.g., 'well done', 'keep up the good work' (level 1). The extent to which the basis for praise and encouragement is explained determines whether it is coded level 2 or 3. Level of detail determines the coding level for the further learning categories.

Note that any one feedback comment from a tutor may be assigned more than one code. For example, a tutor may acknowledge and correct a factual error (Ce2) using negative words or phrases (DMn). Similarly, a tutor may acknowledge the presence of irrelevant material (Ci1) and also correct it because it is erroneous as well (Ce2). There is also a high degree of subjectivity involved in assigning codes to comments and so any analysis using the code provides pointers to strengths and weaknesses in feedback practice, not precise diagnoses.

Applying the classification system to analyse written feedback to students

The classification system was used in 2003 to analyse the tutor feedback on 112 student assignments at the OU, covering six different biological and physical sciences modules. The assignments were authored by module-team full-time staff but the students' work was assessed by teams of part-time tutors (associate lecturers), guided by a common mark scheme and accompanying tutor notes. The work of 83 tutors was involved.

This section explores how the outcomes for the analysis as a whole, and for two of the modules specifically, were used to diagnose strengths and weaknesses in the feedback provided. This enabled the module team to assess how well some of the feedback conditions were being met and how well the principles of good feedback were being applied (Tables 6.1 and 6.2). Two modules have been singled out because the analyses also demonstrate how the nature of assessment tasks may influence the feedback given. S204: *Biology: Uniformity and Diversity* and S207: *The Physical World* are both 60 Credit Accumulation and Transfer Scheme (CATS) credit-point modules at higher education (England, Wales and Northern Ireland) Level 6. S204 involved the analysis of 20 assignments, representing feedback from 20 different tutors; S207 involved 17 assignments with feedback from 10 tutors.

The mean score for the 112 assignments, marked using a linear scale of 0–100, was 71 (just above the class 2(i)/2(ii) borderline) and the total number of codes assigned was 3580, an average of about 32 per assignment. The mean score for the S204 assignments was 60 (class 2(ii)), and the total number of codes assigned was

805, an average of about 40 per assignment. The mean score for the S207 assignments was 76 (class 2(i)) and the total number of codes assigned was 410, an average of about 24 per assignment.

In Figure 6.1 the proportions of the different categories of feedback for S204 and S207 are compared with the data for all the modules analysed and a high degree of uniformity can be seen.

Strengths identified across all modules

The students received a reasonably large amount of motivational feedback (the vast majority in the form of praise) and very little of the feedback was de-motivating. This feedback was likely to encourage positive motivational beliefs and self-esteem, thereby increasing the likelihood that students might act upon it.

Weaknesses identified across all modules

The majority of the feedback was content-focused, relevant to the topics that were assessed. Interviews with the 112 students whose assignments were analysed revealed that they did not act on this feedback to improve their work, although they valued it most, because the topics studied had moved on and the students felt that they were unlikely to be revisited. The feedback, therefore, was not provided quickly enough to be useful to students, despite a relatively short turn-round period of only three weeks.

Skills feedback, which students felt did feed forward to future work, and feedback designed to encourage them to engage in further learning were poorly represented. These weaknesses suggest that most of the feedback served to reinforce the summative nature of the assignments. It was marks-focused, justifying the students' marks by telling them 'what counted' (Boud, 2000): i.e., it fed *back* far more than

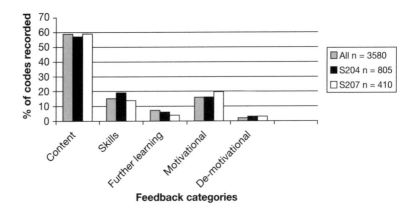

Figure 6.1 Analyses of the different categories of feedback for S204 and S207 compared with all modules

it fed *forward* and so did not fulfil the formative function of helping them to improve their work and learning.

A comparison of S204 and S207

A more detailed analysis of the types of content feedback (Figure 6.2) showed that the ratio of omissions to errors was an order of magnitude higher for S204 (5.0:1) than for S207 (0.4:1).

The S204 assignment was largely discursive and interpretive whereas the S207 assignment was dominated by calculations. Most marks for S204 were awarded for specific points students were expected to make rather than for students' achievement of broader criteria, so students found it difficult to map their own answers onto those indicated by the tutors' mark schemes: 'I was not sure what was expected by the questions' (S204 student interview). Consequently the tutors' comments were largely to do with material omitted from answers (average fourteen codes/script) and little to do with factual errors or misconceptions (average two codes/script). Thus, while the feedback was linked to the purpose of the assignment, there was no link to criteria.

By contrast the S207 students had little difficulty in understanding what their assignment questions expected (omissions – average 3.5/script) but were prone to make more mistakes, largely due to the high mathematical content (errors/ misconceptions – average 8/script).

An analysis of the depth of feedback given revealed a further difference between S204 and S207. In common with all other modules *except* S204, most of the feedback on errors/misconceptions and skills for the S207 assignment was at the level of simply the acknowledgement of a weakness or the correction of the weakness (levels 1 and 2) (Figures 6.3a and b). Less than a third involved explanation

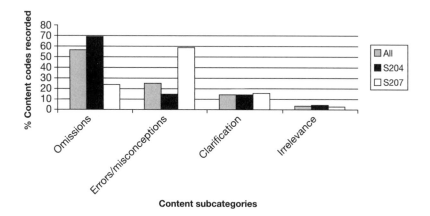

Figure 6.2 Analyses of the subcategories of content feedback for S204 and S207 compared with all modules

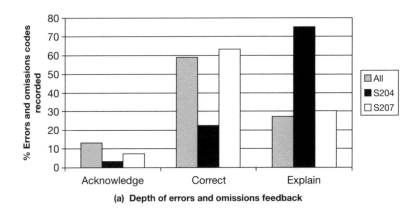

(a) **Depth of errors and omissions feedback**

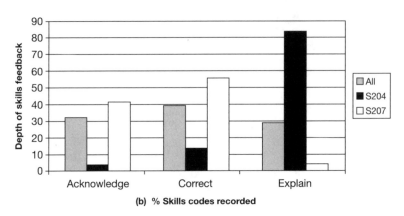

(b) **% Skills codes recorded**

Figure 6.3 Analyses of the levels of feedback on (a) errors and omissions and (b) skills for
S204 and S207 compared with all modules

(level 3). By contrast, around three-quarters of the feedback for S204 involved
explanation. Similarly, where praise was given it was mostly unexplained ('good',
'excellent', 'well done'), except for S204 where more than half of the instances
explained the basis for the praise.

The S204 assignment tasks had a large number of questions requiring analysis
and evaluation, asking students to explain 'how' or 'why' in drawing conclusions.
The marking notes supplied to tutors also encouraged the provision of explanations
to students (level 3 feedback), enabling students to make the connections between
the feedback and their own work so they were given ample opportunities to close
the gap between their current and desired performances.

The problems of levels 1 and 2 feedback

The predominance of levels 1 and 2 feedback used in the other modules suggests that students studying these may not have been able to make the connections between their work and the feedback, especially the less able students, and so they may not have been able to understand how to interpret it or what to do with it. In other words, they may not have been able to act upon it.

Improving the quality of feedback and the student response

The feedback analysis enabled the module teams to identify weaknesses in the type and quality of feedback that inhibited students' engagement with their feedback to improve their later work or learning. These are the lack of:

- Feedback that fed *forward*, providing students with the incentive to engage with it, thereby enabling them to improve future work.
- Feedback designed to encourage further learning, especially the lack of the sort of dialogue that facilitates the development of reflection in learning.
- Clear assessment criteria shared by tutors and students.
- Feedback that enabled students to make connections with their own work and so able to close the gap between their current and desired performances.

As a result, various changes have been made by different module teams which address some of these deficiencies, for example:

- Permitting students to receive formative-only feedback on their work before submitting it for summative assessment. This eliminates the focus on marks and encourages the students to engage with the feedback to improve their work and learning.
- Providing exemplars (specimen answers) for students with explanatory notes that stress skills development and the relevance to future work (S204).
- Encouraging tutors to highlight aspects of the student's strengths and weaknesses that have relevance for future work (S207).
- Generating assessment tasks in which the feedback from one assignment is relevant to subsequent tasks.

Even small changes may lead to worthwhile improvements in the quality of feedback. In 2004 we analysed the feedback provided on the equivalent S207 assignment to that analysed in 2003 (Figure 6.4). This analysis involved six tutors and fifteen student assignments. The mean assignment score was 83 (a high class 2(i)) and the total number of codes assigned was 413, an average of 28 per assignment. The proportion of feedback encouraging further learning had more than trebled.

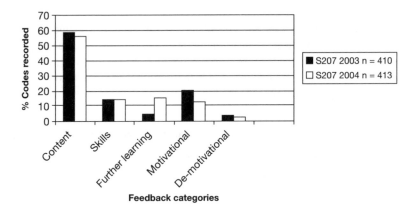

Figure 6.4 Analyses of the different categories of feedback for S207 in 2004 compared with 2003

Conclusion

The feedback coding system provides a potentially valuable tool to help teachers at all levels to reflect on the quality and effectiveness of the feedback they are giving their students. It enables the strengths and weaknesses of the feedback to be identified in relation to both the principles of good feedback practice (Nicol and Macfarlane-Dick, in press) and the conceptual framework for improving students' learning of Gibbs *et al.* (2003). Once weaknesses have been identified it is possible for teachers to search for the causes and to put into effect changes to the type of feedback given and/or assessment tasks set that will lead to improvements in the quality of the feedback and increase its potential to help students' learning.

References

Bales, R. F. (1950) 'A set of categories for the analysis of small group interactions', *American Sociological Review*, 15 (2): 257–63.

Black, P. and Wiliam, D. (1998) 'Assessment and classroom learning', *Assessment in Education*, 5 (1): 7–74.

Boud, D. (2000) 'Sustainable assessment: rethinking assessment for the learning society', *Studies in Continuing Education*, 22 (2): 152–67.

Brown, E., Gibbs, G. and Glover, C. (2003) 'Evaluating tools for investigating the impact of assessment regimes on student learning', *BEE-j* 2 (November). Available at <http://bio.ltsn.ac.uk/journal/vol2/beej-2-5.htm> (accessed 4 April 2005).

Brown, E., Glover, C., Freake, S. and Stevens, V. A. M. (2005) 'Evaluating the effectiveness of written feedback as an element of formative assessment in science'. *Proceedings of the 12th Improving Student Learning Symposium: Diversity and Inclusivity*, Chris Rust (ed.) The Oxford Centre for Staff and Learning Development: 470–8.

Cooper, N. J. (2000) 'Facilitating learning from formative feedback in level 3 assessment', *Assessment and Evaluation in Higher Education*, 25 (3): 279–91.

Gibbs, G. and Simpson, C. (2004) 'Does your assessment support your students' learning?', *Learning and Teaching in Higher Education*, 1(1): 3–31. Available at <http://www.glos.ac.uk/adu/clt/lathe/issue1/index.cfm> (accessed 19 August 2005).

Gibbs, G., Simpson, C. and Macdonald, R. (2003) 'Improving student learning through changing assessment – a conceptual and practical framework'. Paper presented at the European Association for Research into Learning and Instruction, Padova, Italy.

Glover, C. (2004) 'Report on an analysis of student responses to a questionnaire given to Year 2 and Year 4 science students at Sheffield Hallam University'. Available at <http://www.open.ac.uk/science/fdtl/pub.htm> (accessed 4 April 2005).

Hyland, F. (2001) 'Providing effective support: investigating feedback to distance learners', *Open Learning* 16(3): 233–47.

Nicol, D. and Macfarlane-Dick, D. (2004) 'Rethinking formative assessment in HE: a theoretical model and seven principles of good feedback practice'. Available at <http://www.heacademy.ac.uk/assessment/ASSO51D_SENLEF_model.doc>

Roberts, D. (1996) 'Feedback on assignments', *Distance Education*, 17(1): 95–116.

Rorty, R. (1989) *Contingency, irony and solidarity*, Cambridge: Cambridge University Press.

Sadler, D. R. (1989) 'Formative assessment and the design of instructional systems', *Instructional Science*, 18: 145–65.

—— (1998) 'Formative assessment: revisiting the territory', *Assessment in Education*, 5(1): 77–84.

Whitelock, D., Raw, S. and Moreale, E. (2004) 'Analysing tutor feedback to students: first steps towards constructing an electronic monitoring system', *Association for Learning Technology Journal*, 11(3): 31–42.

7 Using formative assessment to improve student learning through critical reflection

Alan Robinson and Mark Udall

Introduction

This chapter presents the goals and principles of a learning and teaching approach designed to improve student learning and success. The approach is underpinned by various educational theories and concepts, but has developed experientially in a number of different contexts as a result of critical reflective and reflexive practice. The approach has been evaluated by the authors and two external researchers, using inventories and a variant of the Delphi technique, in terms of student perceptions and the quality of the learning outcomes achieved.

The approach is based on a conceptual model and practical framework (Robinson and Udall, 2003), which together promote the design of an aligned teaching, learning and assessment strategy. The focus is on increasing the quality and quantity of formative assessment activities, but within a manageable overall assessment workload for students and teachers.

In our approach learners engage with the curriculum through progress recording, self-assessment against outcomes, identification of questions, and critical reflection. Taken together these provide an environment within which learners can make their own judgements about both the extent of their engagement and their likely level of attainment. The approach enables learners to instigate and sustain conversations about the quality of their learning, becoming active stakeholders in formative assessment rather than passive recipients.

Previously, in the more traditional curriculum, students were asked to undertake specific tasks either in a classroom context or independently. There was an 'act of faith' involved here, in that the learner had to believe that in some way each of these tasks had some meaning and held some potential benefit through its completion. In addition the teacher was making the judgements about the quality of the outputs from these tasks. Also, greater effort was being placed in describing the tasks compared to the effort devoted to making the expectations of the qualities and standard of the outputs explicit. Taken together, these placed the power with the teacher in the teacher–learner relationship.

Student responses to such tasks were sometimes: 'Does this count?', 'I don't see the point of doing this . . .', 'I don't understand . . .' or 'I couldn't do it . . .'. However, on closer scrutiny it was found that these students had made no real attempt. This more in-depth questioning took time and also meant that the teacher was the one driving the learning process. We propose that from the learners' viewpoint 'doing without perceived purpose' combined with the teacher-centric balance of power discourages modern students from fully engaging in learning.

This case study draws on previous work of the authors and details how the above issues have been addressed. In general, the approach places a strong focus on outcomes and provides an easily implementable framework within which learners can make judgements about their performance. Outcomes and criteria form a central element of the conversations that take place about student learning. These outcomes are not, however, just a target; they bring conceptions of purpose and potential benefit. This is reflected in the higher degree of student engagement experienced through the use of the approach. In evaluations learners report strong perceptions of both what they are expected to do and what the expected result should be. This approach represents an innovation in terms of the way in which the learning experience itself is conceptualised. In this context learners are enabled to work independently by equipping them with the skills to monitor, make judgements and critically reflect on their performance in relation to intended outcomes. Through this shift in focus, students are encouraged to take responsibility for what and how they learn.

Formative learning activities

The approach is designed to encourage and progressively develop the learners' ability to identify, structure and articulate questions about their own growing understanding. Key to this is the design of formative assessment activities that provide learners with feedback on their progress towards achievement of the intended learning outcomes for the unit (module) being studied (Biggs, 2003; Knight, 1996).

Quality feedback is well recognised in the literature as promoting 'good' learning (Black and Wiliam, 1998). This feedback is most useful when it is regular and timely and closely related to the outcomes of learning activities (Chapter 2, this volume).

However, our experience is that if the feedback process is driven by the teacher, even when integrated into the learning experience, then students fail to engage fully with the meaning of that feedback. Where the feedback process is driven by the learners' own enquiry, through critical reflection (Brockbank and McGill, 1998), their focus becomes the progress they are making towards the intended learning outcomes of the unit of study.

However, there is a range of difficulties and challenges associated with the design of formative assessment activities (Gibbs and Simpson, 2004):

- Students may simply fail to engage fully with the activities.
- Students may not use the feedback to great effect.
- Formative assessment can place an increased workload on teachers.

- The feedback when coming from the teacher may have little meaning to the learner and can be seen as a judgement on them rather than their work.

Self-assessment judgements

To overcome these problems our approach to formative assessment is designed to promote and encourage each learner in making their own regular and structured self-assessment judgements on their progress. This assists the learners in identifying any difficulties and in formulating and articulating questions to test their own constructed understanding. Through the ensuing 'learning conversations' a greater degree of ownership and responsibility is developed, which leads to greater independence and autonomy in their learning.

The two-way positive and shaping feedback engaged in also enables appropriate interventions to be applied according to the specific, individual learning needs of the student. This is achieved without the workload associated with traditional formative assessment approaches, as the learner drives the feedback process.

Structural aspects of the approach

The work of Sadler (1989) is useful in introducing the key concepts associated with our approach. Sadler identifies three key factors in establishing good-quality formative assessment:

- The ability to understand the goals being aimed for.
- Some way of comparing the actual performance with the goals.
- The skills to engage in activities which close the gap between the two.

Further, Sadler identifies formative assessment as comprising not only feedback but self-monitoring. Our approach focuses on the latter in developing an independent approach to learning and is based on a conceptual model and generic framework (Robinson and Udall, 2003) that realises each of these three factors.

The generic framework is characterised by:

- Specific outcomes associated with each learning activity.
- Learning activities that allow students to assess their own learning and identify areas of uncertainty or problems.
- A method that allows students and teachers to record engagement and achievement in these learning activities.

The approach structures the learning experience as a series of activities, each having clearly defined intended learning outcomes. These outcomes are explicit in the description of the activity given to the student. Each outcome contributes to the richer set of intended learning outcomes, for a unit of study as a whole. The outcomes are an important aspect of the approach as they are used to articulate what is expected of the student and also provide the basis of engagement with the criteria used for feedback, reflection and later summative assessment.

Activities can be situated in any type of learning context from a lecture through to a facilitated small group session. However, the student is expected to undertake some form of preparatory work before they attempt each activity.

The purpose of these individual, fine-grained outcomes is to place the learner's focus on 'what must be achieved' rather than 'what must be done'. Where there is a focus on task rather than on outcome, there is a danger that learners feel that they are achieving purely by virtue of completing the task. However, this does not necessarily mean that they have 'learned' or indeed that they are capable of repeating and transferring the learning to another context. The focus on outcomes also provides a sense of a capability gained and, critically, it provides a framework within which students can make their own judgements about their performance. These may be very binary judgements about meeting or not meeting the outcome, or may be more sophisticated, focusing on the achievement of the outcome in terms of its structural complexity. It is important here to appreciate the difference in effect on the students between the teacher making the judgement (no matter how sensitively) and the students making their own judgement.

However, the provision of the outcome statements does not in and of itself establish a clear sense of goals with the learner (Price *et al.*, 2001). There must be regular engagements about the meaning of the outcomes and these must be supported by criteria that can be used to make the judgements about attainment. It is recognised that in order to engage in a process of reflection, there must be a framework within which the associated judgements can be made (Boud, 1995). However, key to the success of our approach is the way in which the 'learning loop' is closed and through which the self-assessment judgements are tested.

Progress recording

The underlying principle of this approach is that learners are led into taking responsibility for and ownership of their own learning. The extent to which students are engaging and their level of attainment need to be explicit to both the learner and the teacher. This is achieved through the learning process supported by our approach.

Each learning activity comprises a number of much finer-grained tasks, including the preparation that leads up to that activity. These are carefully designed so that the learner must produce some form of output by virtue of engaging with the tasks. These outputs build over time into a personal learning resource, for example a portfolio, logbook or reflective log, depending on the subject discipline being studied. This learning resource is used as validating evidence of the extent of engagement. However, it may also contribute in some way to the summative assessment.

Students maintain a summary 'progress record' sheet (Robinson and Udall, 2004a) on which they indicate the tasks completed and hence the extent to which they have engaged with the learning process. They also record their perceived level of achievement of the outcomes for each activity. The 'progress record' is an important motivator in encouraging learner engagement as it provides a simple but powerful 'visualisation' of the learner's development and likelihood of success, for both the student and teacher. Additionally, it is the first step in the self-assessment and reflective process and also forms a focal point for conversations between learner and teacher. The evolving evidence in the 'portfolio' can be used to align teacher and learner perceptions of the degree of engagement and attainment.

Each activity provides an opportunity for the learner to assess their own constructed understanding and formulate specific questions around problem areas. These questions are then used to instigate subsequent conversations at a deeper level. It is through this process of self-assessment, questioning and reflection that the learner takes ownership of the feedback process. The question-based approach requires the learner to think carefully about the nature of the questions and the language that is used to express them. The intention is that by 'owning' the question the learner also 'owns' the answer and the feedback as a whole takes on greater meaning.

The language adopted when the learner articulates their questions can be used as an indicator of the quality of learning (Robinson and Udall, 2004b). From a SOLO Taxonomy perspective (Biggs, 2003), some learners construct and articulate highly relational questions whereas others, with a less sophisticated understanding of the subject area, tend to pose unistructural or multistructural questions. This provides a quick diagnosis that allows the teacher to respond in different ways with different learners to reflect their level of development.

As a result of the conversations about attainment, students who undertake all of the required activities and who claim a high level of attainment in their self-assessment are offered additional supplementary activities that are designed to broaden and deepen their understanding in the subject area further. Those students who claim a low level of attainment in their self-assessment or who have not completed all of the tasks without help are offered additional complementary activities, as appropriate, designed to improve their understanding and reinforce their learning. By following this process groups of students of widely differing experience or understanding can work at effectively their own pace.

It is important that the cycle of recording, self-assessing and reflection becomes a routine part of the learning experience from the very start. In order to achieve a reliable and effective learning process some degree of repetition and reinforcement of the technique is necessary.

The developing 'picture' of engagement and perception of achievement makes it difficult for students to 'hide' if they are not engaging in the learning process sufficiently, as the evidence of their own work is always central to the learner–teacher interactions. Important dimensions of this approach are the link created between engagement and success and the alignment of perception with reality. Making explicit the tasks that should be undertaken and having a recording method that allows students to recognise the extent to which they are engaging with these tasks is even more important for some students, as it prevents any delusions about the amount of work that they are doing.

Furthermore, the approach provides the opportunity for a student to develop good study habits. The two-way feedback facilitated by our approach develops the student's ability to assess their own learning and supports the student in identifying the nature of any problems that need resolving in order to close the 'gap' between their actual performance and the intended outcomes. Most importantly, it is the student who initiates the feedback rather than the feedback coming as judgement from the teacher.

Evaluation

Analysis of units (modules) prior to adopting our approach showed that there were some students who had the tendency to 'slow start', not completing early formative tasks, resulting in a lack of understanding of the early material. This formed a poor foundation for following more complex concepts, resulting in poor performance in the summative assessment later in the unit. Further, the dialogue about the quality and quantity of student learning in process was mainly initiated by the teacher. Essentially, the teacher was answering questions that the students themselves had not even formulated.

Units in which this approach was applied showed notable improvements both in engagement and attainment. Also, the students quickly became more proactive in raising questions that were more sophisticated and not of the 'I don't understand' type. Students particularly focused on the way in which the structured activities and corresponding specific outcomes were made explicit and how these provided a way in which they could make judgements about their own performance. As a student explained as part of the evaluation, 'More units should adopt this technique as it makes it far clearer what is expected of me and I find it easier to learn the subject.' Learners also felt that they had a much better understanding of how well they were doing as they progressed through their studies and the summative assessment did not come as a 'big surprise'. Some of these learners felt that the approach reduced anxiety and improved their motivation for study generally. From a tutor perspective, there was clear evidence of a higher-quality, learner-driven dialogue about learning. The conversations were more readily instigated by the learners and comprised of richer and deeper questioning.

A formal evaluation has been made to determine student perceptions of the impact of the approach on their learning experience. There were two key findings from this study. First, although students were initially averse to the 'progress recording', there was broad recognition that this encouraged them to engage and complete the tasks associated with activities. Student groups reported, 'this made us do the work when we would not normally have done'. This was directly attributed to the 'way you can see how much you've done and how much you haven't'. Students also identified that there was no escaping their lack of engagement. Second, students identified the approach as conveying clear expectations: 'it's clear what we are expected to do' and 'it's clear what we should be able to do when we have finished'. In the evaluation, students reported that 'it is easy to tell how well we are doing' and 'if there are problems we have a means by which we can get them answered'.

The approach is being used in three universities involving hundreds of students on more than ten different units, at various levels, in three subject areas, by ten teachers. Not all these have been formally evaluated. However, the normal annual course and unit monitoring processes report positive student comments and improved levels of attainment. Two new funded learning and teaching projects are proposed in order to provide a comparative study between the implementation of the approach in the different contexts.

Conclusions

Students are often unable to make realistic judgements about their own learning. As a result they may be surprised by the outcomes of summative assessment. Our goal has been to develop a systematic approach that provides, via the design of appropriately challenging and timely formative assessment activities, a 'visualisation' (an ongoing indication) for students and teachers of the quality and quantity of learning in process. This visualisation is used to initiate conversations through which students and teachers can develop a common understanding and critically reflect upon not only the subject-related intended learning outcomes but the process of learning in which they are engaged. Learners develop a questioning and reflective approach to their studies, promoting higher degrees of student engagement and attainment.

The overall strategy is concerned with 'learning and not just passing'. Activities are designed on the basis of 'what the student does' (Biggs, 2003) (or doesn't do) and 'how they perceive' what they are doing. This perception is most important. Prosser and Trigwell (1999: 81) have argued that the 'way students perceive their learning and teaching situations is central to the quality of their learning'. Our approach makes the link between engagement and success while avoiding the potential for the adoption of a surface approach to learning (Biggs, 2003). The approach stimulates a feeling that assessment (formative and summative) is integral to the learning process and something that students 'take part' in rather than something that is 'done to them'. This corresponds to the self-knowledge conception of assessment identified in Shreeve *et al.* (2003) rather than the lower-order correction conception. The approach is powerful in aligning teacher and learner perceptions of the degree of engagement and attainment and in moving the focus of responsibility from teacher to learner.

References

Biggs, J. (2003) *Teaching for quality learning at university*, 2nd edn. Buckingham: Society for Research into Higher Education, Open University Press.

Black, P. J. and Wiliam, D. (1998) 'Assessment and Classroom Learning', *Assessment in Education: Principles and Practice*, 5, 1, pp. 7–73.

Boud, D. (1995) *Enhancing learning through self assessment*. London: Kogan Page.

Brockbank, A. and McGill, I. (1998) *Facilitating reflective learning in higher education*. Buckingham: Society for Research into Higher Education, Open University Press.

Gibbs, G. and Simpson, C. (2004) 'Conditions under which assessment supports students' learning', *Learning and Teaching in Higher Education*, 1, pp. 3–31.

Knight, P. (1996) 'Assessment reform and transforming higher education'. Different Approaches: Theory and Practice in Higher Education, Proceedings HERDSA Conference, Perth, Western Australia.

Price, M., O'Donovan, B. and Rust, C. (2001) 'Strategies to develop students' understanding of assessment criteria and processes', in C. Rust (ed.), *Improving student learning. 8: Improving student learning strategically*. Oxford: Oxford Centre for Staff and Learning Development.

Prosser, M. and Trigwell, K. (1999) *Understanding learning and teaching: the experience in higher education*. Buckingham: Society for Research into Higher Education, Open University Press.

Robinson, A. and Udall, M. (2003) 'Developing the independent learner: the Mexican hat approach'. Proceedings of the IEE 3rd International Symposium on Engineering Education, Southampton, UK.

—— (2004a) 'Developing the independent learner', LTSN Engineering Case Study, May 2004, ISBN 1–904804–17–9. Available at <http://www.ltsneng.ac.uk/downloads/resources/independent.pdf>.

—— (2004b) 'A framework for formative assessment: initiating quality learning conversations', *Learning and Teaching in Higher Education*, 1, pp. 112–15.

Sadler, D. R. (1989) 'Formative assessment and the design of instructional systems', *Instructional Science*, 18, pp. 145–65.

Shreeve, A., Baldwin, J., and Farraday, G. (2003) 'Variation of student conception of assessment using learning outcomes', in C. Rust (ed.), *Improving student learning. 11: Theory, research and scholarship*. Oxford: Oxford Centre for Staff and Learning Development.

8   Improving performance through enhancing student understanding of criteria and feedback

Margaret Price and Berry O'Donovan

Introduction

As has been argued throughout this book, to realise their full potential in any assessment, students need to understand the assessment task, criteria and expected standards, and subsequently their feedback so they can develop their learning and improve future performance. Assessment must convey clear and high expectations concerning standards. Knowledge of standards guides students on the quality of their work and progress, and facilitates self-assessment, enabling them to become more independent learners. This chapter discusses a cost-effective approach to enhancing students' understanding of standards that goes beyond that conveyed by explicit description. The discussion is set in a framework of evidence and the context of a changing higher education environment. The chapter concludes by considering the application of a social constructivist approach to all aspects of the assessment cycle and how this might support improvement in student learning and performance.

Initiatives in the HE community aimed at improving students' understanding of assessment have largely focused on the provision of explicit description of assessment standards and criteria; for example, learning outcomes, programme specifications, grade descriptors. While such descriptions have merit in being easily available to the increasing numbers entering higher education their apparent transparency can be illusory. It is clear that sharing standards is not easy. Evidence suggests that there are considerable difficulties in achieving a useful shared understanding of standards if ways of sharing are based on explicit description alone. Precise articulation of standards is very difficult. Sadler (1987) argues that fuzzy levels are unavoidable in standards specified in linguistic terms. What is, for instance, 'highly evaluative' or 'reasonably coherent' depends on the assessor's expectations and knowledge of the context. Consequently, such terms are relative rather than absolute and require clear anchor points to communicate definitive standards. However, the construction of precise and comprehensive anchor definitions can quickly become self-defeating, as precision is bought at the expense of utility (Yorke, 2002) in terms of both development time and transferability. Notwithstanding these difficulties, prior research also demonstrates that interpretation of such explicit descriptions varies widely between individual staff, let alone between students and staff (Webster *et al*., 2000). In practice, a description that is considered precise and clear by the author will be viewed very differently by recipient students.

Context

University business schools have been experiencing a high demand for their courses for more than a decade; consequently places on business courses have been increasing. As a result, first-year modules that provide the foundation for a range of business courses are very large, having been in triple figures for many years and, at Brookes Business School, now at more than 600. Such large numbers present a problem for effective use of traditional approaches to transferring knowledge of standards as these largely depend on discussion and dialogue with staff in small groups or one-to-one. Such a large body of students also inevitably increases the range of knowledge and experience of education and assessment standards that students bring with them. Students enter a course from a variety of routes: academic; vocational; or business experience. Accordingly, their ability to understand the expectations of higher education immediately is not automatic.

The business courses at Brookes University have responded to the changing environment of HE (as detailed in Chapter 1 of this volume) through the development of an interdisciplinary curriculum with an emphasis on learning processes and skills development integrated with disciplinary knowledge. The school has always striven to maintain and enhance a reputation for high-quality learning and teaching and a culture of innovation and experimentation.

First steps

The authors, who were the course director of the undergraduate business courses and the module leader of a large introductory business module, were well placed to develop new approaches to assessment designed to elucidate assessment standards and requirements. Initially the team focused on the effectiveness of using explicit descriptors of standards through the development of a criterion-referenced assessment grid. The grid (currently still used across the school) has thirty-five criteria plotted in matrix format against grades resulting in 'grade definitions' detailing levels of performance for each criterion at each grade. Staff select appropriate criteria for any given assessment to create a 'mini-grid' (see Figure 8.1 for an example). Originally, it was hoped that such a comprehensive marking criteria grid would help establish common standards of marking and grading for advanced-level undergraduate modules (those normally taken by second- and third-year students) across the business programme. Thus enabling consistency in marking, easier moderation and providing guidance to students (resulting in better subsequent work), and facilitating feedback focused on criteria.

Although the grid has some benefits, it does not appear to establish common standards understood by all stakeholders. In particular, students, while recognising the potential of the grid and what it is trying to achieve, consider it of limited

7029 Placement Search and Preparation – Feedback Sheet

ASSIGNMENT 1

Student Name: . . . .   Student Number: . . . .

	CRITERION	A	B+	B	C	Refer / Fail
1	Presentation of assignment	Shows a polished and imaginative approach to the topic.	Carefully and logically organised.	Shows organisation and coherence.	Shows some attempt to organise in a logical manner.	Disorganised/ incoherent.
7	Attention to purpose	Has addressed the purpose of the assignment comprehensively and imaginatively.	Has addressed the purpose of the assignment coherently and with some attempt to demonstrate imagination.	Has addressed the main purpose of the assignment.	Some of the work is focused on the aims and themes of the assignment.	Fails to address the task set.
27	Self-criticism (include reflection on practice)	Is confident in application of own criteria of judgement and in challenge of received opinion in action and can reflect on action.	Is able to evaluate own strengths and weaknesses; can challenge received opinion and begins to develop own criteria and judgement.	Is largely dependent on criteria set by others but begins to recognise own strengths and weaknesses.	Dependent on criteria set by others. Begins to recognise own strengths and weakness.	Fails to meaningfully undertake the process of self criticism.
28	Independence/ Autonomy (include planning and managing learning)	With minimum guidance can manage own learning using full range of resources for discipline; can seek and make use of feedback.	Identifies strengths of learning needs and follows activities to improve performance; is autonomous in straightforward study tasks.	Can work independently within a relevant ethos and can access and use a range of learning resources.	Can undertake clearly directed work independently within a relevant ethos and, with some guidance, use the standard learning resources.	Unable to work independently, needing significant guidance on methods and resources.

(Please tick boxes)

Comment: . . . .

Marker: . . . .   Mark: . . . .

Figure 8.1 Sample 'mini-grid' marksheet

practical use if presented in isolation without the benefit of explanation, exemplars and the opportunity for discussion. Arguably, the imprecision inherent in passively presented explicit verbal description (interpreted differently by each recipient) requires that consideration be given to other ways of achieving shared understanding of criteria and standards.

'Useful' knowledge of standards

Polanyi (1998) and Tsoukas (1996), among others, argue that the transfer of useful knowledge involves the transmission of both explicit and tacit knowledge. Consequently, a single-minded concentration on explicit knowledge and careful articulation of assessment criteria and standards is not, in itself, sufficient to share useful knowledge of the assessment process. 'Tacit knowledge', in this context, is defined as something that we know but find impossible or, at least, extremely difficult to express. Unlike explicit knowledge 'that can be expressed in formal and systematic language' (Nonaka *et al.*, 2002: 43), tacit knowledge is highly personal and hard to formalise. Deeply rooted in action and often in an individual's commitment to a profession, tacit knowledge consists partly of technical skills based on professional experience, and in a more cognitive dimension in our ingrained mental models, beliefs and perspectives (Nonaka, 1991). It is a type of knowledge that can be said to underpin the established normative, 'connoisseur' model of assessment – illustrated by the phrase 'I cannot describe it, but I know a good piece of work when I see it', most often likened to the skills of perfume or tea blending and 'pretty much impenetrable to the non-cognoscenti' (Webster *et al.*, 2000: 73).

Knowledge of this kind is experience-based and can be revealed only through the sharing of experience – social and active learning processes involving observation, imitation, dialogue and practice (Nonaka, 1991; Baumard 1999). So, over time, discussion and shared experiences of marking and moderation among staff enable the sharing of tacit knowledge resulting in more standardised marking. It follows that inviting students to participate actively in this shared experience should also enable more effective knowledge transfer of assessment processes and standards to them. Such transfer methods are consistent with social constructivism where learners through active learning techniques involving practice and dialogue construct their own representation of knowledge. Social constructivism is becoming more widely accepted as an effective approach to learning, and its use in developing students' understanding of disciplinary knowledge is becoming commonplace. HE still largely relies on written explanation to explicate criteria and standards to students, yet surely acquiring knowledge and understanding of assessment processes, criteria and standards needs the same kind of active engagement and participation as learning about anything else (Rust *et al.*, 2005).

Our action research has shown that engaging students in activities designed to support the social construction of knowledge of assessment criteria and standards can significantly improve student performance, but need take only a very modest amount of contact time to implement.

Pre-assessment intervention

A pre-assessment intervention was designed to involve students in the assessment process through marking practice and self-assessment. The intervention takes place in the final three weeks of students' first term in a large introductory business module (600-plus students). It involves students in preparation for and voluntary participation in a workshop prior to the submission of a self-assessment sheet with their coursework handed in at the end of their first term (three weeks after the workshop).

The detail of this intervention is as follows:

1   A week before the workshop all students on the module are provided with two sample assignments and marksheets including assessment criteria and grade definitions. Students are asked to complete the marksheets individually, providing a grade, marks and rationale/feedback for each of the assignments before coming to the workshops.

2   Workshops (ninety minutes long) are offered to all students in groups of forty. (Student attendance at these workshops is optional.) However, only those who undertake the preparation (see 1 above) are allowed to attend the workshop.

The workshops are structured in the following way:

   i   student discussion in small groups of their initial individual marking of the two sample assignments;
   ii   feedback of small groups' agreed grades and rationale to plenary;
   iii   tutor-led comparison of provided rationales with criteria; looking at inconsistencies and reliance on 'visible' criteria (e.g., presentation; structure);
   iv   tutor explanation of each criterion;
   v   small groups' review of assessment and grade in light of tutor explanation;
   vi   final report from small groups to plenary of grade for each piece of work;
   vii   tutor provided annotated and marked versions of samples and discussed tutor assessment and mark.

(The small group discussions allow students to compare and justify their initial assessment of the work against that of others as well as allowing the declared grade to be the responsibility of the small group.)

3   Three weeks later, students submit their coursework along with a completed self-assessment sheet. There is no indication on the coursework whether students have participated in the intervention.

(The marksheets used for the sample assignments, for the students' submitted work and for the students' self-assessment are the same.)

Results

Over a three-year period the effects of this intervention have been measured using a range of techniques including student responses and gauging staff perceptions, the main one being the effect on student assessment performance.

Table 8.1 Improvements in student performance

Immediate results	Participants' average mark	Non-participants' average mark
Cohort 1 (99/00)	59.78	54.12
Cohort 2 (00/01)	59.86	52.86
Cohort 3 (01/02)	55.7	49.7
Results 1 year later		
Cohort 1	57.91	51.3
Cohort 2	56.4	51.7

Findings replicated annually over a three-year period show that students who attend assessment workshops achieve significant improvements in performance with that improvement sustained at a significant level one year later (see Table 8.1). Note a baseline comparison of participants' and non-participants' performance undertaken prior to workshops has found, for three years running, no significant difference in the performance of the two groups (see Rust *et al.*, 2003 for full details).

This simple intervention, taking a relatively small amount of course time, can have an effect that can last over time and be transferred. (Admittedly the follow-up module was deliberately chosen because of the similarity of the nature of the assessment task and the assessment criteria used – so no claims for transferability can be made on this evidence.)

Looking more closely

Arguably, the pre-assessment intervention supports the transfer of tacit knowledge through the use of exemplars, marking practice and the opportunity for dialogue between staff and students to complement explicit knowledge provided through the verbal explication of assessment criteria by staff and in written format embodied within the grid. While the pre-assessment intervention is constructed to use both explicit and tacit knowledge transfer processes, the findings point to the significant factor in knowledge transfer and sharing being the active learning processes focused on in the workshop. Given that all students are provided with samples of work (to mark) prior to the assessment workshop, and annotated versions, given out at the workshop, are widely circulated among the whole student group, the workshop remains the distinguishing aspect of the process. Only those students taking a full part in all the activities have been found to perform to a significantly better standard than the rest of the cohort. Evidence from the literature on peer marking using model answers (Forbes and Spence, 1991; Hughes,1995) would also suggest that being engaged with the process of marking as well as seeing examples of other work significantly contributes to the students' subsequent improvement in performance.

The provision of sample assignments (particularly the marked and annotated versions) is likely to benefit non-participants as well as participants. This supposition is borne out by staff perceptions of the work of Cohort 1 when they signalled that the standard of student coursework as a whole had risen from standards prior to the introduction of the intervention on the module. This being the case, the comparison of performance by participants and non-participants will have understated the effect of the whole intervention on the participants.

Applying a social constructivist approach to the complete assessment cycle

If you buy into the rationale that all learning requires active participation and engagement on the part of the learner, then it seems reasonable to suppose that this approach should be taken to all aspects of the assessment cycle, including feedback.

A review of the literature indicates that feedback is the most important part of the assessment process in its potential to affect future learning and student achievement (see, for instance, Hattie, 1987; Black and Wiliam, 1998; Gibbs and Simpson, 2002). Yet, how often have we all harboured in our offices at the end of the year boxes of uncollected marked coursework? This apparent lack of interest on the part of students does not, however, tally with research findings that show students want more, and more effective, feedback (O'Donovan *et al.*, 2001; Higgins *et al.*, 2002). So perhaps the problem does not lie with the students but in the way we 'give' them feedback as passive recipients in the process rather than as active participants. Clearly, peer assessment confers on students an active role in the feedback process, but many teachers in the UK are wary of methods that empower students to award marks that contribute to final accredited awards or provide feedback to peers that may be misleading or inaccurate. One way we have engaged students with the feedback process without relinquishing control of 'the mark' is through a process designed to engage students actively with their tutor feedback that is used in conjunction with the pre-assessment marking intervention. Sadler (1998) identifies three conditions for effective feedback. These are: knowledge of the standards; having to compare those standards to one's own work; and taking action to close the gap between the two. The second and third conditions both require the student to engage actively with the feedback: 'students should be trained in how to interpret feedback, how to make connections between the feedback and the characteristics of the work they produce, and how they can improve their work in the future. It cannot simply be assumed that when students are "given feedback" they will know what to do with it' (p. 78).

These conditions underpinned the design of a 'feedback workshop' which takes place following the return of undergraduate students' first marked assignment. Using a proforma in a ninety-minute workshop students 'decode' their tutor feedback by translating it into their own words. They then compare their feedback with their own self-assessment (submitted with their coursework), evaluate it and benchmark their work against an A-grade piece. The final activity involves students developing a brief, three-point action plan for future assignments.

Even though the process has raised some issues that mirror those reported in the research literature and need to be explored further, students have evaluated the process on end-of-module evaluation surveys as being very useful and worthwhile. Taking this approach can perhaps provide a win–win situation. Feedback becomes more meaningful and useful, and perhaps ultimately we will need to spend less time giving feedback by making sure that the feedback we *do* give is more effective.

Putting it all together results in a complete assessment cycle underpinned by a social constructivist approach (see Figure 8.2).

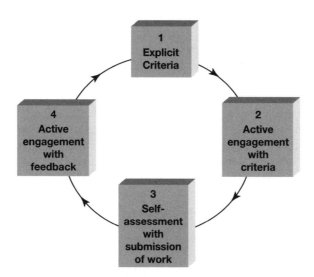

Figure 8.2 Constructivist Assessment Cycle

Managing innovation and change

Within the school's culture of innovation in learning and teaching the introduction of these activities was relatively straightforward. The team has experience of running large and diverse modules with established integrated skills development programmes. Clearly, a prerequisite of such an assessment cycle is a well-designed assessment task with relevant criteria and descriptors and agreement among staff on the interpretation of the criteria and standards. (Indeed, an unanticipated benefit has come from the development of the sample assignments which have helped to build a common understanding of standards within a staff team.) The workshops receive a small amount of resourcing as part of a student orientation programme that does not reduce class contact for the established module disciplinary content.

The introduction of the feedback workshop did raise a number of issues that limited its impact on student engagement. Most of these pertained to the quality of feedback provided by the markers (a group of twelve staff, some full time, some part time). Mirroring reported research, our students experienced difficulty in interpreting their tutor feedback (Lea and Street, 1998). Particular difficulties included the use of jargon, illegibility, inexplicable ticks and lack of feed forward and positive comments. All of which meant it was far more difficult for students to understand and engage with the feedback provided or to act on it in future assignments. These issues are being addressed through staff development and discussion but as the course team can change each year this is an ongoing problem.

Conclusion

The widespread use of explicit criteria and descriptors now firmly established in the HE sector has led to a strong faith among staff that these alone achieve transparency of standards for students. However, the continued emphasis on explicit articulation of assessment criteria and standards is not sufficient to develop a shared understanding of 'useful knowledge' between staff and students. Active learning processes are necessary for tacit knowledge transfer to occur.

Traditional methods of knowledge transfer in higher education place reliance on complex and resource-intensive processes based on practice, imitation, feedback and discussion, often on a one-to-one or small-group basis in a tutorial system. However, for most institutions, reliance on these relatively expensive methods is difficult if not impossible in the context of today's rapid expansion of student numbers and cuts in the unit of resource (see Chapter 1 in this volume). It does appear, though, that through relatively simple interventions incorporating a combination of explicit articulation and social active-learning processes a considerable amount may be achieved in developing shared understanding and, consequently, in improving student performance – and that this improvement may last over time and be transferable, albeit possibly only in relatively similar contexts.

References

Baumard, P. (1999) *Tacit knowledge in organizations*. London: Sage Publications.

Black, P. and Wiliam, D. (1998) Assessment and classroom learning, *Assessment in Education*, 5 (1), pp. 7–74.

Forbes, D. A. and Spence, J. (1991) An experiment in assessment for a large class, in R. Smith (ed.), *Innovations in engineering education*. London: Ellis Horwood.

Gibbs, G. and Simpson, C. (2002) Does your assessment support your students' learning? Available at <http://www.brookes.ac.uk/services/ocsd/1_ocsld/lunchtime_gibbs.html>.

Hattie, J. A. (1987) Identifying the salient facets of a model of student learning: a synthesis of meta-analyses, *International Journal of Educational Research*, 11, pp. 187–212.

Higgins, R., Hartley, P. and Skelton, A. (2002) The conscientious consumer: reconsidering the role of assessment feedback in student learning, *Studies in Higher Education*, 27 (1,) pp. 53–64.

Hughes, I. E. (1995) Peer assessment, *Capability*, 1 (3), pp. 39–43.

Lea, M. and Street, B. (1998) Student writing in higher education: an academic literacies approach, *Studies in Higher Education*, 23(2), pp. 157–72.

Nonaka, I. (1991) The knowledge-creating company, *Harvard Business Review*, November–December, pp. 96–104.

Nonaka, I., Toyama, R. and Konno, N. (2002) SECI, Ba and leadership: a unified model of dynamic knowledge creation, in S. Little, P. Quintas and T. Ray (eds), *Managing knowledge*. London: Sage Publications.

O'Donovan, B., Price, M. and Rust, C. (2001) The student experience of criterion-referenced assessment (through the introduction of a common criteria assessment grid), *Innovations in Education and Teaching International*, 38(1), pp. 74–85.

Polanyi, M. (1998) The tacit dimension, in L. Prusak (ed.), *Knowledge in organization*. Boston: Butterworth Heinemann.

Rust, C., O'Donovan, B. and Price, M. (2005) A social constructivist assessment process model: how the research literature shows us this should be best practice, *Assessment and Evaluation in Higher Education*, 30(3).

Rust, C., Price, M. and O'Donovan, B. (2003) Improving students' learning by developing their understanding of assessment criteria and processes, *Assessment and Evaluation in Higher Education*, 28(2), pp. 147–64.

Sadler, D. R. (1987) Specifying and promulgating achievement standards, *Oxford Review of Education*, 13(2), pp. 191–209.

—— (1998) Formative assessment: revising the territory, *Assessment in Education*, 5(1), pp. 77–84.

Tsoukas, H. (1996) The firm as a distributed knowledge system: a constructionist approach, *Strategic Management Journal*, 17 (Winter Special Issue), pp. 11–25.

Webster, F., Pepper, D. and Jenkins, A. (2000) Assessing the undergraduate dissertation, *Assessment and Evaluation in Higher Education*, 25(1), pp. 72–80.

Yorke, M. (2002) Subject benchmarking and the assessment of student learning, *Quality Assurance in Education*, 10(3), pp. 155–71.

9 Using core assessment criteria to improve essay writing

*Katherine Harrington, James Elander,
Jo Lusher, Lin Norton, Olaojo Aiyegbayo,
Edd Pitt, Hannah Robinson and Peter Reddy*

Introduction

In this chapter we discuss the implementation and evaluation of a programme of writing workshops designed around the concept of 'core' assessment criteria. The workshops had two aims: helping undergraduates improve their essay writing and promoting deep approaches to learning. Essay assignments continue to be valuable as a way of both assessing (Prosser and Webb, 1994) and promoting deep approaches to learning (Scouller, 1998), despite trends in some disciplines towards alternative forms of assessment (MacAndrew and Edwards, 2003). Students often find essay writing difficult and struggle to know exactly what writing a good essay requires, partly because their understandings of the criteria that are applied to essays differ from those of their tutors (Merry *et al.*, 1998). We therefore devised a programme of formative learning opportunities that focused on a small group of centrally important criteria for essays, and linked the meaning of those criteria to relevant disciplinary knowledge and understanding. We hoped this approach would increase the likelihood that students would adopt a deeper approach to learning through writing essays, and encourage strategically focused students to reach a more advanced understanding of the discipline.

The work took place in departments of psychology at three UK universities as part of Assessment Plus, a HEFCE-funded FDTL4 project (<http://www. assessmentplus. net>). The evaluation drew on student feedback and measures of student performance as well as focus groups with each group of students and tutors. We found the programme facilitated a deep approach to learning and improved performance for some students, but that those benefits were limited by low levels of student attendance and variability between tutors in how well the workshops were delivered. We conclude with recommendations for those considering running similar programmes.

Core assessment criteria

The criteria that are employed in the assessment of essays vary between institutions and disciplines, just as individual tutors vary in what they see as the most important qualities in students' written work. However, some criteria are commonly employed across different disciplines and institutions, and appear to have a central role in the shared perception of what constitutes a good student essay (Elander *et al.*, 2004). These include the following criteria: addressing the question, demonstrating understanding, developing argument, using evidence, structuring, critically evaluating, and using language well. A recent review of theory and evidence concluded that many of these core criteria describe properties of the outcomes of adopting a deep approach to learning (Elander *et al.*, 2006). The concept of core criteria, however, does not exclude other criteria, nor does it restrict the meanings of the criteria, for each is open to interpretation in the context of the discipline in which it is used, as Lea and Street (1998) have shown. Our core criteria are a small set of criteria that are centrally important in written work in the social sciences and specify some of the outcomes of taking a deep approach to learning.

The use of core criteria can support a student-centred approach to learning and teaching by:

- channelling assessment-oriented students towards deeper approaches to learning;
- providing straightforward and manageable focal points for students and staff to develop a shared understanding of assessment criteria and standards;
- facilitating students' ability to generalize and apply what they have learned from one assignment to the next and from one module to the next;
- facilitating a coherent departmental approach to marking and feedback procedures.

In this chapter we are concerned with the first two of these potential benefits. The approach is similar to that of other work on the benefits of interventions designed to engage students actively with understanding assessment criteria (e.g., Price *et al.*, 2003). The findings we report focus on the experiences of psychology students, but the approach of identifying core criteria and providing writing workshops built around those criteria is applicable across a range of disciplines where essays are assessed.

The workshop programme

Full workshop protocols are available at <www.assessmentplus.net>. We summarize below the ways the programme was implemented and evaluated differently in the three institutional contexts, before going on to an appraisal of the successes of the programme and the obstacles we encountered.

At Liverpool Hope University College and Aston University, the programme consisted of workshops that mixed discussion and practical exercises, with an emphasis on hands-on activities and interaction between students, which were offered as optional support for first-year psychology students. There were five workshops on the following themes:

- What are assessment criteria?
- Addressing the question and the importance of structure.
- Demonstrating understanding and developing argument.

- Evaluation and using evidence.
- Applying the assessment criteria to your own work.

At London Metropolitan University, the programme was adapted and compressed into a four-workshop series and embedded in a third-year health psychology module that was assessed by essay-style examination answers. The workshop strategy was to use the core criteria to facilitate discussion about how material that had been covered in lectures could be used to construct high-quality examination answers. Students also had opportunities in the workshops to apply the criteria themselves in marking exercises in which they assessed specimen essays.

At Liverpool Hope, the workshop tutor was a psychology lecturer who was one of the designers of the programme. At Aston and London Metropolitan, the workshops were facilitated by specially trained postgraduate psychology students. At each institution students completed an end-of-programme evaluation questionnaire, and at Liverpool Hope students completed an evaluation questionnaire after each workshop. Students and tutors at each institution also took part in focus groups.

What we have learned: the successes

The evaluation of the workshop programme was guided by three questions: Were students helped to understand the assessment criteria? Were they helped to write better essays? Were they helped to learn psychology?

Helping students understand assessment criteria

Students were generally appreciative of the workshops and the focus on facilitating an understanding of the meaning of assessment criteria, as this comment made by an Aston student illustrates: 'Yeah, there have been extra study sessions that explain them in quite a lot of detail. [They were about] what they mean by evidence, what do they want as evidence, what does "analyse" mean. We get told what each word means because not everybody knows.' At Aston and Liverpool Hope, the end-of-programme evaluation questionnaires included rating scales where students indicated how strongly they agreed or disagreed with statements about whether the workshops had helped them understand the assessment criteria (see Table 9.1).

Table 9.1 Proportions of students who agreed/strongly agreed with statements about understanding assessment criteria in the end-of-the-programme evaluation questionnaire

The workshops helped me to understand . . .	Aston (n=11)	Liverpool Hope (n=11)
How to address the question	91%	100%
How to structure	91%	91%
How to demonstrate understanding	82%	91%
How to develop an argument	100%	82%
How to use evidence	82%	100%
How to evaluate critically	82%	100%

Table 9.2 Proportions of Liverpool Hope students who responded in different ways to statements in evaluation questionnaires after workshops 2, 3 and 4

	Yes definitely	Not sure	No definitely not
Workshop 2: Addressing the question and the importance of structure (n= 20)			
I understand the importance of the introduction.	100%	–	–
I understand the importance of the conclusion.	100%	–	–
I have a good idea of how to structure my essay to ensure it addresses the essay title.	70%	25%	5%
I have a clear idea of strategies I can use to stay focused on the essay title.	60%	40%	–
I feel confident that I can use an essay plan to help me structure my essay.	60%	35%	5%
Workshop 3: Demonstrating understanding and developing argument (n =17)			
I know what my tutors are looking for when they judge whether I understand the issues I am writing about.	100%	–	–
I understand that argument in an essay involves examining the pros and cons of an issue rather than providing just one side.	94%	6%	–
I understand that building arguments in psychology depends on supporting claims with evidence which can be accepted or criticized.	94%	6%	–
I have a clear idea of what strategies I can use to help build an argument in my essay.	88%	12%	–
I have a clear idea of how I can demonstrate understanding of theories and concepts in my essays.	76.5%	23.5%	–
Workshop 4: Evaluation and using evidence (n=14)			
I understand what is considered appropriate and inappropriate evidence in my subject.	93%	7%	–
I feel confident that I can cite and reference material correctly.	71%	21%	7%
I know how to evaluate the quality of a book.	50%	50%	–
I know how to evaluate the quality of a journal.	29%	64%	7%
I know how to evaluate the quality of an internet source.	43%	57%	–
I know how to evaluate the quality of the information in a book.	50%	50%	–
I know how to evaluate the quality of the information in a journal.	43%	50%	7%
I know how to evaluate the quality of the information in an internet source.	29%	64%	7%
I know how to detect bias in written sources.	50%	43%	7%

The evaluation questionnaires completed at Liverpool Hope after each workshop asked students about the specific learning objectives for each workshop, and Table 9.2 shows the results for Workshops 2, 3 and 4, which focused on specific criteria. The most positive student response was for Workshop 3, on demonstrating understanding and developing argument.

Helping students write better essays

Table 9.3 shows the proportions of students who responded in the end-of-programme evaluation that they agreed or strongly agreed with statements about how the workshops helped them with essay writing. Responses from the third-year (London Metropolitan) students were notably less positive than those from the first-year students at Aston and Liverpool Hope. This probably reflects less confidence among first years about what university writing requires.

Responses to several of the questionnaire items that Liverpool Hope students were asked after each of the workshops (Table 9.2) also provided insights into students' perceptions of whether and in what way the workshops helped them to write better essays. Comparisons between items with very high (90–100 per cent) and those with lower levels of positive endorsement reveal that students felt the workshops helped them to know what is involved in good essay writing, but were less sure about how to produce that writing. For example, after Workshop 2, all the students believed they understood the importance of an introduction and conclusion in an essay, but substantially fewer were confident about how to structure an essay, what strategies they could use to stay focused on the title, and using an essay plan. Similarly, after Workshop 4, nearly all students felt they understood what was considered appropriate and inappropriate evidence in their subject, but far fewer believed they knew how to evaluate the quality of that evidence. Those findings suggest there is a need for practical writing sessions with tutor feedback, allowing students to gain experience of writing to assessment criteria without being summatively assessed.

Table 9.3 Proportions of students who agreed/strongly agreed with statements about essay writing in the end-of-programme evaluation questionnaire

The workshops . . .	*London Metropolitan (n=50)*	*Aston (n=11)*	*Liverpool Hope (n=11)*
Will help me write better essays	55%	82%	100%
Will help me achieve a better grade in future essays	45%	82%	100%
Will help me make better use of feedback from tutors	36%	60%	100%
Helped me feel more confident about writing	N/A	55%	100%

Helping students learn psychology

Table 9.4 shows student responses to the items in the end-of-programme question-naire that specifically addressed the issue of engaging with the discipline of psychology. The figures indicate that the first-year students (at Aston and Liverpool Hope) found the workshops more valuable than did the third-year students (at London Metropolitan). This is perhaps surprising considering that it was at London Metropolitan that the workshops were embedded within a module but may reflect more negative perceptions of 'study skills' sessions among third-year students.

To explore that issue in more detail, students' qualitative responses to the open-format question 'What was good about the workshops?' were content analysed and assigned to one of three categories: 'deep-related', 'strategic-related' and 'unclassified'. Responses categorised as 'deep-related' included those referring to understanding the subject and the benefits of engaging with different points of view. An example of this type of comment was: 'Gave insight to psychology and aspects of psychology.' The 'strategic-related' category focused on the essay-writing task itself, without reference to broader issues of learning and understanding in the discipline. An example of this type of comment was: 'The essay planning was explained pretty clearly.' The third category of 'unclassified' included any comments that were vague or were not attributable to either of the other categories. An example was: 'I learned so much.' Comments falling into the third category were not included in the final analysis, which showed that 43 per cent of London Metropolitan students' and 44 per cent of Aston students' comments were 'deep-related', compared with 57 per cent and 56 per cent, respectively, classified as 'strategic-related'. The slightly higher numbers in the latter category are disappointing; however, it is nevertheless encouraging that nearly half of the (analysed) comments to an open-ended question about the benefits of the workshops seemed to reflect a perception that they encouraged a deep approach to learning.

At London Metropolitan it was possible to examine workshop participation in relation to performance in the module examination. There was a significant positive correlation between the number of workshops attended and examination grade ($r = .25$, $p < .01$), so that students who attended more workshops obtained significantly higher grades (see Figure 9.1). Multiple regression analyses showed that attendance affected achievement, rather than vice versa. That is, attendance

Table 9.4 Proportions of students who agreed/strongly agreed with statements about subject learning in the end-of-programme evaluation questionnaire

The workshops . . .	London Metropolitan (n=50)	Aston (n=11)	Liverpool Hope (n=11)
Helped me understand my subject	48%	64%	73%
Helped me study more effectively	30%	70%	64%

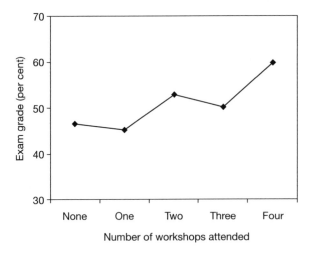

Figure 9.1 Mean module examination grades for students attending different numbers of workshops at London Metropolitan

predicted examination grades, but examination grades did not predict attendance, which means that the correlation between attendance and achievement was not simply the result of more able students attending more workshops (Lusher, 2004).

What we have learned: the obstacles

Attendance

Workshop attendance was poor at each institution, and especially at Liverpool Hope and Aston, where the workshops were an optional programme outside timetabled teaching. At Liverpool Hope, 33 students (10 per cent of the total cohort of first-year psychology students) attended at least one workshop, and at Aston the figure was 35 (16 per cent of the total cohort of first-year psychology students). At London Metropolitan, where the workshops were timetabled as part of a module, 80 per cent of the 111 students enrolled in the module attended at least one workshop, but only 19 per cent attended all four. The low participation rate affected the impact of the workshops on students who did attend, whose comments included: 'Poor attendance, therefore little chance for discussion'; 'Few numbers meant that when I did turn up, I was the only one and was given the worksheets, then sent away.'

The 'remedial' perception

Poor attendance and commitment is a common problem for workshops associated with study skills, especially when the workshops are optional. One reason may be that there is a perception among students that such programmes are remedial. As one third-year London Metropolitan student said: 'If you need extra help, they are useful.' One of the London Metropolitan tutors commented: 'A subgroup of students was really enthused and found content relating to essay-writing skills extremely useful. Some others felt such study groups would have been more helpful in the first year.'

These reactions were not confined to third-year students and their tutors. Some of the Aston students felt the workshops were not pitched at the right level: 'A lot of the stuff was quite simplified. I already knew it'; 'Sometimes it took a lot of time to get through something relatively simple.'

One of the Aston tutors thought that the workshops appealed more to those who were anxious or unprepared for studying psychology:

> For the core few that attended regularly they were overall very pleased with the workshops as these were students who were very concerned or anxious with taking degree-level psychology and how to go about writing in psychology. Typically these students had either taken a few years out, or had never done A-level or year 0 psychology.

It should be noted, however, that not all students fitted that tutor's view. One Aston student, who had done A-Level psychology, commented: 'If we hadn't had study skills at the beginning, it would have been like walking through treacle. It has been, a bit, anyway, but there's been some things to help.'

Nevertheless, the attendance figures as well as several comments from students and tutors do indicate that the 'remedial' perception is generally widespread and appears to be an unfortunate consequence of provision that is not explicitly and primarily concerned with subject learning. Many students did not see the sessions as a worthwhile investment of their time, including this Aston student: 'I haven't gone because it's on a Monday for an hour and it takes me an hour to get here and an hour to get back. There's nothing else on so it's just not worth it.'

Variability between workshop tutors

Another important issue to emerge from our analysis of the evaluation questionnaire and focus group data was that the approaches to the workshops taken by the tutors at both Aston and London Metropolitan varied considerably. The following comments were made in a focus group with the Aston students: 'The person who was doing them didn't seem to know what they were talking about, they were just too simple'; 'I was really lucky, mine was great.' This awareness of variability among tutors and a feeling that one has to rely on being 'lucky' in order to receive useful instruction was also a prominent feature of student comments at London Metropolitan.

This problem did not emerge at Liverpool Hope, probably because one individual, who was a full-time lecturer in psychology, was the tutor for all five workshops. At London Metropolitan and Aston, by contrast, the workshops were delivered by trained postgraduates. Delivery by a single tutor seems to have provided a level of consistency that was unattainable with teams of tutors, and the fact that the tutor was a full-time lecturer may also have lent additional credibility to the workshops.

Conclusions and recommendations

We had hoped the workshop programme would deliver some of the benefits of engaging students with assessment criteria while enhancing their learning of the discipline. Positive indicators were that first-year students appreciated the workshops and felt that they:

- helped them understand the assessment criteria;
- helped them understand their discipline;
- helped them study more effectively;
- helped them understand better what their tutors are looking for in essays.

And among third-year students, attendance at the workshops was associated with:

- higher grades in the module in which the workshops were embedded.

Based on the main obstacles we encountered, we recommend that workshops:

- be as deeply embedded in subject teaching as possible, in order both to promote links with disciplinary knowledge and raise expectations about attendance;
- be run by a small number of tutors who can establish a consistent approach based on a shared understanding of the purpose of the workshops.

Acknowledgements

We would like to thank all the students and staff who took part in the workshops and focus groups.

References

Elander, J., Harrington, K., Norton, L., Robinson, H., Reddy, P. and Stevens, D. (2004) 'Core assessment criteria for student writing and their implications for supporting student learning', in C. Rust (ed.), *Improving Student Learning. 11: Theory, Research and Scholarship*. Oxford: Oxford Centre for Staff and Learning Development.

Elander, J., Harrington, K., Norton, L., Robinson, H. and Reddy, P. (2006) 'Complex skills and academic writing: a review of evidence about the types of learning required to meet core assessment criteria', *Assessment and Evaluation in Higher Education*, 31, 1: 70–90.

Lea, M. R. and Street, B. V. (1998) 'Student writing in higher education: an academic literacies approach', *Studies in Higher Education*, 23: 157–72.

Lusher, J. (2004) 'How study groups can help examination performance', unpublished report, London Metropolitan University.

MacAndrew, S. B. G. and Edwards, K. (2003) 'Essays are not the only way: a case report on the benefits of authentic assessment', *Psychology Learning and Teaching*, 2: 134–9.

Merry, S., Orsmond, P. and Reiling, K. (1998) 'Biology students' and tutors' understandings of "a good essay"', in C. Rust (ed.), *Improving Student Learning: Improving Students as Learners*. Oxford: Oxford Centre for Staff and Learning Development.

Price M., Rust, C. and O'Donovan, B. (2003) 'Improving students' learning by developing their understanding of assessment criteria and processes', *Assessment and Evaluation in Higher Education*, 28, 2: 147–64.

Prosser, M. and Webb, C. (1994) 'Relating the process of undergraduate essay writing to the finished product', *Studies in Higher Education*, 19: 125–38.

Scouller, K. (1998) 'The influence of assessment method on students' learning approaches: multiple choice question examination versus assignment essay', *Higher Education*, 35: 453–72.

Part III
Stimulating learning

10 Online instantaneous and targeted feedback for remote learners

Shelagh Ross, Sally Jordan and Philip Butcher

Providing feedback on assessment in distance education

The challenge of this project was to develop assessments for a distance-learning course in 'maths for science', such that no hand-marking was required, students were given immediate feedback tailored to their own answers and multiple attempts at each question were permitted.

The importance of feedback for learning has been highlighted by a number of authors, emphasising its role in fostering meaningful interaction between student and instructional materials (Buchanan, 2000: 199), its contribution to student development and retention (Yorke, 2001), but also its time-consuming nature for many academic staff (Chapter 1, this volume). In distance education, where students work remotely from both peers and tutors, the practicalities of providing rapid, detailed and regular feedback on performance are vital issues. Four of Gibbs's 'eleven conditions' under which assessment supports student learning (Gibbs and Simpson, n.d.; Chapter 2, this volume) are particularly worthy of examination in the distance education context:

- the provision of sufficient feedback (in terms of both frequency and detail);
- the provision of timely feedback;
- the delivery of feedback in such a way that students have to engage with it;
- the provision of feedback that can be acted upon by the student in future learning tasks.

The nature of assessment in relation to its 'formative' and/or 'summative' purpose is also important. As noted by Brookhart (2001) and others, these terms are not used consistently in the literature. Most authors subscribe to Sadler's (1998: 77) definition of formative assessment as being explicitly 'intended to provide feedback on performance to improve and accelerate learning', with the further, often unstated, implication that such assessment is not used to allocate grades. Our usage here conforms to both the explicit and implicit parts of this description, with the proviso that formative assessment involves each student's answers being independently checked (whether by a person or a computer program), thus distinguishing it from *self*-assessment, in which students draw their own conclusions by comparing their own answer with some kind of specimen answer. Summative assessment, on the other hand, counts towards an award.

As noted by Gibbs in Chapter 1, at the Open University (OU) the tutor-marked continuous assessments have always been seen as a crucial element of learning and the principal means by which individual feedback is supplied to students during the course. The majority of courses in the OU's Science Faculty last for eight months, with students typically submitting assignments every six to eight weeks. These are annotated by a tutor with corrections, comments and suggestions to help with future elements of the course, as well as a grade. Since these assignments fulfil both formative and summative purposes they conform to Boud's (2000) characterisation of 'double duty' assessments. Such tutor-marked assessment can satisfy the first and fourth of Gibbs's conditions above. Whether the third condition is met depends largely on the extent to which students are willing to work through feedback that necessarily relates mainly to a task that has already been completed. The second condition is only partly satisfied by tutor-marked assessment, in that each assignment relates to study carried out over a period of many weeks and the marking process itself usually takes several weeks. This turn-around time makes feedback via hand-marked continuous assessment unsuitable for courses lasting less than about three months.

Partly for reasons of turn-around time, and partly due to their expense, tutor-marked assignments have not been considered suitable for the Science Faculty's programme of 'short courses'. Instead, credit for these 10 CATS-point courses is awarded on the basis of a single open-book, untimed, end-of-course assessment (ECA) that students do at home. The development of a new Level 1 course entitled 'Maths for Science' within this programme brought a number of the issues raised above into sharp focus. Presented four times a year, it has recruited large numbers of students: currently about 900 complete the course in each calendar year. Students work on printed course material and a CD-ROM at home, without face-to-face tuition or meetings with fellow students. However, they do have telephone and asynchronous computer conference access to specialist advisers and other students.

The team developing the course was very aware of the fact that the majority of the students would be at or near the beginning of their OU studies, and that many such mature learners bring emotional 'baggage' arising from previous negative experiences of maths. It would therefore be particularly important to build students' confidence, despite the lack of continuous assessment to provide ongoing support. Furthermore, in the case of Maths for Science the inevitable delays associated with hand-marking and administration of large numbers of ECA scripts were considered unacceptable: students need rapid feedback on their mathematical strengths and weaknesses before proceeding to other science courses. For the distance-education market, it was felt that the best way of providing this kind of immediate and personalised feedback would be to use an interactive web-mediated format.

A web-based assessment strategy

The rationale for the project was to build a complete teaching strategy in which feedback on both formative and summative parts of the web-based assessment would be a crucial part of the learning process. Figure 10.1 shows one example of the kind of teaching comment that may be provided.

The feedback aims to simulate for the student a 'tutor at their elbow'. To this end, an entirely formative 'practice' assessment (PA) can be accessed throughout the course, as many times as the student wishes, with the option of generating different numbers and variables for each question on each visit. As well as providing subject-specific practice, it was hoped that that the PA would help to reduce anxiety by allowing the students to become familiar with the computer system (Sly, 1999). The summative ECA is available for the second half of each presentation of the course. The PA and the ECA have the following features in common:

- They provide individualised, targeted feedback, with the aim of helping students to get to the correct answer even if their first attempt is wrong. Thus in the example shown in Figure 10.1, the student is told that they have taken the wrong tack, and given a reference to the relevant section of the course material. This feedback appears immediately in response to a submitted answer, such that the question and the student's original answer are still visible.

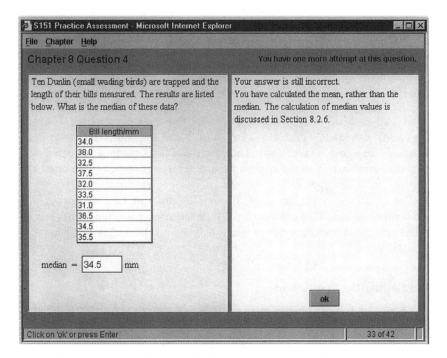

Figure 10.1 An example of targeted feedback, showing the combination of a response-specific explanation of the student's error with a pointer to the course material

- They allow students to make up to three attempts at each question, with an increasing amount of teaching feedback being given after each attempt. Figure 10.1 shows feedback provided after a second attempt.

This instantaneous feedback, together with the opportunity to use it immediately (Boud, 2000: 158) by amending answers if necessary (Clariana, 1993), is designed to encourage students to engage with the feedback and to learn from it actively (OLTC, 1996).

Formats for interactive feedback and multiple-try answers had previously been developed in other OU science courses for formative assessments presented on CD-ROM. However, in pedagogic terms, this assessment strategy was different from anything that had preceded it, in that it:

- continues the *teaching* feedback through the ECA, helping students to amend their answers even *during the process of summative assessment*;
- allows *partial credit* with the mark awarded decreasing with the number of attempts and thus with the amount of feedback given. This is not a replication of the partial marks typically awarded during script-marking. Rather, the strategy is based on answer-matching and feedback that helps the student to make another attempt if necessary;
- allows students to form a reasonably accurate picture of their strengths and weaknesses across the subject matter, both from ongoing feedback and from a final summary screen. If at this point they are not satisfied with their own performance, they can choose not to submit their ECA for credit, but to defer and take a new ECA with the next cohort. If they choose to submit the ECA immediately, the feedback informs them of weaknesses, which they may then address before starting their next course.

As well as fulfilling the pedagogic aim for this particular course, the Open University also saw the introduction of a web-based assessment system as institutionally desirable in other ways. The expense of hand-marking large numbers of scripts is removed. In principle, a bank of templates and question types can be built up. When appropriate, random-number generation can produce many similar questions at minimal cost. Barriers to study of time and geography are further reduced. However, many of these perceived advantages have to be balanced against important design issues and against the requirements for very robust systems.

Developing the assessments

The design of the assessments had to satisfy five main drivers:

1 *Interactive feedback*: both the formative PA and the summative ECA had to provide students with response-specific comments that would help them correct their misunderstandings and learn while doing the assessment.

2   *Easy to use and robust software*: given the nature of the course, many students are inexperienced internet users, with fairly low-specification machines, dial-up rather than broadband connections, and a wide range of software and ISPs. The assessments must sit robustly on top of this variety of hardware and software. Students must be able to take a break (or suffer a dropped connection) and be returned on reconnection to the exact point reached on their last visit.

3   *Simple input*: it is widely acknowledged (e.g., Beevers and Patterson, 2002) that finding an easy way for students to input mathematical expressions is a significant challenge for computer-aided assessment in mathematics. For example, superscripts were enabled by the provision of a button, as illustrated in Figure 10.2.

4   *Minimal use of multiple-choice formats*: Although inputting problems can be avoided by setting multiple-choice questions, there are well-recognised difficulties inherent in such formats (see, e.g., Lawson, 2001). Especially important for the context described here is the fact that multiple-choice questions do not easily assist in the diagnosis of many student misconceptions: the question setter can write distractors based on common errors, but cannot anticipate all possible answers, and of course a student may pick the correct answer simply by guesswork. Multiple-choice formats were therefore used only when answer formats would have been too difficult for students to input.

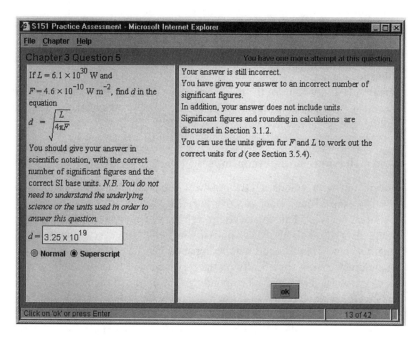

Figure 10.2 A partially correct answer requiring a superscript, with targeted feedback.

Note: In this case, feedback and pointers to course material both cover two independent mistakes in the student's second attempt to answer the question

5   *Institutional record-keeping*: every attempt at a question had to be securely recorded, despite any breaks in communication, and marks transferred to the university's examination data-handling system.

The practice assessment is a cornerstone of the overall pedagogic strategy, and has to fulfil a number of purposes. Its main aims are:

- to engage students during their work on the course, by giving them additional questions for practice in a format in which they receive *specific* feedback (e.g., 'you appear to have calculated the first rather than the second derivative'), as opposed to the printed self-assessment questions which have full answers but may not help students to diagnose their own difficulties or misconceptions;
- to build learners' confidence in the course and themselves by receiving immediate positive feedback on questions they have tackled successfully;
- to ensure that students appreciate all the elements of a 'correct' answer (e.g., not just a value, but a value given to appropriate precision with units of measurement included, as illustrated in Figure 10.2);
- to provide students with an objective formative assessment of their performance, counteracting the tendency of many students to delude themselves in self-assessment. We have seen many examples in pre-course diagnostic maths tests and in tutorial sessions of students believing they have only made a slip when in fact it is a fundamental error, and not engaging with questions they think they can do. Colleagues in other universities report similar attitudes to paper-based solution sheets, whereby students don't fully analyse the answers, or think 'I could have done that' only to discover when it comes to an exam that they cannot;
- to provide a 'dry-run' for the ECA in terms of ensuring that students have the necessary software in place, understand the input mechanisms and have confidence in the technology.

Student behaviour and perceptions

In accordance with standard OU practice, the first intake of students was surveyed by a postal questionnaire, covering all aspects of the course. A very small number of students in a later intake completed the general Assessment Experience Questionnaire (AEQ) discussed by Gibbs in Chapter 2. However, the most detailed information came from a cohort numbering about 500 selected to receive a postal questionnaire focusing specifically on the assessment; 270 completed questionnaires were returned. As well as responding to multiple-choice questions, these students were encouraged to write freely about aspects of the assessment format that they particularly liked or disliked.

Despite many respondents' relative inexperience with technical internet issues, the software proved suitably user-friendly. Responses from those who did not complete the ECA confirmed that while a very small number of students are prevented from submitting by technical difficulties (and alternative provision can be made available when technical problems prove insurmountable), the main causes for non-submission are of the kind revealed in every OU retention study, with lack of time the most reported.

The pedagogical drivers for this assessment format were the immediate teaching feedback and the summary screen that would enable students to make a realistic assessment of their mathematical competence before submission and ahead of entry to other science courses. It was slightly disappointing that the latter was mentioned far more often than the former in students' written questionnaire responses. It seems that for a significant number of students the importance of 'feedback' relates mainly to performance in terms of their idea of the pass/fail divide (what Higgins *et al.* (2001) term 'strategic consumerism'), rather than to learning.

Nevertheless, it was a vindication of the strategy that 74 per cent of respondents who had submitted the ECA agreed with the statement that 'the interactive feedback associated with the ECA questions helped me to learn' and only 5 per cent disagreed. Seventy-nine per cent agreed that the feedback had helped them to amend their initial inputs to obtain the correct answer at a subsequent attempt, with only 6 per cent disagreeing. Eighty-eight per cent agreed that the immediate acknowledgement of correct answers increased their confidence, again with just 6 per cent disagreeing.

Tied up with students' comments about their overall performance are their perceptions of the marking process. Some students are convinced they would gain significantly better marks if they got credit for 'working'. Given that a proportion of the questions are essentially 'one-liners', and that others are likely to be done wholly on a calculator, this assumption is not valid in all cases. It also ignores the fact that many students manage to correct their initially wrong answers and get credit for having done so. This issue probably becomes most contentious when answers have several elements (e.g., value, plus the precision to which it is quoted and/or units of measurement), though some students clearly have an erroneous belief that they would not be penalised by a human marker for what they regard as 'minor errors'. In fact, since every input made by a student is recorded, borderline ECAs and those with unusual distributions of responses are manually reappraised.

Although it had been hoped that the PA would help students both to learn and to distribute their effort sensibly throughout the course (see 'condition 2' in Gibbs and Simpson, n.d.), roughly three-quarters of them accessed it for the first time just before starting the ECA. This is consistent with the fact that most students said they used the PA mainly as a 'mock' for the ECA, rather than as a bank of additional questions. It has become very clear that students are much more likely to submit the ECA if they have previously accessed the PA. This may be due to various factors operating in combination, as with the findings of Sly (1999) that students undertaking formative practice tests significantly improved their mean mark on summative tests compared to those who did not do the practice tests. Those submitting are a self-selected group, so may include all the 'better' or more motivated students who would naturally choose to do the PA. Students who have done the PA may approach the ECA with more confidence in their ability to handle both the subject matter and the computer interface.

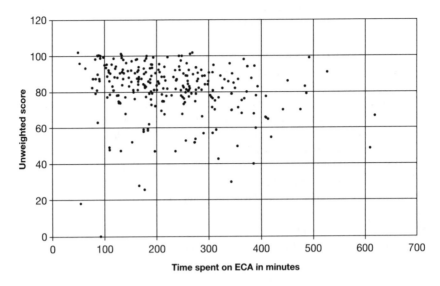

Figure 10.3 Time spent on the summative ECA by one cohort of students

The time spent by students on the PA and the ECA varies widely, in terms of both the total number of hours and the number of online sessions over which their effort is distributed. This time range is illustrated in Figure 10.3, which also shows that there is no clear correlation between time spent and success in the ECA.

Conclusion

The effort required to devise and program these assessments was substantial, although this has been justified by the large student enrolment over a number of years and the longer-term saving in staff time. The project may be considered a success in terms of the student approval of both the interactive feedback and the multiple-try format. However, students' appreciation of the feedback within the summative component was focused more on their attainment standard than on its learning function. Every input to the assessments made by every student is electronically stored and available for analyses that would not be possible for script-marked or multiple-choice assignments. From a teaching point of view, this is contributing substantially to our understanding of common student misconceptions.

Acknowledgements

We thank Spencer Harben, Greg Black, Peter Mitton, Pat Murphy, Isla McTaggart and Stuart Freake for their contributions to the project. A grant of £20,000 from the eOU Strategy Group towards development costs is gratefully acknowledged.

References

Beevers, C. E. and Patterson, J. S. (2002) Assessment in mathematics, in P. Khan and J. Kyle (eds), *Effective teaching and learning in mathematics and its applications.* London: Kogan Page.

Boud, D. (2000) Sustainable assessment: rethinking assessment for the learning society, *Studies in Continuing Education*, 22(2), 151–67.

Brookhart, S. M. (2001) Successful students' formative and summative uses of assessment information, *Assessment in Education*, 8(2), 153–69.

Buchanan, T. (2000) The efficacy of a World-Wide Web mediated formative assessment, *Journal of Computer Assisted Learning*, 16, 193–200.

Clariana, R. B. (1993) A review of multiple-try feedback in traditional and computer-based instruction, *Journal of Computer-Based Instruction*, 20(3), 67–74.

Gibbs, G. and Simpson, C. (n.d.) Does your assessment support your students' learning? Available at <http://www.open.ac.uk/science/fdtl/documents/lit-review.pdf> (accessed April 2005).

Higgins, R., Hartley, P. and Skelton, A. (2001) Getting the message across: the problem of communicating assessment feedback, *Teaching in Higher Education*, 6(2), 269–74.

Lawson, D. (2001) Computer assisted assessment (CAA) in relation to learning outcomes. Available at <http://ltsn.mathstore.ac.uk/articles/maths-caa-series/oct2001/index.shtml> (accessed April 2005).

OLTC [Open Learning Technology Corporation] (1996) Learning with software: pedagogies and practice: operant conditioning. Available at <http://www.educationau.edu.au/archives/cp/04j.htm> (accessed April 2005).

Sadler, D. R. (1998) Formative assessment: revisiting the territory, *Assessment in Education*, 5(1), 77–85.

Sly, L. (1999) Practice tests as formative assessment improve student performance on computer-managed learning assessments, *Assessment and Evaluation in Higher Education*, 24(3), 339–43.

Yorke, M. (2001) Formative assessment and its relevance to retention, *Higher Education Research and Development*, 20(2), 115–26.

11 Improving student experience through making assessments 'flow'

Sean Gammon and Lesley Lawrence

Introduction

At the heart of this innovation in assessment is the utilisation of flow theory in HE assessment design, process and experience. Flow refers to the optimal experience that often occurs in situations that bring deep enjoyment, satisfaction and irresistible spontaneity (Csikszentmihalyi, 1975). When experiencing a state of flow, there are: a balance between challenge and skill; clear goals and immediate feedback; a merging of action and awareness; deep concentration; a focus on the processes of a given activity rather than its outcomes; and a sense that time has accelerated. Using approaches primarily adopted in positive psychology, Csikszentmihalyi's flow model was developed from research on individuals participating primarily in leisure activities and in certain work settings. It is acknowledged, however, that flow can be experienced in 'a wide variety of activities and settings' (Mannell and Kleiber, 1997: 90). Although the usefulness of introducing and applying flow within an educational context has been mooted (Csikszentmihalyi, 1997a and 1997b), little active research and/or discussion has analysed the benefits of introducing flow in HE.

This chapter describes a project that developed and evaluated the application of flow to student and lecturer assessment strategies (Gammon and Lawrence, 2003). The project (designed in three phases) was possible through LTSN funding for two years (Subject Centre for Hospitality, Leisure, Sport and Tourism). Might the introduction of flow reduce student anxiety, increase enjoyment and ultimately their experience of assessment? Might introduction to the principles of flow theory help increase lecturer awareness of assessment impacts and thus improve the student experience? The findings suggested that adopting or at least considering flow positively affects the assessment experience of both lecturer and student.

Flow

Our initial hypothesis several years earlier was that applying flow to the learning process would make learning more enjoyable for many students (Gammon and Lawrence, 2000). So what exactly is flow? In recent years many leisure scholars and practitioners have placed greater emphasis on understanding leisure as an experience as opposed to more traditional temporal, spatial or activity-based inter-pretations. One of the most referred to authors is Csikszentmihalyi (1975 and 1992). His work primarily aims to identify and describe the optimal experience, known as flow, which he believes occurs when an intrinsically motivated individual experiences fun and deep enjoyment. Much of Csikszentmihalyi's contribution to leisure psychology stems from his research into enjoyment, identifying feelings of flow in activities that are perceived as enjoyable.

> The experience of enjoyment, or flow, as we came to call it, is characterised above all by a deep, spontaneous involvement with the task at hand. In flow, one is carried away by what one is doing and feels so immersed in the activity that the distinction between 'I' and 'it' becomes irrelevant. Attention is focused on whatever needs to be done, and there is not enough left to worry or to get bored and distracted. In a state of flow, a person knows what needs to be done moment by moment and knows precisely how well he or she is doing. In flow, a person usually does not worry about the consequences of his or her performance. The sense of time becomes distorted: hours seem to pass by in minutes, but afterward one might feel that an eternity has elapsed. The ego that surveys and evaluates our actions disappears in the flow of experience. One is freed of the confines of the social self and may feel an exhilarating sense of transcendence, of belonging to a larger whole.
>
> (Csikszentmihalyi, 1997a: 82)

The theory of flow (or the optimal experience) can be more easily understood when broken down to what Csikszentmihalyi (1992) identifies as the key 'conditions of flow':

- challenging activity requiring skills;
- clear goals and immediate feedback;
- merging of action and awareness;
- concentration on the task at hand;
- the paradox of control;
- loss of self-consciousness;
- transformation of time;
- the experience is autotelic.

Csikszentmihalyi's (1975) flow model was originally developed through research on individuals participating in leisure activities such as rock climbing, dance, chess and basketball and in certain work settings. While leisure settings are recognised as potentially the best sources of flow experiences, any activity can be adapted and enhance life by making that activity more enjoyable and meaningful (Csikszentmihalyi, 1992). A growing bank of researchers over the last thirty years have applied Csikszentmihalyi's model in both leisure and non-leisure settings. Establishing flow-type conditions in a teaching situation is not new – for example, Csikszentmihalyi himself has remarked upon the usefulness of introducing and applying flow to university students and schoolchildren (Csikszentmihalyi, 1997a and 1997b). He also used flow in advocating the enhancing of creativity, linking this to various domains, including teaching and learning (Csikszentmihalyi, 1996). More recently Salmon (2002) suggests consideration of the concept of autotelism by those creating and e-moderating their 'e-tivities'.

The emergence of the research idea

The idea of relating flow theory to the student learning experience arose several years previously in a third-year module at Luton ('Leisure in Mind') that evaluates philosophical and psychological debates within leisure, focusing particularly on the work of Csikszentmihalyi. The conditions of flow (see above) were introduced to the students who were asked to apply them to their own learning. Their initial cynicism was soon replaced by curiosity and controlled enthusiasm. The significance of the 'paradox of control' – i.e., not focusing upon the implications of a particular activity or task – was emphasised and reinforced by asking students to trust in their own abilities and skills, to set regular and reachable goals, and to reflect upon skills required to meet the challenge. We cautiously concluded that incorporating autotelic (self-goal) structures within course delivery in HE might appreciably improve the learning experience; individuals applying flow in their learning should be:

- unphased taking on new or complex challenges;
- intrinsically motivated to learn;
- empowered and informed concerning their ability to improve their own learning experiences;
- confident in their own learning abilities;
- relaxed about completing assessments;
- reflective regarding the applicability of flow in other areas of their lives (Gammon and Lawrence, 2000).

When a funding opportunity appeared on the LTSN website a year later, we reviewed the preliminary study and decided to focus on an element of the student experience that had emerged and interested us: namely, assessment strategies employed by both student and lecturer. On investigation of the literature, relatively little attention had been paid to anxiety and confidence levels linked to assessment strategies employed by students, nor to possible interventions through which anxiety may be reduced, confidence maximised and the process made more enjoyable. This was worrying given 'anxious students perform particularly badly. They adopt over-cautious strategies' (Gibbs and Habeshaw, 1989: 38). Anxiety in an assessment context should not be perceived as inevitable, and thus not the concern of the lecturer. As is contended, lecturers should be doing everything they can to reduce the anxiety from assessments (Ramsden, 1992). The project set out to investigate the impact of flow upon assessment strategies and experiences.

Project design and findings

Phase One included a review of student attitudes towards assessment (questionnaire completed by 130 students on three undergraduate modules). Levels of anxiety were relatively high, with students most anxious about examinations, then presentations. Students considered anxiety might be reduced with greater lecturer support and more preparation on their own part, being refreshingly honest about their own shortcomings. Lecturer assessment attitudes and strategies were determined from questionnaire responses (n=28). Feeling competent in assessing, just over half classed themselves as 'largely traditionalist and occasionally an innovator' when designing assessments (see Table 11.1). The one 'real innovator' had become disillusioned and had returned to traditional methods of assessment due to a perception of over-bureaucratic institutional practice that resulted in 'linear, unadventurous, documented modes of assessments suited to its prosaic systems'.

Phase Two evaluated the application of flow theory to student in-course assessments in two modules (co-ordinated by one of the authors). Questionnaires were completed by students in these modules prior to the application of flow intervention and then after the intervention (at the end of the module) together with student focus groups and lecturer interview. Students were found to have generally received a positive experience and many found the assessments more interesting and enjoyable; confidence had been retained throughout; and support was perceived as good.

Student and lecturer guidelines were developed including a student checklist to be incorporated into the assessment brief. Workshops were held to enable other lecturers to apply flow theory to assessment design and practice in their modules; ascertaining whether flow theory could be effectively introduced to lecturers who had *not* encountered the theory was critical. Participants in the workshops (n=5) were informed that a new approach would be introduced, designed to make the assessment process enjoyable to both lecturer and student. After being introduced to the concept of flow, participants were encouraged to personalise flow by reflecting upon their own experiences and considering how flow could be applied in assessment design. Could their usual approaches be augmented or changed to create more flow-like experiences in their students? Post-workshop interviews revealed both interest and stimulation resulting in a review of current assessment practice, and enthusiasm and confidence to experiment. One lecturer was looking forward to 'trying things out' when designing assessments and 'could not wait'. In another

Table 11.1 Lecturer – innovator/traditionalist designer?

Type	% (n=28)
Pure traditionalist: i.e., rely on tried and tested methods of assessment	0
Largely a traditionalist, but occasionally an innovator	53.6
Both equally	28.6
Largely an innovator, but occasionally a traditionalist	14.3
A real innovator: i.e., try different types and be creative	3.6

instance, greater understanding of current working practice was seen to be explained by flow theory: 'This is what I do. It seems to work. That [flow intervention] explains why it works'.

For Phase Three all five lecturers agreed to have their attempts to introduce flow monitored over a semester and for their students to participate in focus groups. Unforeseen circumstances resulted in two dropping out due to long-term sick leave and employment in another institution respectively, though compensating for this the remaining participants applied the intervention in several modules rather than in just one, as was originally planned. Trying to incorporate only some of the elements of flow worked best – all chose to focus upon the autotelic, skills/challenge, paradox of control and 'goal and feedback' elements. Focus-group students appreciated the interventions employed, in particular the supported creativity allowed in the assessment task. The change in lecturer practice most evident was redesigning assessment tasks to allow students greater freedom, and in many cases greater enjoyment was an outcome. One student intimated that an assessment had been 'enjoyable but bloody hard'. Another appreciated the greater opportunity to talk to the lecturer about 'how we were getting on with our assignment. I knew I was on the right lines so I was able to relax and enjoy putting it together.'

Using flow in assessment design

As the project unfolded, a model incorporating elements of flow was developed (see Figure 11.1) to aid lecturers in the design of in-course assessments. Brief descriptions of the shaded boxes follow, representing those considerations more closely related to flow. The three unshaded boxes are key elements in assessment design but are not directly associated with flow theory (learning outcomes visited/ revisited; the assessment; reflection). The thin arrows direct assessment designers to related factors to be considered during the design process.

Model elements (flow-related)

Skill(s) and challenge

Lecturers should consider skills possessed and required. Is the challenge (for example, a question, a problem or time/word limits) likely to be perceived by students as neither too simple (low = boredom) or well beyond their capabilities (high = anxiety)? Maintaining an appropriate balance between skills and challenges is an ongoing process that ultimately determines whether enjoyment features in the activity or task. Lack of confidence is a barrier to experiencing flow (Jackson and Csikszentmihalyi, 1999) and entering into flow is very much dependent upon the skill being equal to the challenge.

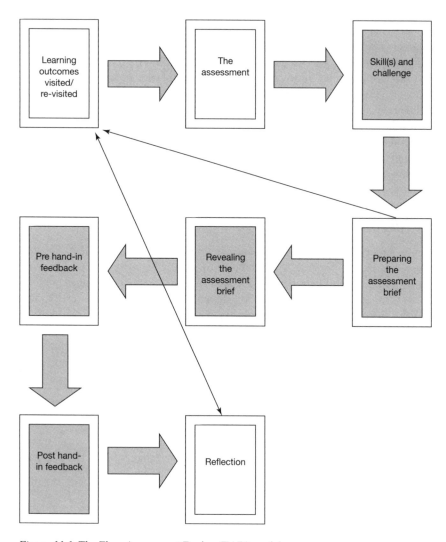

Figure 11.1 The Flow Assessment Design (FAD) model

Preparing the assessment brief

A vital feature of the optimal experience is it being an end in itself, a state Csikszentmihalyi coined as 'autotelic'. For 'when the experience is autotelic, the person is paying attention to the activity for its own sake; when it is not, the attention is focused on its consequences' (Csikszentmihalyi, 1992: 67). Where possible, students should be given the impression of choice within the assessment process, creating a more positive, autotelic experience. This could be achieved by incorporating, for example, either question or case-study choices, or by emphasising that several approaches could be used for successful completion. The task should not be completely open-ended, however, and students left to 'get on with it'; requirements should be clear and students encouraged to set regular and realistic goals.

The *paradox of control* is arguably the most intriguing ingredient of the flow experience, underlining the importance of not focusing upon possible consequences of actions. Students should be encouraged to 'let go of the ledge', to trust in their abilities and skills and not focus upon their potential grade. Therefore, while there should be an unambiguous explanation of what is required to complete the assessment successfully, details of what is necessary for specific grades should not be given. By reducing the saliency of the grade students should focus more on the assessment itself and less on the consequences, though not entirely – hence the paradox.

Revealing the assessment brief

Assessing an optimal time to reveal assignments to students has been scantily covered in the HE literature. Yet, if taking flow into account, the timing and nature of the 'revealing' are critical. The assessment brief should not be divulged too soon or late – for example, distributing the assessment at the beginning of the module with full details can generate anxiety due to a perception of lacking the skills to meet the challenge presented. Revealing the general nature of the assessment(s) – i.e., group presentation, report, etc. – at the beginning of the module, however, helps to inform students and prepare them without divulging too much information.

Pre hand-in feedback

Self-feedback should be encouraged with a checklist formatted to help students reflect on progress. In addition, further to encourage feedback – e.g., 'Am I on the right lines?' – and to discuss ideas, a meeting between lecturer and student (halfway into the assessment preparation) can be written into the assessment brief.

Post hand-in feedback

The importance of clear, supportive oral and written feedback to students' work is unquestionably a vital element of student learning and progression (Stefani, 1998). Effective feedback should be above all things informative, identifying where marks were gained and lost.

Conclusion

We are now more convinced of the benefits of lecturers utilising the principles of flow, having seen workshop participants enjoy some success in doing so; the workshops led to a reappraisal of approaches to assessment and a confidence to experiment with the ideas introduced. Yet why do many lecturers not trust more in their abilities as teachers? Potentially the job can become more enjoyable even in a relatively high-pressure culture. For flow to be effectively applied, the lecturer's attitude is fundamental as is student–lecturer interaction and reciprocity, for example in the feedback element. A potential obstacle for innovations being adopted more widely is unwillingness to change attitudes and practice. We are not deluding ourselves that all lecturers would be as open and enthusiastic or indeed give up their time as freely as our participants; many lecturers do not 'have the time for new initiatives because they are fully committed trying to do everything else that they have been allocated' (Davis, 2003: 253). We are not advocating wholesale changes, however; our evidence suggests that even minor changes can make a difference, for example if some thought is given to the timing and nature of revealing the assessment brief.

From the student perspective, if lecturers adopt some of the suggestions in our model, students can have more positive, enjoyable experiences with anxiety levels reduced. This is particularly important when more are entering HE with non-traditional qualifications. Many of the elements of flow introduced seemed to give students greater confidence and reduced anxiety when working on and submitting an assessment – for example, students given checklists (own goals and feedback), 'How well am I doing'? as part of the assessment brief. Students were also willing to try new approaches and 'let go of the ledge'. Two outcomes of introducing principles of flow are students acquiring greater self-awareness and control over their own learning processes and learning to reflect realistically on their progress, key goals in the UK's 'personal development planning' era.

Arguably, being able to make any part of the educational experience enjoyable must be the *raison d'être* of those delivering courses in HE. The application of flow is certainly one means of achieving such positive outcomes. More specifically, we firmly believe, and have some evidence to suggest, that the experience of adopting or at least considering flow affects the assessment experience of both lecturer and student, and this, of course, may have weighty implications for performance, retention and lifelong learning.

References

Csikszentmihalyi, M. (1975) *Beyond boredom and anxiety*. San Francisco: Jossey-Bass.

—— (1992) *Flow: the psychology of happiness*, London: Rider.

—— (1996) *Creativity – flow and the psychology of discovery and invention*. New York: HarperPerennial.

—— (1997a) Intrinsic motivation and effective teaching: a flow analysis, in J. L. Bess (ed.), *Teaching well and liking it*. Baltimore, MD: Johns Hopkins University Press, pp. 73–89.

—— (1997b) Flow and education, *NAMTA Journal*, 22, 2, pp. 3–35.

Davis, M. (2003) Barriers to reflective practice – the changing nature of higher education, *Active Learning in Higher Education*, 4, 3, pp. 243–55.

Gammon, S. and Lawrence, L. (2000) Using leisure in learning to re-focus student motivation: 'Letting go of the ledge', *University of Luton Teaching and Learning Conference Proceedings*, pp. 99–110.

—— (2003) *Developing and evaluating the application of leisure-related psychological theory (the concept of flow) to student assessment strategies in higher education (summary of the final report)*. LTSN. Available at <http://www.hlst.ltsn.ac.uk/projects/lawerence_summary.pdf>.

Gibbs, G. and Habeshaw, T. (1989) *Preparing to teach – an introduction to effective teaching in higher education*. Bristol: Technical and Educational Services.

Jackson, S. A. and Csikszentmihalyi, M. (1999) *Flow in sports – the keys to optimal experiences and performances*. Champaign, IL: Human Kinetics.

Mannell, R. C. and Kleiber, D. A. (1997) *A social psychology of leisure*. State College, PA: Venture Publishing.

Ramsden, P. (1992) *Learning to teach in higher education*. London: Routledge.

Salmon, G. (2002) *E-tivities: the key to active learning*. London: Kogan Page.

Stefani, L. A. J. (1998) Assessment in partnership with learners, *Assessment and Evaluation in Higher Education*, 23, 4, pp. 339–50.

12 Confidence-based marking

Towards deeper learning and
better exams

A. R. Gardner-Medwin

Introduction

This chapter looks at confidence-based marking (CBM) at University College London over the last ten years. The CBM strategy was initially introduced to improve formative self-assessment and to encourage students to think more carefully about questions in objective tests. It became known as LAPT (London Agreed Protocol for Teaching: <www.ucl.ac.uk/lapt>) through collaboration between a number of medical schools now mainly subsumed within UCL and Imperial College London. We have recently developed web-based tools for dissemination and evaluation in other institutions and new disciplines, and since 2001 we have been using CBM at UCL for summative (years 1 and 2) medical exams. CBM is seen by our students as simple, fair, readily understood and beneficial. They are motivated to reflect and justify reasons either for confidence or reservation about each answer, and they gain by expressing true confidence, whether high or low.

Experience with students suggests that many of the stronger ones find they can do well by relying on superficial associations, with little incentive (on conventional right/wrong mark schemes) to think rigorously or understand the issues thoroughly: the first thing they think of is usually good enough. At the same time, weaker students try to emulate this with diligent rote learning, rejecting deeper learning as unnecessarily challenging. A properly designed scheme for CBM ensures that in order to get the best marks students must discriminate between responses based on sound knowledge or understanding and those where there is a significant risk of error. The essence of such a motivating scheme is that confident answers gain more marks if correct, but at the risk of significant penalty if wrong; low confidence benefits the student when there are reasons for reservation, because the penalties are proportionately less or absent. We shall see later how these constraints on the design of a proper marking scheme can be understood in graphical terms (Figure 12.1), but the essential feature is that the students who benefit are those who can identify the basis for justification or reservation, not those who are consistently confident or unconfident.

This chapter will refer to previous publications where specific points are covered there in more detail (Gardner-Medwin, 1995; Issroff and Gardner-Medwin, 1998; Gardner-Medwin and Gahan, 2003). Readers are strongly encouraged, before thinking far about the issues, to try out confidence-based marking for themselves on the website (<www.ucl.ac.uk/lapt>) using any of a range of exercises in different fields. Experience shows that students approaching CBM as learners seem to understand its logic instinctively through application, much more readily than through exposition and discussion. The website also provides access to prior publications and authoring tools.[1]

Confidence-based marking has been researched quite extensively, but mostly before computer-aided assessment was practical on much of a scale (see, for example, Ahlgren, 1969; Good, 1979). Our experience is, we believe, the largest application to routine coursework, and differs from most research studies in that students have had extensive online practice before use in formal tests. We use a three-point confidence scale (C = 1, 2 or 3). Whenever the answer is correct, the mark (M) is equal to its associated confidence level: M = 1, 2 or 3. If the answer is wrong, then at the higher confidence levels there are increasing penalties: –2 marks at C = 2 and –6 marks at C = 3. This scheme is set out in Table 12.1. For example, a student asked whether Russia has a Baltic coast would need either sound knowledge or a convincing argument to risk C = 3.

Confidence levels are deliberately identified by numbers (C = 1, 2 or 3) or neutral descriptors (low, mid, high) rather than by descriptive terms ('certain', 'very sure', 'unsure', 'guess', etc.), because descriptions mean different things to different people and in different contexts. A transparent mark scheme must be defined by rewards, penalties and explicit risks, not by subjective norms.

The rationale of CBM: the student's perspective

Several qualitative features of pedagogic importance are immediately clear to a student when thinking about answering a question with CBM. These relate directly to the second and fifth 'principles of good feedback practice' (reflection and motivation) set out in Chapter 5.

1   To get full credit for a correct answer you must be able to justify the answer, to the point that you are prepared to take the risk that – if wrong – you will lose marks. This makes it harder to rely on rote-learned facts, and encourages attempts to relate the answer to other knowledge.

2   Equally, if you can justify reasons for reservation about your answer, you also gain credit, because with a higher probability of error you will gain on

Table 12.1 The normal LAPT confidence-based mark scheme

Confidence level	C = 1 (low)	C = 2 (mid)	C = 3 (high)	No reply
Mark if correct	1	2	3	(0)
Penalty if wrong	0	–2	–6	(0)

average by lowering your confidence. This is the *motivating* characteristic of the mark scheme (Good, 1979).

3 A lucky guess is not the same as knowledge. Students recognise the fairness and value of a system that gives less credit to a correct answer based on uncertain knowledge than to one that is soundly justified and argued. Teachers should recognise this, too.

4 A confident wrong answer is a wake-up call deserving penalty. When studying, this triggers reflection about the reasons for error, and particular attention to an explanation. In exams, it merits greater penalty than a wrong answer that is acknowledged as partly guesswork.

5 To quote comments from an evaluation study (Issroff and Gardner-Medwin, 1998): 'It . . . stops you making rush answers'; 'You can assess how well you really understand a topic'; 'It makes one think . . . it can be quite a shock to get a –6 . . . you are forced to concentrate'.

These points encapsulate the initial reasons for introducing CBM. Unreliable knowledge of the basics in a subject, or – worse – lack of awareness of which parts of one's knowledge are sound and which not, can be a huge handicap to further learning (Gardner-Medwin, 1995). By failing to think critically and identify points of weakness, students lose the opportunity to embed their learning deeply and to find connections between different elements of their knowledge. It is distressing to see students with good grades in GCSE mathematics struggling two years later to apply half-remembered rules to issues that should be embedded as commonsense understanding – such as the percentage change when a 20 per cent fall follows a 50 per cent rise.

Students benefit by learning that there are different ways to solve problems, and that efficient learning and rigorous knowledge involves the skill of always testing one idea against another. Only then can one be said to have 'understanding' of a subject. What is more, the ability to indicate confidence or reservation about opinions to others, explicitly or through body language, is an essential skill in every discipline and walk of life. These skills may nevertheless remain largely untaught and untested in assessments before final undergraduate or graduate tests, when they become crucial in viva situations and in demanding forms of critical writing.

Is there a correct CBM mark scheme?

A student's best choice of confidence level (C = 1, 2, or 3) is governed by two factors: confidence (degree of belief, or subjective probability) that the answer will be correct, and the rewards (or penalties) for right and wrong answers. The average marks obtained with our scheme (Table 12.1) are plotted in Figure 12.1 for each confidence level against the probability of being correct.

One always stands to gain the best overall score by choosing a confidence level (C = 1, 2 or 3) for each answer that corresponds to whichever line is highest on the graph, above the point showing one's estimated probability of being correct. It is best to opt for C = 1 if this probability is less than 67 per cent, C = 2 if it is

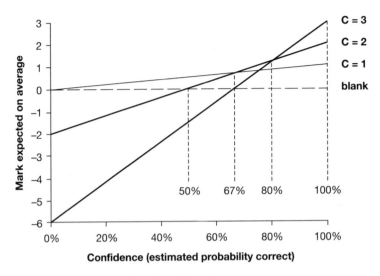

Figure 12.1 Rationale for a choice of confidence level.

Notes: The average mark, expected on the basis of a student's estimated probability of an answer being correct, is shown for each confidence level and for a blank reply, with the mark scheme in Table 12.1. The best choice for a particular estimated probability of being correct is the one with the highest graph

67–80 per cent, and C = 3 if it is greater than 80 per cent. It doesn't pay to misrepresent one's confidence. This is the motivating characteristic of the mark scheme, rewarding the student's ability to judge the reliability of an answer, not their self-confidence or diffidence. CBM is quite unlike games such as poker, in which misrepresentation of confidence can gain advantage.

At UCL we have used this scheme mainly for questions with true/false answers. With just two possible answers, the estimated probability of being correct can never be less than 50 per cent, since, if it were, then one would obviously switch choices. The three confidence levels cover the possible range of probabilities (50–100 per cent) fairly evenly. For questions with more options (a typical MCQ question, or one requiring a numeric or text entry), a preferred answer may be given with an estimated probability of being correct that is lower than 50 per cent. For such questions we have experimented with a scheme similar to Table 12.1, but with lower penalties: –1 at C = 2 and –4 at C = 3. The graphs for this scheme (Figure 12.2a) show it also to be properly motivating, with incentives to use C = 1 when confidence is low (less than 50 per cent) and C = 3 when it is high (more than 75 per cent). This gives more uniform coverage of the full probability range, from 0–100 per cent. Data show that students can adapt confidence judgements with multiple-choice questions to whichever mark scheme is employed,[2] so the better strategy in the future may be to avoid complexity by keeping to a single mark scheme (Table 12.1) for all question types.

Not all CBM schemes in the literature have been properly motivating schemes (see discussion in Gardner-Medwin and Gahan, 2003). Figure 12.2b shows a

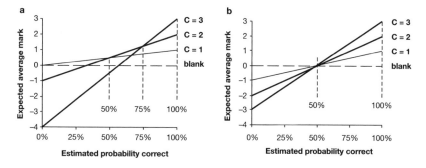

Figure 12.2 Characteristic graphs for different CBM schemes.

Note: These graphs are equivalent to Figure 12.1 but for a scheme used on a trial basis in LAPT for questions with more than two possible answers and for a non-motivating scheme used elsewhere

superficially similar scheme (incorrectly attributed to LAPT by Davies, 2002) with penalties (–1, –2, –3) instead of (0, –2, –6). This scheme has the merit of simplicity. However, inspection of the graph shows that it is always best either to opt for high confidence (C = 3) or not to answer at all. This shows the importance, if one is devising a new CBM scheme, of plotting such graphs. Students who use confidence levels 1 or 2 on this scheme may be following their teachers' advice, but would be quite disadvantaged. They would gain lower scores than students who were brash, or who saw that this strategy was never sensible. Though such a scheme could have some of the benefits of CBM by encouraging students to reflect, and by reducing the weighting of unconfident answers, it could never be seen as fair, given that it benefits students who only use C = 3. It could not survive once the best strategy became known.

The schemes used in LAPT at UCL are not the only ones that are properly motivating, but they are simple, easily remembered and well understood. They were also chosen because the scores with T/F questions (Table 12.1) correspond about as closely as can be achieved with a three-point scale to the correct measure of knowledge as a function of subjective probability that derives from information theory (Figure 1 in Gardner-Medwin, 1995). A more complex scheme was devised and used by Hassmen and Hunt (1994) with five confidence levels and marks for correct answers (20, 54, 74, 94, 100) and for wrong answers (10, –8, –32, –64, –120). This scheme is in principle motivating (Gardner-Medwin and Gahan, 2003) but it is hard to remember and understand. Perhaps because of this, it has sometimes been used without the student being aware of the marks associated with different confidence levels.[3] Again, it may encourage reflection, but lacks the simplicity and transparency that seem critical if one is to obtain full engagement of students in a system designed to improve study habits and assessment.

Students rarely describe their choice of confidence level in terms of explicit probabilities, even after the principles are explained. Watching students (and particularly staff) in a first encounter with CBM, it is common to find some who initially regard anything less than C = 3 as a diminution of their ego. In group working, confidence is often determined by one person, until others start to realise that a little thought can do better than a forward personality! Brashness does not long survive a few negative marks, nor diffidence the sense of lost opportunities. Despite their intuitive approach, students on average come to use the confidence bands in a nearly optimal fashion to maximise their scores. In exams, few students have percentages correct in the three bands that are outside the correct probability ranges (Gardner-Medwin and Gahan, 2003). This is consistent with the general finding that though people are poor at handling the concept of probability correctly, they make good judgements when information is evident as clear risks, outcomes and frequencies (Gigerenzer, 2003). This is perhaps the chief benefit of a simple, transparent scheme. However, our data do suggest that students initially vary more widely in their ability to calibrate judgements according to the mark scheme. Formative practice with feedback is therefore essential. Our system ensures that in addition to immediate feedback after each answer to assist reflective learning, students receive a breakdown of percentage correct at each confidence level whenever they complete an exercise.

Concerns about CBM: why don't more people use it?

Despite the clear rationale for CBM, its student popularity and statistical benefits in exams (see below), CBM has surprisingly little uptake in the UK or globally. In our dissemination project (<www.ucl.ac.uk/lapt>) we provide tools for new institutions and teachers to experiment with their own materials and students, and to interface with their own VLE. An interesting feature of dissemination within UCL has been the stimulus to uptake within medical science courses that has come from the students themselves – often a much more potent force for change in a university than discussion among staff. However, it is worth addressing misconceptions that sometimes emerge in discussion.

It is sometimes thought that CBM might unfairly favour or encourage particular personality traits. In particular, it is suggested (though usually vigorously rejected by students) that CBM may lead to gender bias, usually based on the notion that it might disadvantage diffident or risk-averse personalities – supposedly more common among females. Several points can be made about this (discussed at greater length by Gardner-Medwin and Gahan, 2003). Careful analysis of data from exams and in-course use of CBM at UCL has shown no gender differences, despite clear differences (in both sexes) between summative and formative use (more cautious use of high confidence levels in exams, with consequently higher percentage correct when using these levels: Figure 12.3). We have correlated exam data also to ethnic status, and again there is no evidence for significant ethnic variation among practised students. Gender and ethnic factors may be present on first encounter with CBM; such transient effects would not have shown up in our analysis. But if, quite plausibly, individuals or groups do have initial tendencies to be under- or over-confident, then this is an objective problem of which they should be aware. CBM offers suitable feedback and training. This is not to say that outwardly diffident or

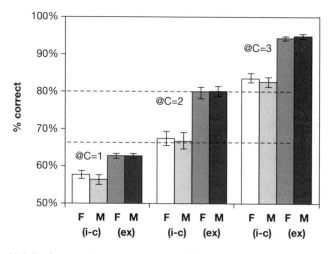

Figure 12.3 Performance broken down by confidence, context and gender.

Notes: Accuracy (mean % correct) is shown at each confidence level for T/F answers entered in voluntary in-course (i-c) exercises (mean 1005 Qs) and in exams (ex) at the end of year (500 Qs), separated by gender (190F, 141M). Bars are 95 per cent confidence limits for the means. Differences between exams and in-course work are significant at each confidence level (P <0.01 per cent) but gender differences are not significant (Gardner-Medwin and Gahan, 2003)

confident personalities are undesirable or unattractive, but rather that in decision-rich occupations such as medicine, miscalibration of reliability is a serious handicap.

A second misconception is that the aim of CBM is somehow to boost self-confidence. Of course, self-confidence should ultimately be boosted by any effective learning tool. Students often say, in evaluation questionnaires, that the LAPT system with CBM has improved their confidence in their knowledge (Issroff and Gardner-Medwin, 1998).[4] But they also say, and this seems pedagogically more important, that it forces them to think more, and reveals points of weakness. CBM places a premium on understanding: on the ability to link and cross-check pieces of information, and therefore to distinguish sound and weak conclusions. The net effect may be to undermine confidence as students come to realise that sound knowledge cannot be based on hunches. But this realisation is itself a step towards academic success and the building of self-confidence.

Some people suggest that CBM may be useful for formative assessment but not for exams, supposedly because what matters are correct answers, not students' confidence in their answers. From an epistemological standpoint, this seems simply wrong: a lucky guess is not knowledge, and a firm misconception is far worse than acknowledged ignorance. My view is that we fail our students if we don't acknowledge this. But we can also regard the issue simply as a psychometric one. Our exam data show improved reliability using CBM,[5] consistent with research data with other forms of CBM (Ahlgren, 1969). Some of this improvement is due to involvement of an extra skill that varies between students: ability to handle CBM. But even if one adopts number correct as the criterion of performance, our data showed that CBM scores are the better predictor of this on a separate set of questions, and are therefore both more valid and more reliable as a measure of knowledge.

Confidence-based marking places a premium on careful thinking and on checks that can help tie together different facets of knowledge. It thereby encourages deeper understanding and learning. It is popular with students, and helps them develop valuable skills. In exams it produces higher-quality data for their assessment. A puzzle remains: why this seemingly sensible strategy for objectively marked tests, which has been known and researched over many decades, is so little employed by teachers or vendors of software.

Acknowledgements

Supported by the Higher Education Funding Council for England, under the Fund for the Development of Teaching and Learning, Phase 4. Some of the software was written by M. Gahan. Data for analysis were provided by D. Bender at UCL and N. Curtin at Imperial College.

Notes

1   For study and revision purposes we employ either dedicated Windows software or a browser-based resource written in Javascript. The browser system now offers equivalent flexibility and more material, in more subject areas; it will be the main platform for future development and collaborations, and can be integrated with grade management in a virtual learning environment (VLE). Other institutions may use the UCL software to run exercises placed on their own or a UCL site. For exams we use optical mark reader (OMR) technology, and for trial purposes UCL currently offers a processing service, saving initial investment in hardware and software, through collaboration with Speedwell Computing Services (<www.speedwell.co.uk>).

2   Data from 10,000 (mostly multiple-choice) answers to practice questions for a biomedical admissions test (see <www.ucl.ac.uk/lapt>), carried out mainly by inexperienced CBM users, gave mean percentages at each confidence level that were within the appropriate optimal bands (Figures 12.1 or 12.2a) when the exercises were made available at different times using the two schemes.

3   E.g., SACAT: Self Assessment Computer Analyzed Testing. Available at <www. hpeusa.com>.

4   Sixty-seven per cent of students rated CBM 'useful' or 'very useful'. Forty per cent said they sometimes changed their answers when thinking about their confidence. Additional comments: 'If [score is] high – gives more confidence'; '[I] revise areas where confidence is weak'; 'Useful guide to level of knowledge and real ability' (Issroff and Gardner-Medwin, 1998).

5   In data from six medical exams, each with about 350 students and 250–300 true/false questions (in groups of five, on related topics), we calculated reliability indices for both CBM scores and numbers correct, using the standard (Cronbach Alpha) measure. These were 0.925 ± 0.007 for CBM (mean $\pm$ SEM, n = 6) and 0.873 ± 0.012 for numbers correct. The significant improvement (P <0.001, paired t-test) corresponded to a reduction of the chance element in the variance of exam scores from 14.6 per cent of the student variance to 8.1 per cent. We also correlated the two types of score on half of the questions (odd numbers) for their ability to predict the number correct on the remainder. CBM scores were substantially better predictors (Gardner-Medwin and Gahan, 2003).

References

Ahlgren, A. (1969) Reliability, predictive validity, and personality bias of confidence-weighted scores. Available at <www.p-mmm.com/founders/AhlgrenBody.htm>.

Davies, P. (2002) There's no confidence in multiple-choice testing. *Proceedings of the 6th International CAA Conference*, Loughborough, pp. 119–30.

Gardner-Medwin, A. R. (1995) Confidence assessment in the teaching of basic science, *Association for Learning Technology Journal*, 3: 80–5.

Gardner-Medwin, A. R. and Gahan, M. (2003) Formative and summative confidence-based assessment. *Proceedings of the 7th International CAA Conference*, Loughborough, pp. 147–55. Available at <www.caaconference.com>.

Gigerenzer, G. (2003) *Reckoning with risk*. London: Penguin.

Good, I. J. (1979) 'Proper fees' in multiple choice examinations, *Journal of Statistical and Computational Simulation*, 9: 164–5.

Hassmen, P. and Hunt, D. P. (1994) Human self-assessment in multiple-choice testing, *Journal of Educational Measurement*, 31: 149–60.

Issroff, K. and Gardner-Medwin, A. R. (1998) Evaluation of confidence assessment within optional coursework, in M. Oliver (ed.), *Innovation in the evaluation of learning technology*. London: University of North London, pp. 169–79.

13 Developing group learning through assessment

Cordelia Bryan

Introduction

This case study documents an innovative approach to assessment designed to encourage students to focus on the process of collaboration. It shifts student attention from focusing almost exclusively on performance and outcomes to attitudes which begin to value co-operation and group dynamics. In so doing, the intention was not only that students might develop and acquire important collaborative skills such as communication, negotiation, self-initiative, resourcefulness and conflict management, but that their ultimate performance grade might consequently be improved when such characteristics were manifest, observed and part of the assessment process.

Although collaboration is often the context of learning within the performing arts, it is rarely a focus of it, due to an almost universal emphasis on individual task objectives and performance.[1] Perhaps unsurprisingly, our research also revealed that students frequently felt that this emphasis on outcomes was 'unfair' as it did not differentiate between group members who contributed positively and those who were 'passengers', or, worse, may have had a generally negative influence on the group.[2] Tutors were often aware of their students' grievance that individual effort and input into group work was not formally recognised, but seemed unable to remedy the situation. This was due either to rigid assessment regulations or, more frequently, to a perceived scarcity of appropriate and fair methods to allocate credit for the processes of group-work-assessed tasks. Where we encountered evidence of tutors applying sound pedagogical theories of learning in teams with successful results (Boud, 1995; Bourner *et al.*, 2001; Brown and Glasner, 1999; Gibbs, 1995; Jaques, 2001; Janis, 1972; Johnson and Johnson, 1994), this was seldom made explicit to students and rarely accrued academic credit.[3]

The challenge

In short, comments expressed by students indicated that they often felt ill prepared to work in groups. Furthermore, when they were expected to work collaboratively without a tutor being present (a frequent occurrence in performing arts), many expressed frustration at the time wasted through arguments and general poor management of the group and the consequent need to seek tutor intervention. The challenge to us then was:

- could we devise assessment methods to assess group processes (as well as outcomes);
- could the assessment differentiate between individual and group contribution;
- could the assessment act as sufficient motivation to improve students' general ability to work as effective group members.

Description of the assessment

After participating in a problem-based learning (PBL) workshop (described later), group participants are asked to rate the following against a mark of 1–5:

- how well the group achieved its task as stated;
- how well you think you contributed to achieve the group task;
- how well the group functioned as a group;
- how well you think you performed as a group member.

Any scale may be used; however, simplicity is recommended to avoid potential confusion leading to discussion about scoring rather than performance. Grading can be further compared and refined by asking participants to give a mark of 1–5 for individual contribution to 'group task' and 'group maintenance' for each of their peers. Group maintenance may include relevant aspects of group dynamics such as how well each individual:

- listened to others;
- extrapolated salient points from muddled contributions;
- enabled shy members to contribute; or
- applied a technique for dealing with unproductive disharmony within the group.

Allocating individual grades for each group member can be time consuming if all the marks are subsequently shared and full discussion of the variances is allowed. However, peer grading offers further scope for refining students' judgement-based learning in and from groups providing that the facilitator ensures the focus of discussion is on feedback, designed specifically to enhance learning.

The assessment proved to work particularly well when two or three participants volunteer (or are selected) to stand outside the group and observe the process, make notes and provide feedback at the end. Participants may be asked to listen to *all* feedback from the observers before being allowed to comment on or justify their behaviour. Utilising this model to peer assess group processes has several advantages. First, it enables the observers to devote their full and undivided attention to the group dynamics. Second, it allows observers to be more objective because they have no vested interest in the task outcome. Third, it offers a model in which students practise giving and receiving feedback as two distinct processes, thus allowing for momentary reflection, before engaging in a dialogue about what may or may not have been intended (Bryan and Green, 2003: 316–25).

If the group or the tutor is relatively new to self- and peer assessment *per se*, or to the idea of assessing group participation, it can be helpful to leave the whole criteria setting and grading process until the end of a session, *after* feedback has been given and discussed fully. If criteria setting is delayed, it should be emphasised that this is not normal good practice (i.e., to impose assessment criteria after the event) but that it is for a particular reason: namely, to raise questions about how participants might have behaved differently, had they known they would be assessed on their collaborative performance. Delaying the discussion about assessment criteria until after the exercise can also demonstrate the importance of matching the mode of assessment to the particular task.

Sufficient time must be allowed for participants to share their feelings as well as their perceptions of assessing and being assessed. Thus a commonly owned and shared mode of assessment may be developed for subsequent workshops where it is proposed to assess the collaborative process as well as the outcome. The pedagogic benefits for requiring students to assess group maintenance as well as group task are summed up by these two student comments:

> I was one of the ones who said how unfair it is not to get marked on how well we work together in our group projects but I had no idea how difficult it is to do it properly. I have learned so much from watching our group and having to articulate the grades I gave.
>
> (Second-year Drama student)

> It's weird how at the beginning we gave very different marks for how well we thought we had worked in the group but after discussing it [group dynamics and different roles] we sort of more or less agreed. Our group work has definitely improved as we now know what things to do if it is going badly.
>
> (First-year English/Drama student)

The following student comment echoes research (Lapham and Webster, 1999) which shows that by engaging collaboratively in the assessment process students gain a group identity, thereby further enhancing the potential learning in groups.

> I notice a real difference working with people who have had to think about and argue how they should be assessed in their group. It's like we have already done quite a lot of ice breaking and can get stuck straight in with our projects.
>
> (Second-year Drama student)

The assessment criteria may be decided by the tutor and explained at the start of the workshop. Alternatively, it might be more appropriate to involve the students in the process of devising their own assessment criteria, thereby also clarifying the objectives of the session. Another advantage of involving students in setting their own assessment criteria is that the students learn to determine what is or is not important in the exercise and consequently how to allocate the weighting of marks.

> At first I couldn't see the point of deciding our own assessment criteria but having done so now on three separate occasions, I realise how it helped the whole group think and agree what was most important and should therefore carry most marks.
>
> (PGCE Drama student)

> Everyone knows the rules if you have to set the assessment together so we don't waste time arguing when we're working without the tutor.
>
> (First-year Jazz student)

The last comment not only sums up student views frequently expressed in our trials but provides a counter-argument to the commonly voiced lecturers' lament that involving students in devising assessment criteria is too time consuming. While it is true that generating assessment criteria collaboratively takes time at the outset, our experience shows that in group work it ultimately *saves* time otherwise frequently spent arguing about fairness of individual effort and contribution to the whole. Agreeing assessment criteria collaboratively helps establish clear rules for how the group will function. When students are expected to work in groups partially unsupervised by the tutor, as is increasingly the case, it would seem that time spent discussing and agreeing assessment criteria is time extremely well spent.

Rationale for the approach

This innovation sought to focus attention on the process of collaboration by adopting a PBL approach utilising group dynamics. Our consortium of nine colleagues from six higher education institutions (HEIs)[4] agreed to work collaboratively as an action research group adopting a PBL approach whenever possible. We recognised that by 'problematising' the assessment of group practice and working collaboratively towards potential 'solutions' we would experience for ourselves the inherent paradoxes expressed by students of having to work collaboratively in what is often a competitive environment. We also recognised an opportunity for our own professional development through adopting a collaborative PBL approach: namely, that we might enhance our own critical, reflective and communication skills and other well-documented qualities associated with PBL and professional development (Boud and Feletti, 1997).

PBL workshop approach

The nine tutors introduced various methods of self- and peer assessment of group work with twelve selected groups of students on diverse performing arts courses. With the students' consent, this was initially introduced as a 'trial' where the marks generated would not contribute to the summative assessment of the module.

However, it was explained to them that should the assessment prove to be practical, fair and transparent, appropriate changes to the module assessment might be considered. The self- and peer assessment focused on both group dynamics and the task in hand. Tutors agreed to select sessions in which some form of group PBL would anyway be taking place because there was a need to have some clearly defined 'problem' which could generate a number of more or less effective solutions capable of assessment. The selected sessions were called 'workshops' and included traditional seminar groups (tutor plus up to thirty students) and tutor-facilitated rehearsals for first- and second-year student productions.

In this initial stage 185 students were involved in nine workshops, each utilising diverse materials adopting a clearly defined PBL approach. Data was gathered using a version of the Delphi technique whereby information was collected from all those participating and then analysed and fed back to the whole group. Further discussion in the light of feedback refined the data which then informed development of the assessment method and identified the need for specific supporting learning materials. This cyclical approach for gathering and analysing student opinions seemed particularly appropriate as it served two purposes. First, it contributed to the development of reflective dialogue and autonomous learning habits as advocated by Brockbank and McGill (2000: 132); and second, it fed directly into the action research cycle of all nine tutors within the consortium. The cyclical process thus enabled students to:

- develop an awareness of group dynamics (in the assessment and in the sub-sequent discussions);
- acquire appropriate language of assessment with which to articulate with their peers;
- begin to understand the sort of discourse of exam boards (and thereby appre-ciate the complexities and problems associated with rigour and fairness);
- engage actively in the design of their own assessment;
- identify their own individual and collective deficiencies; and consequently
- articulate quite specific needs for the improvement of their performance as group participants.

The Delphi method for reaching consensus as applied in the workshops also acted as a vehicle for students to make valuable contributions to curricular alignment of teaching, learning and assessment in group work. The consortium functioned and progressed as an action research group (McGill and Beaty, 1992), developing and trialling its assessment innovations both internally and externally (Bryan, 2004a: 52–64).

Collaboratively we developed practical approaches and materials which would support the areas of weakness the students (and staff) had identified by engaging in the assessment. These approaches included:

- how to apply basic group dynamic theory in differing contexts;
- how to give and receive feedback so it would contribute to future learning;

- how to deal with 'difficult' group participants;
- how to assess individual and group contributions to both task and process.

All materials are available in easily downloadable form from the project website at <http://assessing-groupwork.ulst.ac.uk>.

Further trialling was conducted using the revised and developed methods of assessment supported by targeted learning materials. Forty-six of the original 185 students and an additional ninety-two 'new' students participated in at least one workshop (in some cases up to three) in which the innovative assessment was employed, making a total of 138 students representing five tutor groups. In one of the five groups, the self- and peer-generated assessment grades were tutor moderated and contributed to the module's final assessment. This had been made possible by a minor amendment to the course assessment structure which was internally agreed and approved by the external examiner.

How and why others might wish to adopt this approach

This assessment innovation, as argued here and supported by student and staff feedback, has demonstrated a positive shift of attention to include the collaborative process. It has been successfully applied in diverse situations, thereby demonstrating its flexibility. It offers a simple yet effective grading system which recognises individual contribution to both task achievement and the collaborative process. In so doing, it reframes assessment as being central to creative and pedagogic practices in group work.

Qualitative data such as module evaluation by tutors and annual subject monitoring reports within the six consortium institutions indicate that there has been a perceived improvement in the quality of student group work.

This is reinforced by staff (350) and student (roughly 700) feedback across twelve institutions where participants actively engaged in some form of assessed PBL workshop. Nowhere did we encounter real opposition to the proposition that students need to learn about group dynamics to take control of their own group learning environment and that *assessing* group skills is key to achieving this. The most frequently expressed reservation was about the difficulty of finding time within an already crowded curriculum to include the assessment of group processes. Participants were reassured and sometimes surprised how feasible this could be once they had participated in an assessed PBL workshop. A particular advantage to them was the fact that the PBL workshop approach is infinitely flexible, allowing for almost any subject matter to be presented as 'the problem'.

Two final staff comments illustrate the sort of shift in practice clearly brought about by the assessment intervention which is so difficult to quantify:

> I thoroughly enjoyed the workshop [Developing Effective Group Behaviour] and want to try it on my students, not because I'm a fan of peer assessment but because the workshop raised so many other critical issues that have been bugging me lately.

Since the workshop over a year ago, a group of us have used various [Assessing Group Practice] materials to raise students' awareness of group dynamics. We are convinced that since we assess the group process the standard of work has improved but also that group work seems to be more fun with participants appearing to feel safe to take more risks.

Acknowledgement

The author (Project Director) gratefully acknowledges the contribution of all other members of the Assessing Group Practice consortium in the development of this case study: Linda Cookson (Chair), Anthony Dean, Debbie Green (Central School of Speech and Drama); Paul Cowen, the late Wendy Johnson (University of Leeds, Bretton Hall campus); John Hall, Simon Persighetti, Catriona Scott, Claire Donovan (Dartington College of Arts); Robert Gordon, Ajay Kumar, Gareth White (Goldsmiths College, University of London); Steve Dixon, Jackie Smart, Tracy Crossley (University of Salford); Tom Maguire (University of Ulster).

I would like formally to thank all the staff and students who shared their experiences with consortium members and who took the time to explain what does or does not work for them.

Notes

1   This paper is informed by field research and case studies conducted as part of a three-year consortium project, Assessing Group Practice, funded by HEFCE's Fund for the Development of Teaching and Learning. The consortium was formed in 2000 to research issues in the assessment of group work in HE performing arts and to identify, develop and share successful practice. The project was led by the Central School of Speech and Drama and also involved the Universities of Leeds, Salford and Ulster, Dartington College of Arts, and Goldsmiths College, University of London. The project was extended by a further six months to trial and evaluate materials with six CADISE institutions (Consortium of Art and Design Institutions in the Southeast of England). At the time of writing aproximately 700 staff and in excess of 1,000 students have engaged with Assessing Group Practice materials and approaches. Further details are available from the consortium website, <www.ulst.ac.uk/assessing-groupwork>.

2   In 2000–1 the Assessing Group Practice consortium interviewed a number of staff and students in our own institutions and conducted a questionnaire survey from thirty-six neighbouring institutions. In addition, 142 tutors in performance and creative arts departments in 61 UK institutions were contacted for information about courses in which group activity formed a major part. Although the response rate was lower than we had hoped (just under a third of the 142 tutors responded), there was considerable congruence in a variety of themes, many of which accorded with the experience of consortium members (Bryan, 2004b).

3   See note 2 above.

4   See note 1 above.

References

Boud, D. (1995) Assessment and learning: complementary or contradictory, in P. Knight (ed.), *Assessment for learning in higher education*. London: Kogan Page in association with SEDA.

Boud, D. and Feletti, G. (1997) Changing problem-based learning: Introduction to the second edition, in D. Boud and G. Feletti (eds), *The challenge of problem-based learning*, 2nd edn. London: Kogan Page.

Bourner, J., Hughes, M. and Bourner, T. (2001) First year undergraduate experiences of group project work, *Assessment and Evaluation in Higher Education*, 26, 1, pp. 19–39.

Brockbank, A. and McGill, I. (2000) *Facilitating reflective learning in higher education*. Buckingham and Philadelphia: Society for Research into Higher Education and Open University Press.

Brown, S. and Glasner, A. (eds) (1999) *Assessment matters in higher education: choosing and using diverse approaches*. Buckingham and Philadelphia: Society for Research into Higher Education and Open University Press.

Bryan, C. (2004a) Assessing the creative work of groups, in D. Miell and K. Littleton (eds), *Collaborative creativity*. London: Free Association Books.

—— (2004b) The case for assessing and developing group practice, in C. Bryan (ed.), *Assessing group practice*, Birmingham SEDA Paper 117, pp. 7–17.

Bryan, C. and Green, D. (2003) How guided reflection can enhance group work, in C. Rust (ed.), *Improving student learning: theory and practice – 10 years on*. Oxford: Oxford Centre for Staff and Learning Development, pp. 316–25.

Gibbs, G. (1995) *Learning in teams: a tutor guide*, rev. edn. Oxford: Oxford Centre for Staff Development.

Jaques, D. (2001) *Learning in groups*, 3rd edn. London: Kogan Page.

Janis, I. (1972) *Victims of groupthink*. Boston: Houghton-Mifflin.

Johnson, D. W. and Johnson, F. P. (1994) *Joining together: group theory and group skills*. London: Allyn and Baco.

Lapham, A. and Webster, R. (1999) Peer assessment of undergraduate seminar presentations: motivations, reflections and future directions, in S. Brown and A. Glasner (eds), *Assessment matters in higher education: choosing and using diverse approaches*. Buckingham and Philadelphia: Society for Research into Higher Education and Open University Press.

McGill, I. and Beaty, L. (1992) *Action learning: a practitioner's guide*. London: Kogan Page.

14 Supporting diverse students

Developing learner autonomy via assessment

Kay Sambell, Liz McDowell and
Alistair Sambell

Introduction

This chapter focuses on two case studies in which lecturers aimed to use assessment as a pedagogic technique to foster learner autonomy. Analysis of the student viewpoint is used to highlight some of the issues that surround the use of assessment to develop autonomy as an outcome, particularly in the context of increasing student diversity.

Formative and summative self-evaluation activities, and the closely related activity of peer-assessment or reciprocal peer feedback situations, are becoming increasingly common in higher education (Brown *et al.*, 1997; Segers *et al.*, 2003). Often this is because they are considered to be valuable activities that develop students' abilities to become realistic judges of their own performance, enabling them to monitor their own learning effectively, rather than relying on their teachers to fulfil this role for them. As such, they are commonly regarded as important tools for learning, frequently linked to the notion of promoting, practising and developing autonomy (Boud, 1995; Hinett and Thomas, 1999; Knight and Yorke, 2003).

Autonomy and learning

Self-assessment in higher education is frequently promoted on the grounds that it develops the capacity to self-monitor by raising consciousness of metacognitive processes and learning-to-learn skills. In this general way self-assessment becomes 'a particularly important part of the thinking of those who are committed to such goals as student autonomy' (Boud, 1995: 14). When more specifically related to learning, however, autonomy and its development is clearly a complex construct. It is typically thought to incorporate several dimensions, including different domains of knowledge (Brew, 1995: 48), cognitive elements, the self and the subject matter being studied.

There are important distinctions to be made between different forms of autonomy, most significantly the distinction between managing learning and handling knowledge, academic ways of thinking and discourse. Ecclestone (2002) calls the first of these 'procedural autonomy'. This relates to the capacity to manage one's studies generally, referring to matters such as organising your time, meeting deadlines, paying attention to requirements and following guidance and instructions. Ecclestone refers to the second as 'critical autonomy'. This relates to ways of thinking, such as being able to look for evidence to build an argument, or consciously searching for meaning when researching a topic. At higher levels it might include seeing knowledge as provisional, seeing knowledge in its wider context, recognising different perspectives and the importance of social and personal responsibility. Such qualities are often seen as generic outcomes of higher education (Perry, 1999).

These definitions can be usefully related to the main concept a learner has of their capacity for exercising control within a specific learning context, and will be used to analyse and illuminate students' views of the two case studies under discussion.

Developing autonomy through formative assessment

The key educational purpose of the assessment methods reported here was to develop student autonomy. A number of formative self-assessment (Black and Wiliam, 1998) activities were introduced to help students:

- understand the nature of high-quality work;
- have the evaluative skill needed to compare their own work to the expected standard;
- develop tactics that help them modify their own work (Sadler, 1989: 119).

Developments were based on the assumption that, as Black and Wiliam argue, if assessment is to be formative for learners they must do more than simply receive feedback. They must actively consider and use the information in some way and so will, at some level, be involved in evaluating and managing their own learning. The formative activities were designed to:

- involve students in self-evaluation;
- inculcate the belief that the learner was in a position to exert significant control of their own learning to improve their own performance.

In addition, emphasis was placed on collaborative activities to draw upon the social learning potential of the student group and to limit both demands and dependence upon the lecturer, fostering autonomous learning within a community.

Case study 1

This took place with first-year undergraduates on an interdisciplinary humanities degree. Lecturers were worried that students misguidedly 'rely too heavily on lecturers to dispense information that they then try to

---

continued

regurgitate in their assignments'. They spoke of wanting to offer 'timely feedback', particularly on productive ways students could read round a topic to inform their academic writing, but did not have time to look at formative pieces of work. For this reason they wanted to encourage students to learn to view peers as learning resources. They sought to involve students in regular formative self-assessment episodes in class time to help them become clear about academic expectations (especially the provisional nature of knowledge in their subject) and how best to approach academic tasks.

To do this they set a series of highly structured activities, including individual and group short-writing tasks, and oral presentations, which students shared on a regular basis. Starting with personal written responses and building up to fully theorised pieces as the module unfolded, these culminated in the self- and peer evaluation of a short conceptual paper written by the students, in which they were asked to explain their understanding of a major concept underpinning the course. During class time students evaluated their own and each other's work in relation to four tutor-prepared student answers, which exemplified 'good' through to 'ineffective' responses. This opened up a two-hour dialogue about the merits and shortcomings of each, so that students became 'clear about standards and expectations and could see how far and in what ways their own piece matched up. The aim was to enable them to offer each other, and more importantly themselves, usable feedback.'

Case study 2

Here students were in their second year of study of an engineering degree. The lecturer was keen to find ways of 'getting students to work on their own' and avoid what he saw as a heavily dependent, reductive approach to learning.

> Before now, this [electronic engineering] module has been summatively assessed by an exam, but I was worried that students tended to question-spot, cram, and attempt to memorise, rather than understand, the material to be learned. I've redesigned it to include interim student presentations on research topics that they carried out during the term, giving students the opportunity to practise understanding, condensing and presenting information, to practise the analytical skills they need, and to discuss their thinking.

After formal lectures that introduced the general field, students were required to conduct independent research on different related topics, which they presented halfway through the term to the group. The presentations were peer and tutor evaluated, each student receiving extensive written feedback. Students were then asked to prepare a final project report in the light of the feedback on the presentations. Their final submission was to be accompanied by a reflective commentary outlining the ways in which they had responded to the formative feedback and anything they had learned from evaluating the presentations. The lecturer explained:

> I particularly experimented with encouraging them to fill in peer feedback sheets to formatively assess the interim presentations, as well as offering each student extensive written feedback on their ideas. I wanted them to reflect on what makes a good piece of work in this area, and we had a lot of discussion about this, and the criteria, before and after the presentation, and well before they had to hand in the final piece of work for marking. I hope they'll be in a better position to approach that final piece as a result.

Research methods

Our research sought to identify students' perceptions of the impact of being involved in self-evaluation methods that were designed to enhance autonomy. Their views were analysed in order to capture and illuminate shifts in student consciousness as a result of their involvement in such assessment episodes. We will report these under key headings, which indicate the range of different views students held about the precise nature of the new levels of control they felt they had learned to exercise. They represent emergent concepts of autonomy. These will be presented below, together with illustrative quotations.

Both studies gathered data chiefly from students, using semi-structured interview schedules to support reflective phenomenographic interviewing strategies (Marton and Booth, 1997). Interviews were conducted at key points throughout the semester and focused on asking students to discuss what they had learned from the activities, and how they felt that had any bearing on how they now went about learning independently, outside the formal classroom environment. This data was complemented by observational data, documentary analysis and interviews with academic staff.

Findings: student experiences

Anxiety surrounding autonomy

Students in the first example, who were in their first semester, were initially interviewed before undertaking the self-assessment activities. Most admitted to harbouring deep anxieties about the levels of autonomy they would be expected to display at university. Many of their earliest comments related to a conception of autonomy that did not appear in the model described at the outset of the chapter. In this dimension independent learning is viewed as being thrown in the deep end, or being left to sink or swim.

> It's so different to college. Because you're a part of the college, it's so structured – everything you do. Like you do an assignment, you hand it in, you get it back, you hand another in, you get it back – so you get complete guidance, you don't have to do anything outside what they tell you. Because of that you feel chucked in at the deep end when you come to uni. (From Case Study 1)

Development of procedural autonomy

In later interviews, after the self-evaluation activities, all claimed to be highly aware of consciously developing their approaches outside the classroom. They all said they had begun to learn how to manage their own time, usually prompted by seeing how others approach academic tasks. Learning from others 'not so much tutors, but people on your level' was key here.

Transformation in time spent

Many said the value of the activities were that they'd learned by becoming more aware of the amount of time you 'needed to spend' on academic tasks. They now said they did more, or at least knew they *ought* to. They saw the benefits of becoming involved in self-evaluation activities as a matter of learning the rules about tutors' expectations: 'It's a bit of an eye-opener 'cos I worked out for every hour I spend here I should be spending two more at home or in the library!' (Case Study 1). Here independent learning was viewed in quantitative terms – seen simply as the need to do more work. This was discussed in terms of time spent and also equated with procedural tasks – locating sources, taking photocopies and so on. Student self-evaluative activity in this dimension related solely to the question: 'How much time have I spent?' 'I found out that I need to put much more reading in – I was trying to do it based on lecture notes, but that's not enough' (Case Study 1).

This view was only evident in Case Study 1.

Transformation in presenting one's work

Many students claimed that the benefits of self-evaluation activities lay in bringing a new awareness about how to approach the assignment in terms of its physical production. They talked of, say, gaining insight into the process of producing work, but this time on the level of technical presentation, with a focus on the generic task in hand, such as 'doing a presentation' or 'writing an essay'. In this dimension students start to ask themselves questions, as a consequence of being exposed to others' ways of working: 'Mine looked most like the second one. And now I know

I have to bring in a lot more reading, if I want to get a better mark – so I know what I have to do.' (Case Study 1).

Mechanisms for self-monitoring here revolve around the question: 'How should I set it out?' 'Before, I only know what I would put in an essay, or what I think should go in. But when you read other people's you think, "Oh well, I'll get to see what they would put in." I suppose you wonder what is best then, so . . . I suppose it makes you think about what are the assessment criteria, really' (Case Study 1).

Development of critical autonomy

Beginning to understand criteria

In this dimension students appeared to believe they could take steps to improve their own learning by becoming clearer about tutors' expectations, and thus get a 'feeling' for how they can apply criteria to their own work, in time to improve it. 'You learn to see what the module tutor is doing – how they mark. You are in that position where you are making decisions, making judgements: who is better at what? So you get a feeling for what the tutor is looking for when they are judging you' (Case Study 2).

The following more experienced learner also talks of becoming 'more aware', but this time that awareness refers to the attempt to judge his own work in relation to that of others, with a view to identifying areas for his own development.

> Having to comment on somebody else's presentation makes you think a lot more, made you more aware. You started to compare your presentation to other people, so by looking at other people you were seeing what you are good at and what you need to improve on, by comparing to the other person. You have developed from each other's experience. (Case Study 2)

For some, this was clearly helpful, and underpinned a new sense of confidence and efficacy in terms of generic approaches to tasks. 'It's quite a new way of writing, to me, and it's certainly new to think about it from the marker's point of view. It was really helpful, seeing how you could write about these things, and what looks good, or less good. So it helped me listen out for my own writing' (Case Study 1).

The comment about 'listening out for my own writing' implies a level of self-evaluation that focuses on the question: 'What can I do to improve the way I present my own learning?'

Transformation in ways of thinking

In this dimension students claimed to be conscious that they were beginning to see the nature of learning differently as a result of the self-evaluation activities. Although still very task focused, here conceptual awareness relating to the task is redefined as calling for a search for meaning and understanding. Instead of simply looking for how to set out their learning, the students here began to discuss their awareness that lecturers expected you to look for meaning – thus moving beyond a purely technical and quantifiable view of what constitutes quality work. Here students talked of beginning to question their own thoughts and views and 'think about things' as a result of being involved in self-evaluation activities

> At college I took a sort of ticky box approach to doing my work. I'd say to myself, right, I've done that, I've measured that, I've read that. There, it's done. Before I just had to find a lot of information and put it in, whereas here it's different. I have to think about how I feel about things, that's the difference. (Case Study 1)

Needing to become analytical and critical

The following student talks of realising she should try to see other constructions of knowledge, and is conscious of moving from a fixed to a relative way of knowing, because she saw 'good' answers presented different perspectives. As opposed to the earlier dimensions, which focused on procedural study habits, this transformation is based on monitoring how far she has personally made sense of subject matter.

> The hardest thing is actually choosing what to put in an assignment, because I think you've got to think about it from a personal point of view. Here you have to read not just on the subject, but round it, which I find hard to do. You see, I think it's testing totally different skills. At college I didn't think of doing that, as it was a yes/no, it either is or it isn't the answer. It can't be in between. You can't have a critical eye when you're looking at stuff like that because there is an answer to it. At college we just got given the chapters and stuff to read and once you knew that you knew everything to write. Here you need to be not methodical, but sort of analytical. To understand how you feel about it and how different everybody else feels. It's a different kind of learning, you know, to see everybody's point of view. (Case Study 1)

This level of critical autonomy was rare in the first-year case study, but more pronounced with the engineers, who all talked of trying to monitor their own understanding of the subject by listening to their peers 'It was very positive, as I really started to understand about communication systems. I was also able to relate to other communication systems; the technical detail, how it is used as opposed to other systems' (Case Study 2).

All the engineers felt that they were better able to develop and assess the level of their understanding in a more sophisticated and integrated way by rehearsing their ideas within a peer community of practice during the peer and self-evaluation activities.

> Because it comes from your own group, it's pitched at the right level for the class. Some lecturers can be just too difficult to follow – this way you can relate to it. You are still learning, but on a level you can understand. Students are

likely to use other forms of expression that the lecturers couldn't. Students can relate it to other modules we've done, that perhaps the module tutor doesn't know about. So we can tie all these modules together through our presentations, and the other students know what we are on about. (Case Study 2)

Capacity to engage in an expert community of practice

Among engineering students autonomy in a subject-specific rather than generic academic sense (Candy, 1991) began to appear as a result of the assessment activities.

> You can pass an exam without knowing anything about the subject at all. Whereas this really is embedded in you – you really learn the subject quite well in-depth. So you feel you can come away with the confidence and talk to the other lecturers in a conversation on a reasonable technical level. If you went and spoke to the same people after an exam, you wouldn't have an idea what they were talking about. (Case Study 2)

This student was conscious of starting to 'think like an engineer', monitoring his own research findings and interpretations against those of others. His experience of developing autonomy seems more connected with the specific subject than with generic study skills.

Discussion

There is a series of well-known developmental models of university students (Baxter Magolda, 1992; Perry, 1999), which illustrate changes in concepts of learning and knowledge, and in the personal capabilities to cope with and make sense of academic learning over time at university. With respect to autonomy in learning, perhaps all students need to work out what is required in a new context. This seems particularly important in the case of an increasingly diverse student population whose prior experiences of learning and assessment have prompted a surface approach to learning in which the learner feels heavily dependent on the teacher to issue instruction. Under these conditions the discourse of autonomous learning being promoted in university can readily result in student resistance to developing autonomy, especially in the early stages of a degree.

Our research into the process of innovation in Case Study 1 highlights some interesting insights into the reasons inexperienced students might appear, from lecturers' perspectives, to display heavily dependent behaviour and require what might seem like 'spoon-feeding'. If, as was the case with the students in this study, learners are anxious and acutely aware of feeling 'lost' in a new, bewildering or threatening learning environment, it is perhaps unsurprising that they consciously seek explicit guidance on the 'new rules'. To meet the needs of such learners means starting to develop procedural autonomy in a fairly directed way, which superficially might seem to be at odds with the learner-controlled principles of autonomy.

It is important to consider the implication that teacher control and provision of structure might not be at odds with developing autonomy in the early stages of a student's academic career. Williams and Deci (1996) suggest learners need teachers who are supportive of their competency development and their sense of autonomy. Our research suggests that Case Study 1 was successful because it allowed students to use peer and self-assessment activities systematically and gradually to build up the skills and concepts of procedural autonomy, by carefully scaffolding their experience and encouraging them to reconceptualise the nature of assessment and learning. Sophisticated views of autonomy take time and experience to develop gradually. As Ecclestone (2002) suggests, students need to develop a sense of procedural autonomy before they are ready to approach subject knowledge in a critically autonomous manner.

Knight and Yorke (2003) make a strong case for actively involving students in self- and peer assessment that, instead of being designed to pin down achievement in terms of grades or marks, takes on a different tone when explicitly used to give students feedback on their performance, for formative purposes which support learning. This view of self- and peer assessment as an important aid to 'assessment for learning' as part of the 'constructive alignment' (Biggs, 1999) of learning, teaching and assessment can therefore be seen as a positive response to the pressures on assessment which currently threaten to squeeze out formative assessment as add-on tutor feedback. Both case studies overcame this pressure by using self- and peer assessment as a method of teaching and learning. In so doing, the locus of control can be seen to shift, albeit gradually, from teacher to learner, as students' concept of feedback gradually shifts during the activities. Our study suggests a move from a reliance on tutors to issue feedback towards a developing awareness that feedback can derive from the learner, by better understanding criteria, standards and goals, and by developing a sense of 'social relatedness' (Boekaerts and Minneart, 2003). What is important, however, is that the context supports their competency development. Students may benefit, paradoxically, from explicit guidance about the process of applying criteria and making effective judgements.

Some studies have made positive connections between student-centred pedagogic methods offering elements of choice, control and responsibility and the development of personal or critical autonomy (Ecclestone, 2002; Baxter Magolda, 1992). Perhaps these techniques should come later, as in the second case study in which students were offered considerably more choice and responsibility, as they require confidence and experience.

The developmental model of autonomy that emerged from our interviews also has interesting resonance with Lea and Street's (1998) developmental model of academic writing. 'Critical autonomy' corresponds to Lea and Street's notion of 'academic socialisation' in which students are inducted into the 'university culture', largely by focusing attention on learning appropriate approaches to learning tasks. Lea and Street highlight how often this is viewed as fairly unproblematic, a process of acquiring a set of rules, codes and conventions, which are often implicit. Many developments in self- and peer assessment have focused on a form of 'academic socialisation': making these codes or 'rules' of the assessment game explicit and transparent to students (Norton *et al.*, 1996; Mowl and Pain, 1995; Orsmond *et al.*, 1996).

On one level this could also be read as undermining autonomy, because it implies coercing students to accept, rather than interrogate, tutors' assessment criteria and judgements. It has little in common with the 'higher' experiences of learning and epistemological development (Perry, 1999) which characterise an ideal learner who is capable of working in an 'emancipatory' manner, with 'the capacity to bring into consciousness the very ways in which . . . knowledge is constructed and therefore to go beyond it' (Brew, 1995: 53). This level of learner control and capacity to challenge also informs the higher levels of the 'academic literacies' approach (Lea and Street, 1998) that emphasises academic writing as a site of ideological assumptions, discourse and power. That being said, the problems of educational practice in Higher Education being driven conceptually by such developmental models as Perry's are highlighted by Pugh (2004), who argues that it is unsurprising that little evidence of the 'higher' levels are found in the more diverse, less privileged undergraduate populations of many universities. In terms of the development of autonomy, then, perhaps we should not frequently expect to see subject-matter autonomy (Candy, 1991). Instead, it might be more helpful to recognise that a prerequisite for such epistemological autonomy might lie in conscious and systematic attempts to develop students' critical autonomy, which arguably needs developing throughout a programme of study.

Conclusion

These innovations worked because they gradually introduced students to situations in which they became involved in self-assessment activities in a purposeful and scaffolded manner. This helped students to develop the necessary skills and concepts that underpin different levels of autonomy in learning. The innovations were possible because the lecturers were committed to the belief that developing student autonomy takes time and practice, and to which it is worth devoting considerable amounts of collaborative time and effort. In both cases, lecturers were open to the idea of completely redesigning the whole of their teaching programme to incorporate self-assessment, not simply as a 'one-off' session, but as an integrated and embedded aspect underpinning the whole course design and curriculum delivery. In practical terms this meant reducing the tutors' control of content delivery and trusting the students to respond to the innovative pedagogical methods and actively engage with the learning material. We know this has been successful because the research studies indicated marked shifts in students' approaches to exercising autonomy. In addition they reported seeing this as a 'much better way of learning than just sitting in a lecture, with everything going way over your head. Let's face it – what do you really learn from that?'

168   *Kay Sambell et al.*

References

Baxter Magolda, Marcia B. (1992) *Knowing and reasoning in college: gender-related patterns in students' intellectual development*. San Francisco: Jossey-Bass.

Biggs, J. (1999) *Teaching for quality learning in higher education*. Buckingham: Open University Press.

Black, P. and Wiliam, P. (1998) Assessment and classroom learning, *Assessment in Education*, 5(1): 7–74.

Boekaerts, M. and Minneart, A. (2003) Assessment of students' feelings of autonomy, competence, and social relatedness: a new approach to measuring the quality of the learning process through self and peer assessment, in M. Segers, F. Dochy and E. Cascallar (eds), *Optimising new modes of assessment: in search of qualities and standards*. Dordrecht: Kluwer, pp. 225–39.

Boud, D. (1995) *Enhancing learning through self assessment*. London: Kogan Page.

Brew, A. (1995) What is the scope of self assessment? in D. Boud (ed.), *Enhancing learning through self assessment*. London: Kogan Page, pp. 48–62.

Brown, G., Bull, J. and Pendlebury, M. (1997) *Assessing student learning in higher education*. London: Routledge.

Candy, P. C. (1991) *Self-direction for lifelong learning: a comprehensive guide to theory and practice*. San Francisco: Jossey-Bass.

Ecclestone, K. (2002) *Learning autonomy in post-16 education: the politics and practice of formative assessment*. London: RoutledgeFalmer.

Hinett, K. and Thomas, J. (eds) (1999) *Staff guide to self and peer assessment*. Oxford: Oxford Centre for Staff and Learning Development.

Knapper, C. K. and Cropley, A. J. (1999) *Lifelong learning in higher education*, 3rd edn. London: Kogan Page.

Knight, P. T. and Yorke, M. (2003) *Assessment, learning and employability*. Buckingham: Society for Research into Higher Education/Open University Press.

Lea, M. and Street, B. (1998) Student writing in higher education: an academic literacies approach, *Studies in Higher Education*, 23(2): 157–72.

Marton, F. and Booth, S. (1997) Learning and awareness. Hillsdale, NJ: Lawrence Erlbaum Associates.

Mowl, G. and Pain, R. (1995) Using self and peer assessment to improve students' essay writing: a case study from geography', *Innovations in Education and Training International*, 32(4): 324–35.

Norton, L. S., Dickins, T. E. and McLaughlin Cook, A. N. (1996) Rules of the game in essay writing, *Psychology Teaching Review*, 5(1): 1–14.

Orsmond, P., Merry, S. and Reiling, K. (1996) The importance of marking criteria in the use of peer assessment, *Assessment and Evaluation in Higher Education*, 21(3): 239–50.

Perry, William G. Jr. (1999) *Forms of intellectual and ethical development in the college years: a scheme*. New York: Holt, Rinehart and Winston.

Pugh, S. (2004) *Models of college students' epistemological development*. Available at <http://www.indiana.edu> (accessed 9 January 2005).

Sadler, D. (1989) Formative assessment and the design of instructional systems, *Instructional Science*, 18: 119–44.

Segers, M., Dochy, F. and Cascaller, E. (eds) (2003) *Optimising new modes of assessment: in search of qualities and standards*. Dordrecht: Kluwer.

Williams, G. C. and Deci, E. L. (1996) Internalization of biopsychosocial values by medical students: a test of self-determination theory, *Journal of Personality and Social Psychology*, 70(4): 767–79.

Part IV
Encouraging professional development

15 Identifying themes for staff development

The essential part of PDP innovation

Sue Williams and Sheila Ryan

Introduction

This chapter presents the findings of a project conducted when the Personal Development Planning (PDP) initiative (QAA, 2000) was being piloted at the University of Gloucestershire (UoG) during 2002–3 (Ryan and Williams, 2003). We recognised that while our teaching had familiarised us with the challenges of designing, delivering and assessing aspects of personal and professional development, many of our colleagues would find themselves in unfamiliar (and uncomfortable) territory. In order to understand the challenges they faced as both personal and academic tutors, we examined what we believed to be two of the crucial factors for success – staff capabilities and readiness. As experienced trainers, we considered the provision of relevant and timely staff development essential for the implementation of PDP for undergraduates. Our main aims were to evaluate the experiences of those staff involved and use the findings to inform effective delivery and assessment of PDP. One UoG tutor told us: 'Higher Education initiatives can be too student centred in their focus, with little recognition of the implications for staff experience and capability' (Ryan and Williams, 2003).

In the following sections, we outline our approach to the project, describe the key themes that emerged and debate their relevance. Finally, we present our conclusions and recommendations for those who plan and evaluate such activities.

Approach and setting

Although PDP is being introduced for undergraduates across United Kingdom higher education by 2006 (QAA, 2000), the need to prepare academic staff for effective participation in this initiative appears to have been sidelined.

PDP is an activity undertaken by individuals in order to reflect upon their own learning and to plan for personal, educational and career development. It should consist of a structured, integrated and strategic process containing a set of interconnected activities:

- doing (learning through an experience);
- recording (noting thoughts, feelings, ideas, experiences, evidence of learning);
- reviewing (making sense of it all);

- evaluating (judging self and determining what needs to be done to develop/improve/move on);
- planning (clarifying objectives, deciding on actions).

(Adapted from Jackson, 2002)

Because personal development is in itself complex, the associated teaching and assessment skills differ in many respects from those required to impart knowledge and assess academic quality in the curricula. The introduction of a programme that is not based within one specified academic discipline, is undertaken over at least three years of study, and aims to be 'personal' to each individual student's development raises a number of questions about the demands this places on tutors. If PDP is to be of real value to students, we consider the tutors' capabilities to be an essential part of its provision.

We therefore identified individuals already involved with the design, delivery and assessment of personal development and obtained their views. We wanted them to reflect on their experiences and expertise and identify issues they considered to be important for the provision of PDP. We sought opinions about relevant skills, their acquisition and the provision of relevant staff training. Initially, we interviewed academic and careers staff involved in the UoG PDP pilot. As our understanding broadened, we extended our investigations to other staff groups. Our findings were then used to identify any 'capability gaps' and recommend areas for staff development and involvement.

The project team members were chosen for their expertise in teaching and researching experiential learning, professional development, human resource development and training. A participative and inclusive approach was agreed, involving people throughout the university who represented different aspects of PDP provision. Interviewees included personal and guidance tutors, academic and career advisers, academic staff developers and co-ordinators and student union representatives. Semi-structured individual and small group interviews enabled us to track staff experiences during 2002–3. During this period, PDP was piloted and evaluated in three faculties and its implementation across UoG planned for 2004. By using collaborative enquiry (Reason and Rowan, 1984) this interactive process helped to promote critical discussion of staff issues. As our data was collated, key themes began to emerge which we have presented in our findings.

Findings

We would emphasise that although our findings have been separated to highlight main concerns, the themes set out below are interrelated. They help to clarify the responses required of an institution, so that staff training objectives are based on defined organisational aims, forming a strategic approach to employee learning and development.

As we asked interviewees to reflect on their experiences, we found they shared a number of concerns, some of which have been highlighted by other authors writing on PDP. We have contextualised our thematic findings with comments from such authors. The concerns of UoG staff are captured by the following themes:

- the perceived purpose of PDP;
- the teaching and assessment of PDP within the curriculum;
- which staff should deliver PDP, their role and effectiveness;
- the provision of training or staff development.

The debates within each theme are summarised in Figures 15.1–15.4 and discussed in more detail below.

Theme 1: Clarifying the purpose of PDP

Defining a clear direction for PDP across an institution (see Figure 15.1) assists in the identification and selection of staff with appropriate skills and experience. These individuals may be newly recruited or currently employed in a 'PDP-related' role. Staff had their own views about the purpose of PDP:

- how it adds value to all HE learning;
- whether PDP should be an explicit contribution to employability;
- what was driving the PDP initiative: government and employers' needs or individual development and potential?

Academic co-ordinators (AC) generally found the defined purpose of PDP too 'narrow', only addressing career prospects, job/employability skills and government targets for HE. One saw this as particularly relevant for the many graduates unclear about future employment. A senior academic co-ordinator (SAC) supported the need to develop realistic self-respect and self-confidence: to know that 'I've got two left feet so I shouldn't really [go] onto the dance floor', adding that students should not be 'too concerned with how they will sell themselves in the world'. A group interview with SACs revealed strong feelings that the fundamental purpose of PDP is to create well-rounded individuals: 'to critically reflect is the hallmark of [good] interpersonal skills'.

   Noble (1999: 122) suggests that the development of skills in HE is as much about the whole individual as it is about employability: 'many of the "skills" identified for employability are not in fact skills, but rather attributes and attitudes of mind'. Staff felt that something so potentially valuable for student development, incorporating reflection and encouraging lifelong learning, could become compressed into an instrumental, mandatory 'chore'. They remained concerned that PDP implementation had been insufficiently debated throughout UoG.

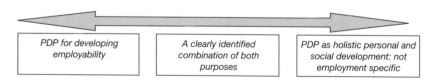

Figure 15.1 The purpose of PDP: skilled employee versus holistic graduate

Theme 2: PDP in the curriculum – integration or separation?

Tutors and academic advisers debated whether PDP should be integrated into subject learning, teaching and assessment strategies or kept separate. This debate ranged along a continuum from total separation to 'bolted on', partial integration, ending with complete integration (see Figure 15.2).

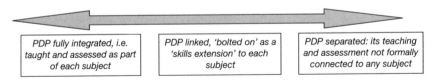

Figure 15.2 The PDP integration continuum

Discussions arose on the position of reflection, reflective practice and learning, and how these should be best incorporated within programmes. We found personal reflection on learning already situated within a subject. One personal tutor said:

> I particularly encourage students to reflect where there's a practical component . . . sports coaching, where I would be looking at their performance. I need them to take the reins of responsibility by reflecting on some of the practical experiences that have been planned very carefully to give them experiences . . . they will have an opportunity based on the feedback to move on and think, 'Yes, I'm doing that well, I'm not doing that well, I'm not sure.'

By comparison, the PDP pilot formed part of a separate study skills programme with a focus on employability and careers assessment unrelated to specific subjects or degree programmes. We were made aware of some UoG examples of subject-based personal learning, including learning logs. Moon's (1999: 27) research identifies such writing as being 'associated with improved capacities for metacognition'.

Interviewees indicated a preference for a more inclusive approach, where students perceive PDP as more relevant and less of a chore or additional workload. It did not appear that these alternative curriculum experiences had been considered in positioning PDP.

Theme 3: Assessment – what are the concerns?

We found staff opinions on PDP assessment varied, ranging from queries about formal, graded assessments to whether PDP should be assessed at all (see Figure 15.3). A number of interviewees were very aware of the problems of how best to capture the significance of this individual, 'personal' learning in a 'public' way. Students' views on PDP assessment were not part of our project remit.

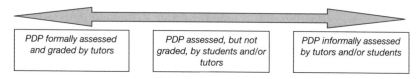

| PDP formally assessed and graded by tutors | PDP assessed, but not graded, by students and/or tutors | PDP informally assessed by tutors and/or students |

Figure 15.3 The PDP assessment continuum

The QAA's proposals offer opportunities for innovation in curriculum and assessment design. One concern voiced by both academic and personal tutors and student representatives was whether UoG's PDP 'product' would be too narrowly defined.

> The success of such assessment practices should be judged by how much the student develops during all stages of the assessment process. Is the student learning while carrying out the assessment, or does the student only learn from the product of assessment?
>
> (Orsmond *et al.*, 2000: 24)

However, as one tutor explained, without an assessment element PDP can be seen as: 'a filing exercise, putting the right bits of paper in . . . it's not embedded within their learning experience'. When debating whether it should be assessed at all, there was a pragmatic recognition of current HE reality from one student representative: 'If it's not assessed, I don't know the take up and commitment you'd get towards it, that's the problem.'

Staff questioned the use of graded assessment and any 'formal' relationship with degree classification. This was strongly connected to HE and institutional desires for quantified and measured 'results outputs'. Many academic tutors viewed this as not only difficult but nigh impossible:

> the assessment-driven HE curriculum so permeates our approach to innovation that there needs to be a critical mass of programmes like this to shake off the belief that everything can be represented and captured in a number . . . I call this syndrome metrimania . . . the overwhelming desire to reduce everything to numbers . . . if you can count it – it ain't it.
>
> (Maughan, 2001)

Staff saw this leading to a 'tick box' approach, counter-intuitive to 'genuine' reflective practice. One student representative observed:

> Because everybody's personal development will be completely different, and maybe if you put it on a scale, say communication skills, and they'll log 'my communication skills have improved', I don't know, a 7, and some-body else might have a 3. Well, the one with a 7 shouldn't necessarily have a higher grade than the one with a 3 if the one with a 3 can justify their skills just as well.

However, learners do find reflective writing difficult, and Moon (1999) suggests that further research in this area could provide more direction on assessment flexibility.

Using PDP to facilitate a more 'free thinking', organic and personally orientated approach led academic tutors and student's officers to question the ethics and 'fairness' of such assessments. One tutor emphasised that assessment of reflective learning by students requires a degree of trust from tutors:

> One hopes that the benefits outweigh the disadvantages but the way we measure that I think is very limited . . . we have to sign things off – that tends to be maybe a bit tokenistic at times. I mean I will have a quick glance. There's a lot of trust going on there.

Another senior academic tutor did not want PDP assessment to repeat his experience with BTEC skills portfolios: 'With some students [we had] these progress files going backwards and forwards . . . hopefully they saw what to do . . . [to] pass but it was so time consuming . . . it really was.'

Another challenge emerging from the BTEC assessment debate arose when discussing the 'final product' of PDP. Staff with previous experience of marking BTEC, NVQ skills portfolios and personal/professional development journals had struggled with the volume of work, the grading of 'evidence' against loosely categorised criteria and to reach agreements with colleagues about percentage grades. Recognising the need to identify an acceptable alternative, the project team looked for existing examples of PDP 'products', selecting the CD-ROM designed by members of the Keynote Project (2002). This provides a student-centred, flexible approach, with the potential to meet a range of PDP purposes. It was also freely available to institutions for adaptation.

Theme 4: Staff – what are the issues?

'So I am very concerned that if it's implemented across the board that it should be done with passion, hopefully, but at least with informed enthusiasm,' said one senior academic co-ordinator. We found both academic and non-academic staff at UoG already contributing to 'personal development' and study skills activities, in addition to their subject tutor or other roles (see Figure 15.4). This contrasted with examples from other institutions, where PDP is seen as exclusively belonging to the academics' terrain. Our interviewees all agreed that they could usefully

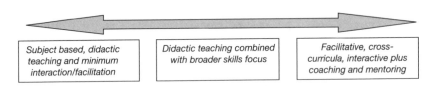

Figure 15.4 PDP tutors' skills and staff selection

contribute to PDP, although there appeared to be little formal recognition of this potential PDP staff resource. Equally, concern was expressed that a 'personal tutor' role was not perceived to be as important as an academic role.

Placement tutors, student guidance officers, careers advisers and learning centre staff could provide students with qualitative feedback on assessment, but we did not find examples in UoG of their involvement with PDP design.

Staff involved in the PDP pilot had not undertaken specific training and were anxious about their own limited experience of reflective practice. Those with some teaching experience of basic skills development felt that providing valuable feedback was 'an enormous task', and, as one former BTEC skills co-ordinator said, 'The academic role as it relates to undergraduates did not include facilitating skill developments, only in a very broad-brushed way.'

PDP changes the ways in which staff are expected to work, moving them from being autonomous, subject-focused academics into a more applied and facilitative role. To understand and then articulate through the written word the aims and progression of one's own technical, emotional and social capabilities is not easy, particularly for students at an early stage of maturity. Students need to be encouraged and 'mentored' rather than admonished, as such capabilities do not lend themselves to being 'taught' and 'assessed' by more traditional methods.

Another view was that staff needed a personal value system that is supportive of PDP ideology. The SACs were clear that encouraging students to reflect on their learning while developing self-knowledge required individual and small group mentoring. They questioned whether the university would be prepared to commit time and resources for this level of tutor support and its progression through levels 2 and 3.

Two of the academic tutors frequently reflected on their practice and evaluated their personal learning. A third undertook these tasks but did not formally record them. All three considered this added value to both tutoring on skills programmes and general student support. Their personal enthusiasms enable them to become effective facilitators of reflection and appear likely to be the necessary ingredient that encourages lifelong learning. A learning support tutor thought: 'One needs to be very supportive, very positive. Clearly there will be times to be critical but essentially one values what they're doing.'

One positive outcome of the Scholarship of Learning and Teaching Project (SoLT) was the introduction of a training programme for all PDP personal tutors at UoG, which included sessions on assessment of personal development and reflection. Tutors were encouraged to share experiences, air their views and identify training needs relevant to PDP provision.

Conclusions and recommendations

As a result of our research, we consider that the staff best capable of effective PDP provision will have the following attributes:

- an ability to be committed, enthusiastic role models for personal development;

- an ability to recognise opportunities for their own and their students' development;
- a positive commitment to students as learners and human beings.

It is not only academic staff that can play a role in PDP. The investigation found a range of examples of PDP, reflective-type activities that could contribute to the successful implementation of PDP.

The tensions identified in the assessment discussions emphasise the need for staff to be comfortable with whatever mix of delivery and assessment methods are chosen. They should then be able to manage the process fairly and consistently. Little was reported about the impact of PDP delivery and assessment on the tutor's role. In developing 'readiness for reflection', the changing nature of the tutor's role must be taken into account by establishing appropriate organisational staff development policies. Trust feeds on support and, in our experience, this is where PDP implementation falls short, failing to appreciate that the support staff need to nurture reflection and personal development. Irrespective of an institutionally defined purpose for PDP, staff training and development need to provide opportunities to explore these issues.

Participants commented that the way we conducted our intervention helped them to reflect on their involvement with PDP and other related professional activities. They had been able to clarify their views and exchange ideas and information, which they later used to progress their practice. One academic co-ordinator revealed: 'you and your colleague are taking it seriously, and devoting time, effort and energy to it . . . quite definitely [this] has encouraged reflection, and the opportunity to talk one to one is very good'.

Finally, in order to determine appropriate policy and processes for staff training, it is important for the institution to have a clear vision of PDP, by defining:

- the purpose of PDP;
- where PDP fits within the curriculum;
- whether and how PDP will be assessed;
- which staff should be involved in delivering PDP.

The provision of training then requires answers to the following questions:

- Which staff do you select?
- Have you defined their involvement?
- Do they have the relevant skills and experience?
- What are the capability gaps and how would these be bridged?

You can't have successful innovation in PDP unless your staff know what they're doing.

Acknowledgements

To the other members of the project team, M. Maughan and C. Hetherington, for their hard work. To Dr A. Ryan for guidance on approach and style. To Dr K. Clegg, our project adviser, who started this process.

References

Allen, D. P. (2002) Keynote Project. The Nottingham Trent University. david.allen@ NTU.ac.uk,

Jackson, N. (2002) *Expanding opportunities for reflective learning. Time to reflect? Promoting reflection among students and staff.* Conference, University of Gloucestershire, Cheltenham, England, February.

Maughan, M. (2001) *Assessing reflection: herding cats, reading palms and fiery hoops to jump through. Workshop to share and reflect on experiences of evaluating student reflection.* LILI conference, Warwick, January.

Moon, J. (1999) *Learning journals: a handbook for academics, students and professional development.* London: Kogan Page.

Noble, M. (1999) Teaching and learning for employability, in H. Fry, S. Ketteridge and S. Marshall (eds), *A handbook for teaching and learning in higher education: enhancing academic practice.* London: Kogan Page.

Orsmond, P., Merry, S. and Reiling, K. (2000) The use of student derived marking criteria in peer and self-assessment, *Assessment and Evaluation in Higher Education*, 25(1), pp. 23–38.

QAA (2000) *Developing a progress file for higher education.* Available at <http:// www.qaa.ac.uk/Heprogressfile/>.

Reason, P. and Rowan, J. (eds) (1984) *Human inquiry: a sourcebook of new paradigm research*, Chichester: Wiley.

Ryan, S. and Williams, S. (2003) *Experiences of delivering guidance on Personal Development Planning for undergraduates: an exploration of academic advisers as role models.* Scholarship of Learning and Teaching (SoLT) Research Project, University of Gloucestershire, England.

16 Assessing learning in a PBL curriculum for healthcare training

Christine Curle, Jim Wood, Catherine Haslam and Jacqui Stedmon

Introduction

The innovation we describe below has taken place within the taught Doctorate in Clinical and Community Psychology (D.Clin.Psy.). Professional training in higher education is accredited by regulatory bodies that usually require the learner to develop, and demonstrate, a range of competencies. Programmes typically include elements of academic study, research skills and placement-based learning, aiming to promote critical, reflective and integrated learning. The D.Clin.Psy. is no exception to this general pattern and, both in teaching and assessment, has tended to be quite traditional in approach.

What is typically assessed for academic requirements – 'know that' – and on placement by practitioners – 'know how' (Eraut, 2000) – introduces a schism between these complementary facets of practitioner development. Using traditional assessments drives students to focus on the transmission of propositional knowledge (Gibbs and Simpson, 2002) whereas they need to apply deep learning to their work with people. As Eraut (2000) indicates, transmission models emphasise academic content and show little evidence of transfer into practice. They are also of dubious utility for assessing competence in health service settings characterised by uncertainty, complexity and an ever-expanding knowledge base.

Through this innovation we were concerned to help students bridge the gap and make professional training mirror the nature and quality of the work they are required to do once qualified, in a coherent and complete manner. We developed the approach as an intrinsic part of a problem-based learning (PBL) curriculum introduced into the academic component of a D.Clin.Psy. programme (see Stedmon *et al.*, in press) to address the challenges, for students, of

- integrating theory and practice;
- managing large amounts of knowledge;
- learning effective team working in the National Health Service;
- being responsible for their own learning as adult learners

while developing their clinical skills.

Description of assessment

The practice

The assessments focus on the learning outcomes (LOs) of the PBL exercises that are part of a 'hybrid' PBL curriculum, which includes a mix of teaching, tutorials and lectures (Armstrong, 1997). We designed the assessment to complement the PBL group process and to form a natural conclusion to it. PBL uses scenarios to generate discussion in small groups who determine both how and what to learn to complete the task. Group members use a range of resources, including past learning and experience to tackle 'the problem'. As part of the group's work students are required to manage the dynamics of functioning in a group and reflect on that process. 'I learned how I am in a group . . . recognising how I present under pressure and affect others' (student).

Each PBL exercise is associated with both a range of generic LOs linked to core competences and an additional set of specific LOs, which may relate to a particular area of knowledge acquisition, such as aspects of working with older adults. We have collaborated with practitioner colleagues in the development of the exercises so that the PBLs encompass a variety of objectives and can be presented in a staged, iterative manner (Barrows, 1986) with sufficient complexity to represent the real world of practice. 'In terms of a learning strategy, it is quite useful as it exposes trainees to clinical problems' (staff).

The assessment is in two parts: first, a group presentation; and second, an individual written reflection on the group's work, following experience on clinical placement. We chose this structure because it has high ecological validity, tapping into a range of core competences for clinical practice. Unlike more traditional assessments, this format allows not only for the assessment of knowledge and reasoning capability, but for the in-vivo assessment of a range of communication and team-working skills. The individual written summary gives us an indication of individual students' development and ability to link theory with clinical practice.

Assessment by group presentation

Students have access to the marking guidelines to orient themselves to key aspects of the assessment. The presentation enables them to demonstrate what, and how, they have learned and is the culmination of work carried out over several weeks. Each group has thirty minutes to summarise their findings and take questions. The presentation is assessed formatively by peers, contributing to a greater understanding of the criteria for assessment (Topping 1998), and summatively by staff, including a practitioner and a senior staff member acting as moderator across all assessments in the cycle. The areas and example criteria for grading the presentations are summarised in Table 16.1A and 16.1C. We inform groups of their grade on the day of the presentation and give a summary of general points and observations. Detailed written feedback is provided subsequently, according to the quality standards for the programme (i.e., within four weeks). The group grade becomes the grade for each student. Our marking scale incorporates a 'referred' category for work that is not up to standard and if this occurs the group would be required to undertake a further presentation within four weeks of receiving feedback. '[N]eed smaller groups to present to, i.e. less than the whole cohort.' '[N]ot helpful for the [learning] process with a deadline' (both students).

Individual written summary

To ensure that students reflect on their work and learn from clinical experience, there is a separate, individual assessment. They are required to submit this after approximately three months on placement when they have gained relevant clinical experience. It comprises a 1500-word account summarising and reflecting on the work of the group. Students are encouraged to focus on one aspect of the group's work and to offer a critique in the light of subsequent learning and practice.

Given the word limit, note and bullet points are acceptable providing the account is clear and coherent. We expect them to include in their reflection learning about the group's process and working approach. This method of individualising assessment around group work encourages personalisation of the learning and reflective cycle (Kolb, 1984) and ensures a measure of discrete autonomy in the approach to clinical work. We have attempted to reduce the likelihood of plagiarism through the timing and structure of the assessment, which should also capture individual differences, discriminating between good or weak performance. The areas and example criteria for this assessment are in Tables 16.1B and 16.1C.

The novel nature of the assessments and the inherent demands in PBL for moving from a competitive to a cooperative framework for learning can lead to anxiety. 'It gets very stressful, having to negotiate with everyone.' 'A lot of stress in the tutor group that seemed to be PBL related . . . tension emerges in the tutorial' (both staff). However, students' initial experiences of these assessments are now structured to reduce stress and promote deep learning. We have done this by starting with a small PBL exercise, formatively assessed, in a tutorial context rather than to the whole year group.

This strategy focuses on the *outcomes* of learning as a means of monitoring the process and product of group work, for the group and for the individual. In order to simulate the complexity and natural history of professional life we require students to work in the same groups for all PBL exercises, experiencing group dynamics and learning to manage group processes over time. We encourage adult learning by reducing tutorial support over succeeding exercises so that assessment implicitly incorporates the results of a high degree of autonomy and self-direction from a basis of collaboration.

Rationale for the approach

This innovation centres on core professional competences required of clinical psychologists (captured in Table 16.1A) who, while autonomous practitioners, are required to work collaboratively. This capability is rarely assessed in the

Table 16.1 Assessment categories and criteria for PBL assessment

A Group presentation

Content	*Process*
• Identification of the problem • Therapeutic alliance considered • Psychological assessment • Formulation and hypotheses • Recommendations for intervention • Evaluation and use of research evidence • Evidence that risk assessment considered • Evidence of reflection	*Organisation* • Task and roles shared effectively • Group working cohesively • Keeps to time limits • Group manages questions and comments well *Presentation* • Articulation and audibility • Posture, eye contact • Quality and use of visual aids • Management of notes and props

B Individual written summary

• Identification of the problem • Identification of specific area(s) for review • Critical reflection	• Outline of the work carried out by the group • Development of work of the group • Learning points for self and others

• Conclusions

C Selected examples of marking criteria from presentation and individual written summary

	Excellent/very good	**Good/satisfactory**	**Requires revision**
Evaluation and Use of Research Evidence (Presentation – *Content*)	A good account is given of the factors likely to influence the outcome of the intervention, based on theory, research and the circumstances of the case. Strengths and limitations of existing evidence bases are offered.	A reasonable account is given of the factors likely to influence the outcome obtained from theory, research or the case.	Limited or lack of scholarship in judging the likely outcome of the intervention.
Task/Role Allocation (Presentation – *Organisation*)	All members of the group clear about their roles and contribute to task.	Members of the group reasonably clear about roles and all contribute.	Group members are unclear about their roles, or task allocation unequal.

continued

Table 16.1 continued

Quality / Use of Visual Aids (Presentation)	High-quality OHPs or Power Point slides used or good use of flipchart.	Good-quality OHPs or Power Point slides used or appropriate use of flipchart.	Poor-quality visual aids, i.e., too detailed, poorly visible or used inappropriately.
Critical Reflection (Individual Summary)	A broad-ranging/ in-depth critique is offered of both the process and results of the exercise. Good understanding of ethical, professional and service user perspectives in complex clinical contexts is evident. Acknowledgement of dilemmas and proposals for solutions are developed.	A satisfactory critique is offered of the process and results of the exercise. A satisfactory understanding of ethical, professional and service user perspectives is evident.	An inadequate or ill-thought through critique of the process and results of the exercise.

academic context. As a collaborative teaching and learning method, PBL encapsulates many of the qualities promoted in professional development (Albanese and Mitchell, 1993) and is well documented in a range of professions (Boud and Feletti, 1997). We have used it particularly to support integration, self-direction and lifelong learning, all necessary elements in training clinical psychologists (Huey, 2001). In promoting social interaction, PBL also meets the criteria Doise (1990) considers necessary to support the development of competence. 'We have really benefited from the variety of ideas and people's input'; 'The learning was to negotiate, respect others and manage difference'; 'Now have transferable skills to take to placement' (all students).

However, even in PBL curricula the current tendency to assess content knowledge through exams and group process by verbal feedback or project work fails to asses learning objectives directly, even though peer and self-assessment are increasing (Macdonald and Savin-Baden, 2004). Our concern was to use an assessment model based on the group's work that was constructively aligned (Biggs, 1999) to match the nature of the outcomes in which we were interested (Ward, 1999). 'Students see clinical thinking in action'; 'It is a good match for teaching in terms of process and content – gets a lot of stuff over' (both staff). 'It develops formulation skills' (student).

Assessing 'know-how'

The development of 'know-how' and professional knowledge (Eraut, 1994) through training is a process for developing clinical reasoning within dynamic and changing circumstances for the individual and the systems of which they are part. Students must integrate prior experience, theory and practice at a sophisticated level. The mature, experienced and highly selected students on doctoral programmes in clinical psychology are highly motivated and committed to training and the profession. The challenge for us was to adopt assessments that facilitated the demonstration of integration of different kinds of knowledge.

An assessment regime that provides evidence of this while encouraging self-direction is essential as a means of modelling elements of future practice. The demands of integrating theory and practice, collaboration, taking multiple perspectives and developing clinical reasoning require learning to be dynamic and constructivist (Bolhuis, 2003; Savery and Duffy, 1995). The group context of PBL supports this in a variety of ways (Hollingshead, 2000; Howe, 2004) and we believe the alternative assessments we have outlined capture these elements more closely than traditional methods. '[I] benefited from the group, sharing and learning'; '[We] learned how useful it is to work as a team' (both students).

Implementation

We were able to implement the approach by carefully integrating the changes within a major revision of the D.Clin.Psy. programme. We rethought our assessment strategies while considering the aims for the programme, the learning and teaching methods, and how LOs might most effectively be assessed as a means of 'closure' for the PBL work. Core programme staff were included in discussions from the outset and helped to shape the overall approach. Careful planning helped to allay concerns: for example, the potential for negative student evaluations that might have an adverse impact on quality assurance monitoring. A crucial aspect of the change was to ensure consistency between the approach of the revised curriculum and the need to provide evidence of relevant competence. '[I] learned about clearer communication'; 'It was client focused and clinically relevant' (both students). 'Making PBLs seem equivalent is fiendishly difficult' (staff).

Does it work?

Three elements help to answer this question: student achievement in terms of pass/ fail; the quality of student competence and performance; and students' perception about the contribution of the approach to their development as clinical practitioners.

Results

Taking the two parts of the assessment together, the achievements of the first cohort demonstrate improvements in meeting the pass standard, at the first attempt, over the complete PBL cycle (Figure 16.1). The results are similar for the second cohort who are halfway through the PBL cycle: i.e., students take time to reach criterion performance (Figure 16.2). Staff feedback on the assessments indicates development is ongoing in all areas, including presentation skills: '[I] have noticed

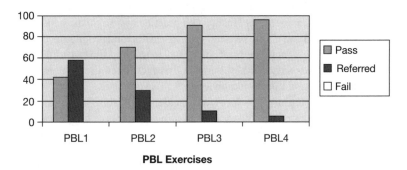

Figure 16.1 Results for the individual written summary – the first PBL cycle

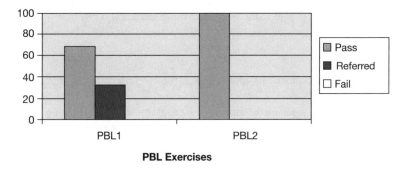

Figure 16.2 Results for the individual written summary – the second cycle to date

Notes: Pass – no resubmission required; Referred – further work to be done; Fail – requires submission of new piece of work

improvement in quality of trainee thinking – in level and resourcefulness' (staff). '[L]ike real life, following things through from assessment to evaluation'; 'Talking to lecturers about the PBL was good, more like adult learning' (both students).

The presentations demonstrate students can reach mastery very quickly. For the first cycle all presentations were at the pass standard whereas one group recorded a 'referred' on the formative exercise during the second cycle. This ceiling effect could be viewed as not providing sufficient sensitivity to difference but there are two indications that this is not so. First, the content of presentations demonstrated increasing sophistication in reasoning, analysis and synthesis. Second, the feedback from students makes it clear that the group condition inculcates a sense of responsibility and commitment. 'There was anxiety about the presentation, whether assessed or not, e.g. letting others down if not good enough' (student). This accords with other evidence of the efficacy of oral and group assessment (Elander, 2004; Joughin, 1999). Furthermore, our rejection of a marking scale in favour of broader categories (to remove competitive effects and increase focus on adult learning/collaboration and competence) masks fine distinctions based on only a few percentage marks.

The pass rate for the individual summary shows the students make steady progress throughout the four exercises. The initial pass rate rose from 42 per cent to 95 per cent, indicating they reached the standard required at the first attempt, by the second exercise. The high number of revisions required for the first PBL shows the early difficulty students had in adapting to different criteria for this kind of work. This is mirrored in the second cycle of PBL exercises to date.

Standards of performance

The guidelines and criteria for assessment provided for students appear to encourage high standards of presentation, for both content and delivery. Over the assessment cycle students demonstrate increasing complexity and sophistication in their explanations of the situation and ideas for practice while becoming more confident in linking their reading to their clinical practice. A content analysis of a random, 70 per cent sample, from the total marked summaries for the second cycle, shows that there is a high degree of reflection and development of theory–practice links. 'If they work with a referral the way they work on the PBL, they will be fine' (staff).

Feedback from students

A focus group of students from our first cohort, held after completion of all PBL exercises, gathered reflections about process, results, benefits, problems and personal response to PBL (Wood, 2004). Feedback suggested that while, in a few instances, students' anxiety could increase through PBL and preparation for the assessment, the overwhelming response was that this approach is preferable and useful in assisting the development of clinical thinking and practice. This view has increased over time, so, for example, individuals who initially disliked the strategy and still find it uncomfortable say it should be retained. Other feedback from tutors and practice supervisors involved in the exercises also supports the general conclusion of the value of the innovation. Given that assessment drives learning (Gibbs and Simpson, 2002), an important concern about the innovation is the impact on learning to practise more effectively. Of course, the more removed from the teaching the more tenuous are any conclusions about improvements in practice that can be linked to it; however, the students do appreciate its 'authenticity' (MacAndrew and Edwards, 2003).

Assessment relevance and effectiveness

In terms of effective use of student time and effort across LOs, this format of assessment has been successful, as is evidenced by both the accomplishments and views of the students. However, some students have struggled to adopt appropriate time-management strategies and driven by the assessments have probably worked harder and for longer than intended by staff. Our students tend to be somewhat perfectionist and are highly motivated, but this effect may also stem from the nature of the whole approach, which seems to engender the desire to learn. 'I learned so much from the PBL by researching things compared with doing it for an essay'; 'takes a lot of time'; 'It is good for learning to cope in different ways'; 'need a "Survival Guide" to PBL – the user perspective' (all students). 'It requires the issue of time and effort to be balanced in some way'; '[I] was aware that at times, in teaching, they wanted you to talk about the PBL case' (both staff).

Students have also recognised the value of learning to work together, listening, respecting different viewpoints and incorporating different styles into the results of the group's efforts. The need to present, in a public forum as a team effort, had the effect of supporting those who could be anxious and increased the sense of responsibility of many students for not letting down the team. From the standpoint of generic and transferable skills, this appears to be an effective way of learning communication, teaching and team skills within the context of assessment and the discipline. 'It was good to see people working in a team supporting each other and allocating work'; 'It can get too focused, instead of thinking about broader issues'; 'The approach to knowledge and skills is an excellent preparation for placement and practice' (all staff).

Summary

The evidence we have gathered about the structure and process of this model of assessment for PBL has led us to develop the approach in other areas of our clinical training programme; for example, in teaching research skills and service evaluation. We have also developed an increasing awareness that in implementing and evaluating educational innovations:

- there can be real gains for HE programmes in understanding both the benefits of new approaches and limits to traditional assessments;
- what is easy to measure may not always be what is important; but evaluation of different kinds of learning (in preference to knowledge accretion) can be done, even if it is not straightforward;
- change that is well considered and coherent *can* be implemented quite quickly;
- learning does not equal, and is much more than, teaching; therefore, we should focus on assessing student learning, not our teaching.

It seems essential to utilise the strengths of the assessment approach to provide information about what is required of students, of the curriculum, and of the learning which links the two. 'Keep it, whatever I say' (student).

Acknowledgement

The project on which this chapter is based is funded by the Higher Education Funding Council for England (HEFCE) and the Department for Employment and Learning (DEL) under the Fund for the Development of Teaching and Learning.

References

Albanese, M. A. and Mitchell, S. (1993) Problem-based learning: a review of literature on its outcomes and implementation issues, *Academic Medicine*, 68, 52–81.

Armstrong, E. G. (1997) A hybrid model of problem-based learning, in D. Boud and G. Feletti (eds), *The challenge of problem-based learning*, 2nd edn. London: Kogan Page.

Barrows, H. S. (1986) A taxonomy of problem-based learning methods, *Medical Education*, 20, 481–6.

Biggs, J. (1999) What the student does: teaching for enhanced learning, *Higher Education Research and Development*, 18, 57–75.

Bolhuis, S. (2003) Towards process-oriented teaching for self-directed learning: a multidimensional perspective. *Learning and Instruction*, 13, 327–47.

Boud, D. and Feletti, G. (1997) Changing problem-based learning: introduction to the second edition, in D. Boud and G. Feletti (eds), *The challenge of problem-based learning*, 2nd edn. London: Kogan Page.

Doise, W. (1990) The development of individual competencies through social interaction, in H. C. Foot, M. J. Morgan and R. H. Shute (eds), *Children helping children*. Chichester: John Wiley.

Elander, J. (2004) Student assessment from a psychological perspective, *Psychology Learning and Teaching*, 3, 114–21.

Elton, L. and Johnston, B. (2002) *Assessment in universities: a critical review of research.* York: LTSN Generic Centre.

Eraut, M. (1994) *Developing professional knowledge and competence*. London: Falmer Press.

—— (2000) Non-formal learning and tacit knowledge in professional work, *British Journal of Educational Psychology*, 70, 113–36.

Gibbs, G. and Simpson, C. (2002) How assessment influences student learning – a literature review. Available at <http://www.ncteam.ac.uk/projects/fdtl/fdtl14/assessment/literature_review.doc>.

Hollingshead, A. B. (2000) Perceptions of expertise and transactive memory in work relationships, *Group Processes and Intergroup Relations*, 3, 257–67.

Howe, C. (2004) All together now, *Psychologist*, 17, 199–201.

Huey, D. (2001) The potential utility of problem-based learning in the education of clinical psychologists and others, *Education for Health*, 14(1), 11–19.

Joughin, G. (1999) Dimensions of oral assessment and student approaches to learning, in S. Brown and A. Glasner (eds), *Assessment matters in higher education*. Milton Keynes: SRHE and Open University Press.

Kolb, D. A. (1984) *Experiential Learning: experience as a source of learning and development*. Englewood Cliffs, NJ: Prentice-Hall.

MacAndrew, S. B. G. and Edwards, K. (2003) Essays are not the only way: a case report on the benefits of authentic assessment, *Psychology, Learning and Teaching*, 2, 134–9.

Macdonald, R. and Savin-Baden, M. (2004) *A briefing on assessment in problem-based learning*. York: LTSN Generic Centre.

Savery, J. R. and Duffy, T. M. (1995) Problem-based learning: an instructional model and its constructivist framework, *Educational Technology*, 35(5), 31–5.

Stedmon, J., Wood, J., Curle, C. and Haslam, C. (in press) Development of PBL in the training of clinical psychologists, *Psychology Learning and Teaching*, 5(2).

Topping, K. (1998) Peer assessment between students in colleges and universities, *Review of Educational Research*, 68, 249–76.

Ward, A. (1999) The 'matching principle': design for process in professional education, *Social Work Education*, 18, 161–70.

Wood, D. F. (2003) ABC of learning and teaching in medicine, *British Medical Journal*, 326, 328–30.

Wood, J. (2004) Unpublished Report of the PBL implementation for D. Clin. Psy. programme, Exeter, 2001 Cohort, Part 3. Exeter: School of Psychology, University of Exeter.

17 ePortfolios

Supporting assessment in complex educational environments

Simon Cotterill, Philip Bradley and Geoff Hammond[1]

Introduction

New challenges and opportunities for assessment have arisen with the increasing complexity of many modern educational environments. This complexity may be in the form of having educational input and assessment from numerous 'suppliers', with formal and informal learning often based in multiple locations, and involving a range of different educational and IT infrastructures. The need to develop and support independent lifelong learners capable of formative self-assessment and personal development planning (PDP) represents a further challenge. In this chapter we report on our experiences and lessons learned from developing and implementing electronic portfolios (ePortfolios) for Medicine in relation to these challenges for assessment. Medicine represents a good example of a complex educational environment as students spend much of their time away from the parent institution, and over the duration of the course they are taught and assessed by large numbers of different educators. As such, it provides a good testing ground for ePortfolio approaches to assessment, and many of the lessons learned here are applicable to the wider HE community. At the University of Newcastle ePortfolios were piloted in 2003–4 primarily for formative assessment and for self-assessment purposes. The ePortfolios applied an innovative design to integrate closely with online curricula and virtual learning environments. They provide a means of evidencing the achievement of learning outcomes, and give the learner a personalised view of their accumulating summative assessment results. This type of ePortfolio approach may have an impact on learning pedagogy and assessment: for example, the technology allows learners to share all or parts of their ePortfolio content with assessors, supervisors and peers, who are then able to add formative feedback. The ability of students and assessors to access ePortfolios over the internet from a wide range of different locations is also a key advantage in supporting the recording and evidencing of achievements for formative assessment in complex educational environments.

Policy drivers

There have been increasing demands for developing independent lifelong learners (Spencer and Jordan, 1999) with the skills and attitudes appropriate for assessment, appraisal and professional revalidation. These are reflected in national policy directives for Medicine (GMC, 2003) and indeed have been a long-standing ethos of the Medical programme at Newcastle. In common with other vocational courses, there are growing demands to assess attitudes and behaviours. These are less amenable to traditional methods of assessment and in this respect portfolios may become an important part of the assessment strategy. In addition, there are national policy requirements in higher education to support progress files and PDP (NCIHE, 1997 and QAA, 2001). It is important that curricula and assessment strategies, including online learning environments, are responsive to these changing policy requirements (Cotterill *et al.*, 2004a).

ePortfolio design and implementation

ePortfolios were developed as part of a collaborative FDTL4 project involving the Universities of Newcastle, Leeds and Sheffield. As part of that project a highly configurable 'generic ePortfolio' was developed at Newcastle (Cotterill, 2004b). This can be configured to support programme-specific learning outcomes and components can be selected by course and year group. The ePortfolios are 'learner centric'; they are owned by the student, who can choose which parts of their portfolio they wish to allow others access to.

The ePortfolio can be used on a 'stand-alone' basis but it was also a project goal to integrate it into managed learning environments (MLEs). At Newcastle, the MLE for Medicine was first developed as part of a previous collaborative TLTP project (Jordan *et al.* 1997; Skelly and Quentin-Baxter, 1997). The MLE includes online curricula, study guides, online assessments (MCQ and EMIs), timetable, communication tools and other features. The ePortfolio was integrated into this MLE (Figure 17.1) and piloting began in September 2003. Below we report two case studies based on the piloting at Newcastle. The first is for Year 1 and 2 students for whom the ePortfolio was non-mandatory; the second is for Year 4 students who were required to complete a portfolio for one of their three student-selected components (SSCs).

Case 1: Piloting of the ePortfolio with Year 1 and 2 students

The ePortfolio was trialled with Year 1 and 2 undergraduate Medical students at Newcastle from September 2003. During the pilot phase students had a choice of completing the online portfolio or equivalent sections in an existing paper-based log book. The portfolio included a learning outcomes log, log of meetings with tutors, action plan, CV and log of patient and family visits. The ePortfolio also included a structured learning diary and planning tool which consisted of a weekly 'outcomes achieved' section and to-do list, as well as an area dedicated to reflection and action plans. The portfolios were not assessed formally at the piloting stage.

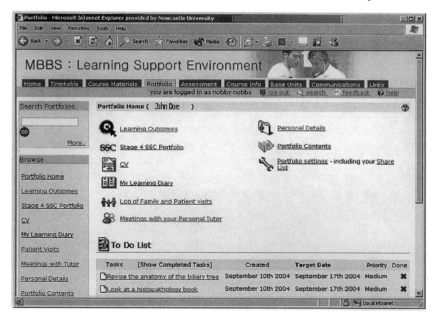

Figure 17.1 The ePortfolio within the MLE (Learning Support Environment) for Medicine at Newcastle

Ethical approval was granted for a study to evaluate student perceptions of the paper log book and ePortfolio used by students in Years 1 and 2. Two focus groups, involving twelve Year 1 students, were facilitated by a Year 4 student as part of their SSC in medical education. Issues raised in the focus groups were used to inform the design of a questionnaire for the wider year cohort. The ePortfolio proved to be acceptable, navigable and easy to use, though some students wanted a more 'quirky' or 'fun' design. Most students thought that the ePortfolio was 'a good idea' but there was a need for better clarity of purpose (i.e., a training issue) and some questioned the motivation to use it when it was not assessed. There was positive feedback on the facility to browse the Learning Outcomes of the curriculum. The structured learning diary was perceived as useful at first but less so over time.

Case 2: Portfolio to support SSCs

Year 4 students were required to complete the ePortfolio for one of their three SSCs running from January to June 2004. In-course summative assessment was provided by the SSC supervisor and in addition students were required to complete three assignments (students allocated one for each of their three SSCs): a poster presentation, an oral presentation and the ePortfolio. The poster and oral presentations were marked by an independent examiner; the ePortfolio was mandatory but was not formally graded, though it might inform borderline cases.

As part of the ePortfolio a structured Learning Outcomes and Action Plan was specifically designed to support the SSCs. Students were required to identify at least three intended learning outcomes (in negotiation with their supervisors). For each outcome students stated how it would be achieved and how their attainment would be measured/quantified (Figure 17.2). During the SSCs students reflected on their learning and achievements for these outcomes. At the end of the SSC both intended and unintended learning outcomes were reviewed. In addition, students could record meetings with their SSC supervisor and make entries in a learning diary. The completed portfolio could then be printed for sign-off and submission to the Exams Office (once submitted the record became 'read only'). Electronic sign-off was not implemented at this time because many SSC supervisors were external to the organisation. There was no requirement for supervisors to view the

---

MBBS Stage 4 SSC Portfolio

Option Details

Name: Carrot Ironfoundsson

SSC: Accident & Emergency Medicine (Middlesbrough General Hospital)

Supervisor: Mr KH Han

Dates: January 6th 2004 to February 20th 2004

Learning Outcomes and Action Plan

Learning Outcome	How will this be achieved?	How will this be measured/quantified?	Action to be undertaken
After completion of the option module, the student should be able to manage multiply injured patients according to ATLS Guidelines	Study of ATLS materials in the department followed by supervised applications of the guidelines to appropriate clinical situations in the A&E department	Direct observation of clinical interventions with A&E patients by Consultant or appointed SpR Viva (formal/informal) to assess knowledge of ATLS guidelines	
After completion of the option module, the student should be able to manage cardiac arrest patient according to ACLS Guidelines	Study of ACLS materials in the department followed by supervised applications of the guidelines to appropriate clinical situations in the A&E department	Direct observation of clinical interventions with A&E patients by Consultant or appointed SpR Viva (formal/informal) to assess knowledge of ATLS guidelines	

Figure 17.2 The initial Learning Outcomes and Action Plan

portfolio online; however, students did have the facility to give their supervisors access to their portfolio if desired.

A questionnaire-based evaluation study using a six-point Likert scale and free-text questions was granted ethical approval and students were asked to provide written informed consent to participate prior to commencing their SSC. Participants were asked to complete questionnaires which were designed to assess potential changes in awareness of learning outcomes, factors influencing use of the ePortfolio, attitudes and perceptions of educational impact, and usability. One hundred and eighty-six students completed the ePortfolio (100 per cent compliance) for their SSCs which ran from January to June 2004. Of those, 157 students completed the questionnaires.

The process of planning learning outcomes was perceived by some students to have had an impact on their approach to learning during the SSC (75 per cent agreed that having clearly defined intended learning outcomes influenced the way they approached the option). This was supported by the qualitative free-text responses:

> It encouraged me to really give thought to what I wanted to achieve during the option, which was especially useful as this was my first option. As a result of the portfolio I think I got much more out of the option than I would have otherwise.

> It made me concentrate on creating aims at the start of the option and allowed me to plan the option with my supervisor in a defined way. Overall it made my learning for the option more organised and focused.

Eighty-five per cent of respondents believed that they had recorded good evidence that they had achieved their intended learning outcomes, and 91 per cent spent time reflecting on what they had learned after completing the SSC. Barriers to using the ePortfolio were limited access to computers (students predominantly used computers at the university, at home or on location at their SSC) and limited time.

The ePortfolio proved to be feasible, acceptable and facilitated the evidencing of learning outcomes. Most respondents perceived it to be beneficial (80 per cent thought it was a useful learning experience). It also had a positive impact on planning and organisation of learning.

Table 17.1 Overview of use of the ePortfolio

Median number of Learning Outcomes recorded	5
Median number of log-ins to the ePortfolio during the SSC	6
Median time taken to complete ePortfolio	3 hours
Locations of computers used	
At the University	77%
At home	59%
On location at the SSC	41%

Discussion

The above case studies give a brief overview of piloting the ePortfolio in under-graduate Medicine during the 2003–4 academic year. The aims of the portfolio were to foster independent learning skills and provide the students with experience similar to that which they will face during their professional careers for processes such as appraisals, assessments and revalidation. The process of completing the Year 4 SSC probably came closest to replicating practices in professional medicine. The emphasis here was on formative processes, rather than summative assessment. The latter requires prior piloting and 'proof of concept'.

Student interface and process

On a technical level, students tended to find the ePortfolio easy to use and navigate. The ePortfolio is accessed via a web-based interface, with which students are already familiar. The structured process involved with the SSC portfolio did have a positive effect in the way that some students approached their learning during the SSCs. The process required students to define and discuss intended learning outcomes with their supervisors near the start of their SSC. This encouraged completion of the ePortfolio during the SSC and not just at the end when it was discussed with the supervisor. On average students logged on to the ePortfolio six times and took a total of three hours to complete it. While it is recognised that student time is limited, this does not compare unfavourably to other forms of assessment.

The process related the ePortfolio directly to the activities of the SSCs, while also encouraging consideration of the programme-level learning outcomes. In contrast, the learning diary used by Year 1 students was more abstract. It was designed to encourage reflection and self-directed learning but did not relate directly to specific aspects of the curriculum. Despite documentation and some training, many students were unclear about the rationale for completing a portfolio by the time the evaluation study was conducted. This indicates that further interventions to reinforce the ePortfolio may be required where it is being used over a sustained period of time.

Staff-development issues

The implementation of the SSC ePortfolio built on existing practice and the student–supervisor relationship. It did not require any significant additional work for supervisors as the portfolio, although mandatory, was not graded. Should the ePortfolio require grading this would have major implications for resourcing and staff development. First, there would be requirements for training in learning pedagogy for those involved in the assessment process (Lonka and Bolander, 2002; Laurillard, 2002). Second, it would require support for the assessors and supervisors, some of whom may be less IT literate than their students (Tenbush, 1998; Cravener, 1999).

ePortfolios for both formative and summative processes

The use of electronic portfolios may potentially reduce the tension between formative and summative processes. The ePortfolio is owned by the learner, who may build up a private collection of evidence and reflection from which they select the parts to be put forward for summative assessment. A key advantage to this approach is avoidance of the need to replicate effort and duplicating data. For example, there may be substantial overlap between preparation for an appraisal and preparation for a job assessment.

Structuring the ePortfolio to evidence learning outcomes

Providing some structure to the portfolio (in this case programme-level learning outcomes) may also help place diverse subjects within a more holistic perspective. They may also help with the assessment of learning outcomes, such as professional attitudes and behaviours which are less amenable to traditional forms of assessment. The ePortfolio should be able to display longitudinal performance in these domains, rather than just at specific points in time. Self-management of portfolio learning is itself an outcome (independent learning).

Supporting lifelong learning

Another potential advantage of the use of ePortfolios is the electronic transfer of data between systems. The technical specifications to support a 'lifelong-learning record' are now coming to realisation. This may encourage the inclusion of prior learning and extracurricular activities as evidence of the achievement of learning outcomes and competencies. During their studies ePortfolios can give the learner a personalised view of their accumulating summative assessment results. After graduation, students can build on their existing portfolio and skills profile, rather than starting with a blank sheet again.

Challenges

Implementing portfolios (either paper-based or electronic) takes many years of refinement and fine-tuning to optimise and align with teaching, learning and assessment strategies. They imply changes in assessment pedagogy, need stakeholder buy-in and may require resourcing if there are significant time demands on learners, tutors and assessors. There are also technical challenges ranging from basic access to IT facilities to integration with online curricula/virtual learning environments (VLEs, such as Blackboard, WebCT, etc.) and management information systems. This 'interoperability' between systems is crucial for ePortfolios for students learning in a multiple-provider environment.

   Where portfolios are used for summative assessment there are validity and reliability issues to consider (Baume, 2001; Friedman *et al.*, 2001). The current emphasis on PDP also raises new challenges. There is a limited amount of evidence to indicate that these processes enhance learning (EPPI, 2003); however, there is a pressing need for further research in this area. The use of IT for both summative and formative assessment raises additional research questions.

Conclusions

ePortfolios provide a means of evidencing the achievement of learning outcomes and have potential for both formative and summative assessment. The case studies here in Medicine are at the explorative stage but have provided some positive evaluation. ePortfolio approaches may help address the increasing complexity of educational environments (multiple process, systems, providers and distance learning, etc.). The ability of students and assessors to access ePortfolios over the internet, from a wide range of different locations, is a key advantage in supporting the recording and evidencing of achievements for formative assessment in complex educational environments.

Note

1   On behalf of the consortium developing 'Managed environments for portfolio-based reflective learning: integrated support for evidencing outcomes', an FDTL4-funded project (<http://www.eportfolios.ac.uk>).

References

Baume D. A. (2001) *Briefing on the Assessment of Portfolios*. York: LTSN Generic Centre, Assessment Series No. 6.

Cotterill, S., Skelly, G. and McDonald, A. (2004a) Design and integration issues in developing a managed learning environment which is responsive to changing curriculum and policy requirements, *Network Learning*, 2004: 409–16. Available at <http://www.shef.ac.uk/nlc2004/Proceedings/Individual_Papers/CotterillSkellyMcD.htm> (accessed 5 April 2005).

Cotterill, S. J., McDonald, A. M., Drummond, P. and Hammond, G. R. (2004b) Design, implementation and evaluation of a 'generic' ePortfolio: the Newcastle experience, *ePortfolios*. Available at <http://www.eportfolios.ac.uk> (accessed 5 April 2005).

Cravener, P. A. (1999) Faculty experiences with providing online courses: thorns among the roses, *Computers in Nursing*, 17: 42–7.

EPPI (2003) The effectiveness of personal development planning for improving student learning: a systematic map and synthesis review of the effectiveness of personal development planning for improving student learning. EPPI Centre. Available at <http://eppi.ioe.ac.uk/EPPIWebContent/reel/review_groups/EPPI/LTSN/LTSN_summary.pdf> (accessed 5 April 2005).

Friedman, M., Davis, M. H., Harden, R. M., Howie, P. W., Ker, J. and Pippard, M. J. (2001) AMEE Medical Education Guide No. 24: portfolios as a method of student assessment, *Medical Teacher* 23: 535–51.

GMC (2003) *Tomorrow's Doctors*. London: General Medical Council. Available at <http://www.gmc-uk.org/med_ed/tomdoc.pdf> (accessed 5 April 2005).

Jordan, R. K., Hammond, G. and Quentin-Baxter, M. (1997) Networked learning processes:

strategic issues and intranet/internet support for the delivery of medical education, in *Proceedings of CTICM Computers in Medicine Conference*. Bristol: CTICM.

Laurillard, D. (2002) *Rethinking university teaching: a conversational framework for the effective use of learning technologies*. London: RoutledgeFalmer.

Lonka, K. and Bolander, K. (2002) Helping university teachers in transforming their ideas of learning: the case of medicine, in *Proceedings of the British Psychological Society's Annual Psychology of Education Section*. London: British Psychological Society.

NCIHE (1997) *Higher education in the learning society: report of the National Committee of Inquiry into Higher Education*, 2 vols. London: HMSO.

QAA (2001) Guidelines for HE progress files, Quality Assurance Agency for Higher Education. Available at <http://www.qaa.ac.uk/crntwork/progfileHE/guidelines/prog file2001.pdf> (accessed 5 April 2005).

Skelly, G. and Quentin-Baxter, M. (1997) Implementation and management of on-line curriculum study guides: the challenges of organisational change, in *Proceedings of CTICM Computers in Medicine conference*. Bristol: CTICM.

Spencer, J. A. and Jordan, R. K. (1999) Learner centred approaches in medical education, *British Medical Journal*, 318: 1280–3.

Tenbush, J. P. (1998) Teaching the teachers. Electronic School. Available at <http://www.electronic-school.com/0398f1.html> (accessed 5 April 2005).

18 Assessment to support developments in interprofessional education

Sue Morison and Mairead Boohan

Introduction

Government (Department of Health, 2000a, 2000b and 2001a), professional bodies (George, 2000; GMC, 2002; NMC, 2001) and higher education providers (CVCP, 2000; Finch, 2000) concur that the development and implementation of effective programmes of interprofessional education (IPE) are essential for healthcare curricula. While it is generally agreed that the aims of such learning should be to help promote collaborative practices, prepare students for effective team working and ultimately improve patient care (Barr, 2000) there remains a need to identify common interprofessional competencies and appropriate assessment methods (Ross and Southgate, 2001). Furthermore, it is essential that these techniques have credibility with each of the professions involved and at all levels – teachers, students and professional bodies. The focus of IPE on skills such as team working, communication and decision-making should also provide a learning and assessment framework that is generalisable to other academic disciplines.

Historically, the relationship between the medical and nursing professions has not always been an easy one (Walby *et al.*, 1994) and recent changes in healthcare practices (Department of Health, 2000b), along with highly publicised reports of failures in professional communication (Department of Health, 2001a and 2001b) have not helped to bring harmony. Moreover, this divergence is reflected in the professions' approaches to education. Medical curricula focus primarily on the scientific aspects of medical practice, while Nursing curricula embrace the art and science of healthcare. This is demonstrated in the traditional assessment strategies of each profession. For example, medicine predominantly employs standardised objective measures such as multiple-choice questions (MCQ) and an objective structured clinical examination (OSCE) to determine competence. Nursing, in contrast, places more emphasis on performance-based and formative assessment that encourages reflective practice and personal development. Developments in IPE must take account of the different expectations of and approaches to assessment, to issues of territorialism and professional identity. Consideration must also be given to the underlying philosophical differences reflected in each profession's approach to curriculum design and delivery, and to the variation in the requirements and standards of professional bodies.

This chapter will examine the assessment methods developed and evaluated in IPE programmes in Queen's University, Belfast (QUB). Funding from the University's Centre for the Enhancement of Learning and Teaching (CELT) and from the Learning and Teaching Support Network-01 (LTSN) enabled two parallel studies to be undertaken. The studies were informed by the findings of a pilot IPE programme introduced in QUB in 2000 (Morison *et al.*, 2003) which identified the clinical ward as the most favourable learning environment, particularly for students who had some clinical practice experience and who had developed an understanding of their own professional roles and responsibilities. A good collaborative relationship between healthcare professionals, university and NHS staff was also found to be essential for successful interprofessional learning, and activities should be assessed in order for students to engage fully with this approach to learning.

Thus, the studies described here focused on the development and evaluation of learning activities and assessment methods appropriate for ward-based interprofessional learning of clinical, teamwork and communication skills. Both studies involved fourth-year undergraduate Medical students from the Healthcare of Children module and third-year undergraduate Nursing students from the Children's Nursing branch. To facilitate collaborative practice, learning and assessments were designed and implemented by an interprofessional team. In addition, the involvement of staff from each profession was necessary to identify the minimum levels of performance required of students on a variety of tasks and to establish standards acceptable to both professions. Using both qualitative and quantitative methods, the studies were formally and rigorously evaluated by the students involved and the results used to inform further development. The discussions during feedback sessions also provided informal evaluation of the programmes.

The studies were underpinned by Gagne's (1985) 'Conditions of Learning' theory, identifying the importance of defining curricula through intended learning outcomes, and the constructivist approach of Biggs (1999), highlighting the importance of aligning learning activities, outcomes and assessment and thereby clarifying knowledge, skills and attitudes valued by teachers, learners and professional bodies. Additionally the selected learning activities and outcomes focused on knowledge, skills and attitudes common to both professions (Morison *et al.*, 2003; Harden, 1998), the recommendations on key transferable skills made by Dearing (National Committee of Inquiry into Higher Education, 1997) and the QAA Framework on Assessment (2000), stressing the importance of developing assessment procedures to support student learning and provide time for reflection.

Study 1 – Interprofessional learning and assessment: using OSCE and role-play to assess clinical, communication and teamworking skills

A small group, problem-based approach was used with interprofessional teams of four to six students during their clinical placement in a teaching hospital. At the beginning of the clinical placement students were given a clinical scenario describing a child who had recently been diagnosed with diabetes and were asked to work as a team to plan, prepare and give an explanation of the condition and its management to the child's parents in an assessed role-play. The team were also asked to liaise with ward staff who were part of the interprofessional teaching team, to organise teaching sessions on the core clinical skill of giving a subcutaneous insulin injection and to gather other information that would help them to learn about diabetes and its management.

Two assessment methods were used to measure students' success in achieving the intended learning outcomes. The clinical skill was assessed by an OSCE, a standardised criterion referenced method traditionally used in medical education where students move between a series of 'stations' with a specific skill and are assessed at each station. Both candidate and examiner are given precise instructions explaining what is required of them at each station (Harden and Gleeson, 1979). In contrast, a role-play was used to assess the students' ability to present information clearly, to communicate effectively and to work in a team.

Both the OSCE and role-play assessments provided an environment similar to that of real clinical practice but where students were safe to make mistakes without real patients being affected. In the OSCE examination some of the students selected the wrong type of insulin, which would have had serious consequences in a real situation. They were, however, provided with immediate feedback and the opportunity to correct and reflect on their mistake. During the role-play, students found that having to provide an explanation to a parent (albeit a role-play parent) was not easy. It was apparent to students and teachers alike that textbook learning did not help students to react to difficult questions or emotional responses from parents. Unexpected questions from parents were also quick to expose gaps in students' knowledge. Those who had worked effectively as a team were able to draw on the support of colleagues in these situations but those who had not had to manage alone.

Awarding grades and setting standards: OSCE

Each student was assessed against predetermined criteria and the marks awarded ranged from zero to 15, with a median score of 12. Having assessed the first team of students (six individual performances), the assessors agreed that all students scoring less than 10 should be invited to undertake further practice in this skill and those students who selected the wrong insulin would score zero. There was no significant difference between Medical and Nursing students' scores. Following the OSCE, a clinical specialist provided each team with verbal feedback and a general summary of strengths and weaknesses. Each team member was given a breakdown of his or her individual marks.

Awarding grades and setting standards: role-play

Each student was assessed against a predetermined checklist of behavioural indicators that were subdivided into three distinct categories. These were clarity of information, communication and teamwork, with each category given equal weighting. The marks awarded to students ranged from 53 to 82 per cent with a median score of 67 per cent. Following assessment of the first team of students, the assessors agreed that all students who scored below 60 per cent should be asked to reflect further on their strengths and weaknesses and discuss these with their clinical tutor. There was no significant difference between Medical and Nursing students' scores.

At the end of the role-play a discussion of the performance took place and this involved the student team, the role-play 'parents' and the interprofessional assessment team providing supportive verbal feedback. The process of preparing for the assessment was also discussed at this feedback session.

Study conclusions

The developmental process was helped by the alignment of learning outcomes, activities and assessment. Teachers and students from both professions deemed the learning outcomes, activities and assessment methods to be appropriate and assessors were confident that these assessments enabled students to achieve a satisfactory level of competence in the clinical, communication and teamwork skills being tested. Moreover, the interprofessional teaching team were able to agree assessment criteria and standards of competence that were acceptable to both professions.

In particular the simulated environment of the OSCE and role-play assessments provided students with an invaluable opportunity to make mistakes without harming patients and to learn important lessons about safe and effective clinical practice and about teamwork. The provision of immediate feedback and the opportunity to reflect on performance were essential to the success of the learning and assessment experience, and participation in the feedback discussion resulted in the assessment process becoming (and being regarded by staff and students as) part of the learning experience. However, a formal awarding of marks for the interprofessional assessments was deemed essential to ensure that all students engaged with the process and took it seriously.

Study 2 Interprofessional learning and assessment: history-taking, problem-solving and reflection

This study also used a small-group teaching approach. Students worked in teams of six and were required to interview (take a medical and social history from) a child recently admitted to a paediatric ward in order to acquire relevant information to help identify medical and related problems and how best to deal with them. One student from each profession conducted the interview while being observed by their peers. On completion of this task each team prepared a joint care plan, which included evidence of how decisions were made about the child's care. An essential component of the care plan was that it should demonstrate students' ability to reflect on the interprofessional aspects of the task, particularly teamworking and communication skills.

Two complementary assessment methods were used. First, each team was required to prepare and deliver a time-limited PowerPoint presentation; and, second, each student submitted a reflective commentary. Although Nursing students were already familiar with the concept of reflection, Medical students had no prior experience of this learning strategy. The teaching team therefore offered a workshop which used the Jay and Johnson (2002) reflection typology. This provided Medical students with a three-stage framework which they could use to guide and direct their reflection.

Presentation assessment and feedback

In the PowerPoint presentation students were expected to describe the joint care plan and present the evidence they had used to prepare it. An interprofessional team of educators assessed the presentations and a standardised marking proforma was used to award each team a mark. Each team of students scored highly on this assessment, marks ranged from 63 to 87, and all teams achieved a satisfactory standard. Verbal feedback was provided on the content and quality of the presentation and students were able to seek clarification on any issues about which they were uncertain. Most teams demonstrated that they could successfully and effectively work in a team to organise the tasks of preparing and giving the presentation. Students found that this exercise helped them to learn to work as a team and improve their communication skills but also provided an opportunity to gain experience of how different healthcare professionals approach the same task.

Reflective commentary assessment and feedback

The reflective commentary required students to outline what they had learned about the roles and responsibilities of different healthcare professionals and to highlight differences and commonalities in the way they obtained information from a patient. Students were also asked to record their perceptions of the influence the IPE experience had on their current learning and may have on future professional practice. Although the commentaries were assessed, and written feedback to facilitate the further development of reflective skills was provided, the teaching team agreed that no mark should be awarded, as the aim of this assessment was to encourage students to provide a personal reflection rather than to satisfy predetermined criteria.

Study conclusions

The assessment methods selected were fit for the purpose as they provided students with an opportunity to learn and work together in teams, and, importantly, to reflect on the relevance of the overall educational experience. Both students and teachers found participation in the project useful in encouraging interprofessional interaction and effective communication. Uni-professional ward-based assessment often excludes some of the staff involved in programme delivery. However, teachers in this study welcomed the opportunity to contribute at all stages of the programme – planning, delivery, assessment and feedback.

Discussion

There are distinct advantages to establishing interprofessional teams of teachers and assessors in all stages of programme planning, implementation, assessment and feedback. Not only did this help to ensure teachers' commitment to the programme but it had the advantage of providing staff with an opportunity to reflect on their habitual modes of teaching and interacting with students from other professions. Teachers from different professions were able to engage in constructive dialogue about profession-specific assessment methods and standards and to identify how these could operate in an interprofessional context. Such an approach provides a useful model for cross-disciplinary developments in areas other than healthcare.

The clinical and history-taking skills were assessed by structured, standardised methods used by most healthcare professions but only in a uni-professional and not an interprofessional setting. Each of the studies described above was able to establish a common level of competence that was attainable by and acceptable to students and teachers from both professions. Similarly, the role-play and presentation assessments were able to establish a set of criteria against which students from both professions could be judged and appropriate standards of performance established. A key feature of this approach was that it recognised the importance of assessors' judgement in validating standards and the need for them to establish confidence in the interprofessional assessment process.

The assessment by presentation was unique in providing a team rather than an individual with a grade. Neither students nor assessors objected to this approach, although persuading professional bodies to accept this as a valid assessment standard may be more problematic. Allocating a group grade allied to an individual grade on an associated task might help to make this more acceptable, and having an interprofessional assessment team would be essential.

There were other disadvantages associated with these assessment methods. They were both time-consuming to plan and deliver, and labour intensive. In the initial stages of developing interprofessional or any innovative assessment method this is unavoidable if assessors and participants are to value and have confidence in the assessment tool. It would be important that curriculum planners and budget holders are cognisant of the implications of this if such assessment methods are to be employed.

Perhaps the most important component of these assessments was the emphasis placed upon feedback and reflection. The feedback session that followed the OSCE and role-play assessment was invaluable in enabling students to reflect on their performance and to examine their own strengths and weaknesses and understand more about working with colleagues and patients. The OSCE enabled students to appreciate the consequences of not following instructions precisely, and the role-play clearly distinguished between effective teams and teams that were simply collections of individuals. Through supportive feedback and discussion students were helped to increase self-awareness, and, importantly, students from both professions were equally adept in this skill.

The reflective commentary, however, demanded a different set of skills and required students to reflect on personal growth and development. Traditionally, in comparison to the Nursing curriculum, the undergraduate Medical curriculum placed little emphasis on this type of reflection and provided students with few opportunities to reflect on personal learning. When required to engage in this process, Medical students found it challenging and needed more support and guidance than the Nursing students, who were used to a curriculum where reflective learning was already embedded. Thus an important outcome from this intervention was that effective learning and teaching strategies employed by one discipline were acknowledged and adopted by the other.

Unlike clinical and presentation skills, the conclusion of this study was that it would be inappropriate to standardise personal reflection and its product (e.g., a reflective commentary). This process is more concerned with personal growth and development than standards of competence, and students need to be encouraged to engage with this, although, paradoxically, without an assessment mark being given, students are less likely to perceive it as important.

During the role-play and at the presentations judgements were made about how effectively students had learned to work in teams, communicate with patients and colleagues and understand about the roles and responsibilities of different members of the healthcare team. Developing and testing criteria to assess this in a standardised way was important, and central to this was the role of feedback and interaction between students and assessors. Students and teachers were able to discuss the appropriateness of both the learning activities and the assessment criteria. Thus, having interactive assessment with immediate feedback made the assessment part of the learning experience.

These developments were based upon the premise that curriculum content, assessment and feedback methods should be constructively aligned (Biggs, 1999). This was particularly important in an interprofessional programme where different professions have their own professional requirements, which are often perceived as unique to that profession. This approach, however, facilitated the identification of common learning activities and appropriate assessment strategies. By establishing learning outcomes at the outset and using these as a springboard to identifying learning and assessment strategies, the educational agenda became paramount and the interprofessional problems were significantly reduced.

Assessing students by methods such as OSCE, role-play, presentation and reflection should not be regarded as exclusive to the healthcare professions as they all have great potential to be adapted and utilised by any discipline promoting teamwork, communication and decision-making skills alongside their profession-specific skills. For example, using role-play to assess communication and teamwork skills may be particularly useful for academic disciplines developing work-based or placement-learning programmes. Further, in implementing the Burgess (Universities UK, 2004) recommendations, all academic disciplines will be required to educate students in the process and practice of reflection, and these case studies provide valuable insights into some of the developmental problems and their solutions. OSCE-type assessment could also be developed in different disciplines to assess students' abilities to perform a specific task and to follow and carry out specific instructions, particularly if this is related to a team task or performance.

Twenty-first-century working practices are increasingly focusing on the ability of employees to be flexible teamworkers with effective communication skills, so it is likely that in future the acquisition of such skills will need to be formally and explicitly assessed. The individually focused feedback mechanisms central to these assessments allowed students to reflect on their own strengths and weaknesses and to identify strategies for improving their performance. This helped to create self-awareness and act as a building block for the development of lifelong learning skills and thus the transition from pedagogy to andragogy.

References

Barr, H. (2000) *Interprofessional education: 1997–2000: A review for the UKCC*. London: UKCC.

Biggs, J. (1999) *Teaching for quality learning at university*. Buckingham: SRHE and Open University Press.

Committee of Vice Chancellors and Principals of the Universities of the United Kingdom (CVCP) (2000) *NHS workforce planning: CVCP response*. Annex 00/96/b (3). London: CVCP.

Department of Health (2000a) *A Health Service for all talents: developing the NHS workforce*. London: HMSO.

—— (2000b) *The NHS plan: a plan for investment, a plan for reform*. London: HMSO.

—— (2001a) *Learning from Bristol: the report of the public inquiry into children's heart surgery at Bristol Royal Infirmary 1984–1995*. London: TSO.

—— (2001b) *Royal Liverpool Children's Inquiry*. London: TSO.

Finch, J. (2000) Interprofessional education and team working: a view from the education providers, *British Medical Journal*, 321: 1138–40.

Gagne, R. (1985) *The conditions of learning*. New York: Holt, Rinehart and Winston.

General Medical Council (GMC) (2002) *Tomorrow's doctors*. London: GMC.

George, C. (2000) *Teamworking in medicine*. London: GMC.

Harden, R. M. (1998) Effective multiprofessional education: a three-dimensional perspective, *Medical Teacher*, 20: 402–8.

Harden, R. M. and Gleeson, F. A. (1979) *Assessment of medical competence using an objective structured clinical examination (OSCE)*. Edinburgh: Association for the Study of Medical Education.

Jay, K. J. and Johnson, K. L. (2002) Capturing complexity: a typology of reflective practice for teacher education, *Teaching and Teacher Education*, 18: 73–85.

Morison, S., Boohan, M., Jenkins, J. and Moutray, M. (2003) Facilitating undergraduate interprofessional learning in healthcare: comparing classroom and clinical learning for nursing and medical students, *Learning in Health and Social Care*, 2(2): 92–104.

National Committee of Inquiry into Higher Education (1997) *Higher education in the learning society: report of the National Committee of Inquiry into Higher Education*. London: HMSO.

Nursing and Midwifery Council (2001) *Fitness for practice and purpose*. London: NMC.

Quality Assurance Agency (QAA) (2000) *Code of practice for the assurance of academic quality and standards in higher education*. London: QAA.

Ross, F. and Southgate, L. (2001) Learning together in medical and nursing training, *Medical Education* 34: 739–43.

Universities UK and Standard Conference of Principals (2004) *Measuring and recording student achievement.* London: Universities UK.

Walby, S., Greenwell, J., Mackay, L. and Soothill, K. (1994) *Medicine and nursing: professions in a changing health service.* London: Sage.

19 Academic professionalism
The need for change

Lewis Elton

Introduction

Professionalism implies a high degree of competence in one's work and a pride in carrying it out (Elton, 1986). In all well-established professions, this requires a combination of training, education and acculturation. This chapter will explore the extent to which the practice of academic staff may be considered 'professional', how this is currently assessed and how perhaps it should be. There is here an implied criticism – that at present much academic work cannot be described as 'professional', and it will indeed be suggested that a development of genuine professionalism requires systemic and personal changes. Such changes should be rooted in good theory, hopefully achievable through appropriate change theory. The approach represents a considerable extension of what is known from current evaluated practice – mostly rooted in particular case histories, some recent and others quite old but still highly relevant, which will be cited and marked with a single asterisk in the References at the end of the chapter.

Academic professionalism

Academic professionalism is multifaceted, corresponding to the multifaceted nature of academic work – teaching, research, leadership and management; plus increasingly nowadays societal and possibly 'business' functions. The evidence is that the majority of academics are most 'professional' in their research function, in that there they have normally received appropriate training and have been acculturated into the research culture. They nevertheless act, and historically have always acted, as if they were either professional in all their other functions or – until recently – considered that there was no need for professionalism in them. Thus, Ashby (1963) castigated his colleagues for their lack of professionalism in the area of leadership and management:

> All over the country these groups of scholars, who would not make a decision about the shape of a leaf or the derivation of a word or the author of a manuscript without painstakingly assembling the evidence, make decisions about admission policy, size of universities, staff–student ratios, content of courses and similar issues, based on dubious assumptions, scrappy data and mere hunch.

But not until he was eighty (Ashby, 1984) did he realise that there was also a lack of professionalism in teaching:

> For many years I taught in universities. Like most academics I assumed that the only qualification I needed was expertise in the discipline taught. It did cross my mind that *how to teach* might be a discipline in its own right, but I never gave it much thought. I marked thousands of examination scripts without examining what the scripts could teach me about my capacity as teacher and examiner.

As Ashby was one of the wisest academics of the past century, this blindness to the need for professionalism in teaching – which he shared and shares with the vast majority of his colleagues – will form the starting point of this chapter. In spite of all that has been written recently in support of professionalism in teaching (see, e.g., Barnett, 1992), it is still relevant in the highly traditional system which constitutes our universities. Nothing that has been written – and there is much – on academic professionalism since has taken due note of either the need for formal professional development[1] as an essential feature of any professionalism or the difficulties inherent in the huge change in the outlook of academics that this implies. Instead, most recent writing has been prescriptive and has ignored all that we know from change theory. Furthermore, the British Higher Education Academy** seems preoccupied with minimum standards for membership, and concentrates, at least at present, on the postgraduate certificate level with the primary aim of enhancing the student experience.[2] While this is indeed suitable for initial training, it often does not rise above the craft level. Staff who have been through such a course then return to their departments often enthusiastic for change but unable to justify such change through any more fundamental understanding, only to be met all too frequently by the scepticism of their traditionalist seniors. Even the agenda of the US/UK Scholarship of Learning and Teaching (SoTL) movement speaks to the converted, without paying due heed to the need for these to become 'fishers of men' (Matthew IV:19) – and women! It may be noted that in the USA, where SoTL started, it would appear that academics need no formal professional development, and the 'transformational agenda' is directed towards change in students:

> [T]he scholarship of teaching and learning is characterized by a transformational agenda. One of [its] publicly stated goals is to foster 'significant long-lasting learning for all students' . . . and the desire to create stronger curricula and more powerful pedagogies . . . The scholarship of teaching and learning might then be defined as scholarship undertaken in the name of change, with one measure of its success being its impact on thought and practice.**

In contrast, the provision of courses at different levels, as provided by the Staff and Educational Development Association (SEDA),** comes closer to a provision for true professionalism, and the course described in the next section was indeed SEDA accredited.

Initial and continuing professional development (CPD) of academic staff[3]

As academics on the whole consider research the most important of their functions, it will clearly be advantageous to base a general model for the initial and continuing professional development of academic staff on their present development in the research function, where *formation* starts with the initial training of research students (see, e.g., Cryer, 1998 and **), and is then continued through an apprenticeship with their supervisors – experienced researchers who also provide acculturation. The *formation* of supervisors is provided by the appropriate SEDA–PDF course.**

A strong indication in the choice of this model is that research should influence *all* academic *formation*, whatever the academic task concerned. It therefore formed the basis of an action research model, which I believe was the first of its kind, and was extensively evaluated (Stefani and Elton, 2002). It has since been developed elsewhere, including at Oxford and DIT Dublin, where I have been external examiner. It is based on participatory action research and depends on five principles: it was experiential, problem based, research based, open and at a distance. Course members proposed the research which they wished to carry out and the associated learning objectives. These, as well as criteria concerning their achievement, were then confirmed through negotiation with the course staff. Structure was provided by the course units, supported by appropriate reading (Cryer, 1992), which covered the various aspects of both traditional and innovative teaching, and the proposed action research programme had to fit that structure. Assessment was on a pass/fail basis, based on qualitative evaluations of the achievement of the declared course objectives. The reason for offering the course at a distance (in essentially pre-electronic days) was that it was judged correctly at that time that no single university would provide a critical mass of course members.

Only ten years ago, probably the most innovative feature of the course was that it was wholly 'student centred', and indeed student driven, through course members having to initiate all negotiations. It also successfully overcame the difficulty that academics see everything essentially from the standpoint of their discipline, while in fact much of what they have to learn is interdisciplinary and generic, by giving the model a structure based on a staff development model (Elton, 1987) first used in the 'Enterprise in Higher Education Initiative' (Wright, 1992), in which the input by a central staff development unit is generic, but this is interpreted along discipline lines by the course members. This model – which implies a synthesis of the 'generic' and the 'discipline specific' – has recently been reinvented at the University of Manchester as a 'hub and spokes' model (Kahn, 2005). It is in striking contrast to the traditional view, accepted by the majority of academics and expressed so ably by Becher (1989), that the academic 'tribes and territories' are divisive and that a synthesis is unachievable.

A feature which was rather fortuitous – i.e., that the course was offered at a distance – should, with the development of the internet, become central, whether such a course is campus or distance based, but experience with the course showed that interactions between participants do not grow naturally and have to be fostered (which they were not in the course under consideration). Such understandings underpin a more recent course in the CPD of medical practitioners (Russell *et al.*, 2005), which also successfully avoided the trap of technology in the driving seat rather than in support.

Assessment of CPD

The student-centred nature of the course which has been described, and indeed of any genuinely student-centred course, cannot rationally be assessed on the traditional positivistic principles of reliability and validity, which both depend on all students being treated the same (Johnston, 2004). Instead, an interpretivist approach is required (Guba and Lincoln, 1989), of the kind familiar from assessment in, for example, arts and design programmes, where examiners cannot have more than a very general preconception of what to expect and 'model answers' do not exist. To prevent utter anarchy, such assessment relies on the 'connoisseurship' of professionally developed examiners – a concept originally conceptualised by Eisner (1985) – who, of course, would have to go through a process of *formation*. Incidentally, such a process ought to be compulsory also for positivist examiners, which at present it is not.

Although the need for interpretivist assessment has been established here only for academic CPD, the fact that the latter must have exactly the student-centred nature that is nowadays increasingly postulated also for student learning indicates that in the latter too interpretivist assessment will be important. The consequences of this for student assessment in general, including the thorny question of the classification of degrees (Elton, 2004), are profound but cannot be addressed within the compass of this chapter.

Initial and continuing professional development of academic management

I next turn to Ashby's other stricture: the *formation* of academic managers. Here, following the Jarratt Report (CVCP, 1985), management by committee has been replaced by essentially top-down management, although these committees have continued to exist! The practitioners of university management at present have mostly not had any formal preparation (i.e, *formation*) for their work, and – in addition – they are even less accountable than are practitioners in corresponding commercial and industrial management, on whom they are largely modelled. In contrast to management in the private sector, it is almost impossible to sack a vice-chancellor. Furthermore, the use of a commercial/industrial model – incidentally of a kind that would be considered inappropriate by much of progressive commerce and industry – clashes with the traditional culture of universities, where academic staff are colleagues and not employees. That this clash is unresolved and causing great damage is indicated by the kind of evidence recently produced by Sommerville (2005) and quoted below. That it has remained unresolved since the Jarratt Report nearly twenty years ago indicates how deep rooted it is.[4] (One wonders whether Jarratt ever read Cornford's (1908) satire. Contrary to Marx's dictum, is the present situation a case of 'first time as farce, the second as tragedy'?)

There would appear to be two ways of resolving this conflict: either by reasserting the collegial nature of academia (see, e.g., Middlehurst and Elton, 1992), which would require a reversal in management structures of the past twenty years; or by successfully changing academics from colleagues to employees. Either change is highly problematic but it can certainly not be achieved without a deep understanding of change processes (Elton, 1999), which would have to be built into any *formation* programmes for managers – from heads of department to vice-chancellors.

The management of change

The need for a scholarly management of change policy is indicated by quotations from the case study of a particular university (Sommerville, 2005), which highlights the continuing unresolved conflict between the traditionalism of academics and the change agenda of top management:

> Like a number of HEIs this university had a commitment to a committee way of managing its affairs: 'Universities are strong on committees and we have a formal committee structure' (Transcript, lines 344–5). However, an aspect of this particular university was that the Vice-Chancellor operated through an informal network which my interviewee referred to as a clique: 'We have a strategy group which is the VC and it's basically the VC's clique and that's not a formal committee of the university but it's probably the most important one and where the big decisions are made' (Transcript, lines 345–7); 'it exists as this strange body called strategy group. And it's not formal in that it doesn't report anywhere or to anyone' (Transcript, lines 350–1); and 'in some ways the informal can be more important. This goes back to what I was saying before about getting decisions made, and the open, transparent move towards Senate but that doesn't always recognize what goes on behind – the persuading and the arm twisting and the informal networks' (Transcript, lines 353–6).
>
> Given what I have said about the perspective on the management of change, it is perhaps ironic that in commenting on the management of change, the Vice-Chancellor in the University's Annual Report of 2002/3 stated:

> How has this change been managed? First, everything must be driven by academic development priorities . . . Second, responsibilities should be devolved as far as possible. Third, experimental new 'units' should be established as the seeds of growth for new activities. Fourth, there is a principle of building creative, cognitive and compunctions capacities . . . Fifth, we would recognize that management is for everybody: clear thinking about his or her own academic objectives by a member of staff – and how to achieve them – is 'management'. But management is not simple: at its heart at corporate levels, it is about reconciling the demands of individual

and various collective interests; of one discipline against another, of new interdisciplinary investment against the disciplinary core. To achieve this without strife demands a sixth principle of management: an open culture – open book accounting and freedom of debate.

There is here evidence of unresolved tensions, between collegiality and top-down management, as well as between traditionalism and innovation, which justifies the reference to earlier evidence, such as in the Ashby quotations.

This ignorance of management of change principles is far less justifiable than the ignorance of innovations in teaching and learning, since, while the latter are new, the former have been developed and their effectiveness evaluated over sixty years (Lewin, 1952; Berg and Östergren 1979; Fullan and Stiegelbauer, 1991; Elton 1999).

Conclusion

This chapter has made a strong plea for creating a truly professional academic profession. The underlying evidence exists, but has perhaps never before been brought together. So the tools for change are there; let academia pick them up and use them in a constructive manner. If they fail to do this, then the current descent into a blind commercialism, with its permanent antagonism between the rulers and the ruled, could destroy the universities.

Notes

1   I shall use the phrase 'professional development' or, alternatively, the French *'formation'*, as English does not have a single word which constructively combines the concepts of training and education, and indeed commonly sees such concept pairs as opposites.
2   ** Denotes websites, which are listed in the References.
3   Including staff engaged in academic staff development; note that the USA uses 'faculty' for 'academic staff' and 'staff' for academic-related and support staff.
4   This clash is incidentally quite separate from conflict within the traditional university culture (Caston, 1977), which arguably persists to this day but will not be pursued here.

References

Printed sources

Ashby, E. (1963) 'Decision making in the academic world', in P. Halmos (ed.), *Sociological studies in British university education*. Keele: University of Keele Press.
——(1984) Foreword, in I. M. Brewer, *Learning more and teaching less*. Guildford: Society for Research in Higher Education.
Barnett, R. (1992) *Improving higher education*. Buckingham: SRHE/Open University Press.
Becher, T. (1989) *Academic tribes and territories*. Milton Keynes: SRHE/Open University Press.

*Berg, B. and Östergren, B. (1979) 'Innovation processes in higher education', *Studies in Higher Education*, 4, pp. 261–8.

Caston, G. (1977) 'Conflicts within the university community', *Studies in Higher Education*, 2, pp. 3–8.

Cornford, F. M. (1908) *Microcosmographia academica*, Cambridge: Bowes and Bowes.

*Cryer, P. (1998) 'Transferable skills, marketability and lifelong learning: the particular case of postgraduate research students', *Studies in Higher Education*, 23, pp. 207–16.

—— (ed.) (1992) *Effective learning and teaching in higher education*, Sheffield: CVCP Universities' Staff Development Unit.

CVCP (1985) *Report of the Jarratt Committee*. London: Committee of Vice Chancellors and Principals.

Eisner, E. W. (1985) The art of educational evaluation. London: Falmer Press.

Elton, L. (1986) 'Quality in higher education: nature and purpose', *Studies in Higher Education*, 11, pp. 83–4.

*—— (1987) *Teaching in higher education: appraisal and training*. London: Kogan Page, pp. 77–8.

—— (1999) 'New ways of learning in higher education: managing the change', *Tertiary Education and Management*, 5, 207–25.

—— (2004) 'Should classification of the UK honours degree have a future?', *Assessment and Evaluation in Higher Education*, 29, pp. 413–20.

Fullan, M. G. and Stiegelbauer, S. (1991) *The new meaning of educational change*. London: Cassell.

Guba, J. M. and Lincoln, V. (1989) *Fourth generation evaluation*. London: Sage.

*Johnston, B. (2004) 'Summative assessment of portfolios: an examination of positivist and interpretivist approaches to agreement over outcomes', *Studies in Higher Education*, 29, pp. 395–412.

Kahn, P. (2005) private communication.

Lewin, K. (1952) *Field theory in social science*, London: Tavistock.

Middlehurst, R. and Elton, L. (1992) 'Leadership and management in higher education', *Studies in Higher Education*, 17, pp. 251–64.

*Russell, J., Elton, L., Swinglehurst, D. and Greenhalgh, T. (in press) 'Using e-learning in assessment for learning: a case-study of a web-based course in primary care', *Assessment and Evaluation in Higher Education*.

*Sommerville, A. (2005) private communication, based on current draft of Ph.D. thesis.

*Stefani, L. and Elton, L. (2002) 'Continuing professional development of academic teachers through self-initiated learning', *Assessment and Evaluation in Higher Education*, 27, pp. 117–29.

*Wright, P. (1992) 'Learning through enterprise: the Enterprise in Higher Education Initiative', in R. Barnett, *Learning to effect*. Buckingham: SRHE/Open University Press, pp. 204–23.

Websites

*Cryer, P. <http://www.cryer.freeserve.co.uk>
Higher Education Academy: <http://www.heacademy.ac.uk/accredited-membership.asp>
SEDA <http://www.seda.ac.uk/pdf/index.htm>
—— <http://www.seda.ac.uk/pdf/supervising_postgraduate_research.htm>
SoTL <http://www.city.ac.uk.edc/Sotlconference.htm>

20 Reflections, rationales and realities

Karen Clegg and Cordelia Bryan

> It serves no useful purpose to lower our educational aspirations because we cannot
> yet measure what we think is important to teach. Quite the contrary, measurement
> and assessment will have to rise to the challenge of our educational aspirations.
>
> (Cross in Crooks, 1988: 470)

Context: the need for innovation

This collection of innovations illustrates that the challenges faced by higher
education practitioners in the UK are echoed by our colleagues in the USA,
Australia and New Zealand. As Gibbs highlights in the opening chapter, the barriers
to innovation in assessment include large student numbers, reward structures that
continue to favour research over teaching and a political agenda that emphasises
product over process. This narrow vision has meant that historically we have seen
assessment as a way of justifying rather than enabling judgements to be made. As
educators we have been conscribed to take a very narrow view of the possibilities
that different assessment modes offer.

> We live in a world obsessed with data; with the collection and dissemination
> of performance indicators, statistics, measures, grades, marks and categories.
> In a world in which it is assumed that quality can be defined, compared and
> certified. And a world in which what cannot be perceived, explained and
> measured is deemed to be either unimportant or non-existent.
>
> (Broadfoot, 2002: 199)

Compounding this vision is a discourse of assessment that emphasises measurement
and grades over opportunity. This discourse is the symptom of modernity and our
concern with accounting and legitimising knowledge. We argue that as eductors
we need to acknowledge the shortcomings of educational assessment and let go of
the idea that we can claim a scientific 'reliability' in what is essentially a subjective
practice. As Broadfoot (2002: 208) highlights, assessment is a 'frail and flawed'
technology. Yet still we cling to the notion of 'objective' assessment, invigilated
exams and online individual assessments. This is due to our desire to be seen to be
'rigorous', our fear of the threat of plagiarism (more of which later in this chapter),
and because until recently, objective tests appeared to serve the purpose.

However, we move on and times change. We live now in what Barnett (1999) describes as, 'a high risk, "super complex" society . . . characterised by uncertainty and unpredictability'. In this context we need to know what, how and the extent to which a student can apply knowledge. As Birenbaum and Dochy (1996: 4) suggest, 'Successful functioning in this era demands an adaptable, thinking, autonomous person, who is a self-regulated learner, capable of communicating and co-operating with others.' This shifting nature of learning and societal requirements is exemplified in the case studies in this book. Note how few are concerned with the assessment of content knowledge and how many focus on the assessment of skills, abilities and capabilities. These qualities are what Claxton refers to as the learner's 'toolkit', which he defines as the three 'Rs': resilience, resourcefulness and reflection. If we can develop these qualities in our students then they will be equipped to cope with the super-complexity of the Western world.

Dochy *et al.* (2004) describe a 'new assessment culture' characterised by a strong emphasis on the integration of assessment and instruction borne out of the need to align learning and instruction more with assessment. They identify five key characteristics emblematic of this 'new culture':

1   students construct knowledge (rather than reproduce it);
2   assessment focuses on the application of knowledge to actual cases – which, they argue, 'is the core goal of the so-called innovative assessment practices' (p. 2);
3   assessment instruments ask for multiple perspectives and context sensitivity – students are required to demonstrate insight into underlying causal mechanisms not just statements;
4   students are actively involved in the assessment process – they discuss criteria and engage in self- and/or peer assessment;
5   assessments are integrated within the learning process and congruent with the teaching method and learning environment.

Peppered throughout the chapters is the idea that good assessment involves active engagement with real-life learning tasks. Researchers such as Birenbaum (2003) and Gulikers *et al.* (2004) maintain that this focus on 'authenticity', as defined by the relationship of the task to the context in which it is set, is what sets innovative assessment apart from more traditional assessments. If assessment tasks are representative of the context being studied and both relevant and meaningful to those involved then it may be described as 'authentic'. This marriage between context and tasks is demonstrated by several case studies and in particular those in Part IV, where the focus is on helping learners in different subject disciplines develop professional knowledge, skills and attitudes. In many UK research-based universities work is being developed to equip Ph.D. students and researchers with a range of skills to enhance their academic practice and performance as researchers.[1] This commitment to the development of future university teachers illustrates a shift in values and a recognition that professional development is not just about meeting a series of assessment criteria to show competence but, as Elton says, is about developing 'connoisseurship'.

At Alverno College (see Mentkowski Chapter 4, this volume) students develop skills and professional dispositions alongside their major field of study. To enable this, Alverno has reconfigured the entire curriculum around the principle of performance-based assessment. Students constantly make judgements about the quality of their own performance and that of their peers in relation to criteria. This development of evaluative skills is what Dochy *et al.* (2004) and Sadler (1989 and more recently 1998) argue is a fundamental characteristic of the new assessment culture and a central aim for higher education. A key consideration to be made of innovative assessment is the extent to which learners are able to self-regulate and engage in 'authentic' assessment tasks.

Assessment and emotion

The emotional impact of assessment has been underrated, but it is central to the motivations and case studies in this collected volume. Being assessed is undoubtedly an emotional business. Having a judgement made about the quality of your work is a potentially humiliating experience, which is why Nicol and Milligan endorse feedback that 'encourages positive motivational beliefs and self-esteem' (Chapter 5). Research shows that events which are highly charged with emotion tend to be well remembered (Cannon, 2002), which would account for the minute details people can recall about sitting their finals, taking a driving test, or going through their Ph.D. viva. For many learners it is the explicit recognition of having done well that drives learning. Of course, there are those who learn for the love of under-standing, but in Western society that learning is verified and celebrated through certificates, post-nominals and promotion. Assessment provides success, status and public accolades. The corollary for those who don't do well is lack of confidence, which can result in student drop-out (Yorke, 2002).

Dweck's work on self-theories explains how learners develop either an entity (fixed) or incremental (developmental) theory of intelligence. Those students who ascribe to an entity view believe that assessment is an all-encompassing activity that defines them as people. If they fail at the task, they *are* failures. Those students who feel that intelligence is incremental have little or no fear of failure. Good assessment then should help students appreciate challenge and shake off the fear of failure (Hinett, 2002). Crooks (1988) and Black and Wiliam (1998) suggest that when designing assessment care should be taken to differentiate what is 'task' and 'ego' involving. Conditions that support task goals include, among other things: 'challenging but attainable tasks, individualisation of tasks, opportunities for student autonomy in learning, use of cooperative learning approaches and little emphasis on summative grading' (Crooks, 1988: 466). Arguably, the more able the student is to separate feedback on work from feedback on themself personally, the more likely they are to pick themself up and try again. It is about developing the kind of resilience that Claxton believes is essential to the learner's 'toolkit'. Helping students to see failure as a natural part of learning and not an indictment of their worth as individuals is one way forward. To achieve this requires a move away from outcome-based assessment and towards more holistic, process-based assessment, such as portfolios (Cotterill *et al.*) and personal development planning (Williams and Ryan). Other options are the online environments discussed by Nicol and Milligan in which students manage their own learning and are free, without risk of public embarrassment, to make mistakes. The more we can develop supportive learning environments that enable students to get things wrong and learn from their mistakes, the less likely they are to adopt an entity view. By developing supportive, authentic learning environments we may also help to reduce the fear of failure that can sometimes prompt students to take desperate measures.

Plagiarism

Without assessment there would be no need to plagiarise. Research into student learning has provided empirical evidence that assessments that reward memorisation and deny the opportunity for reflction promote surface approaches to learning. Similarly, it teaches us that assessments that are related to real life, are relevant to the subject and provide appropriate assessment are likely to produce more sophisticated learning (Entwistle and Ramsden, 1983). Why then do we continue with such practices and blame technology and students for the shortcomings of assessment, when they are entirely our creation? We cannot legislate for the determined students intent on doing well at the expense of others but we can address poorly designed assessment such that the majority of students are inspired enough not to compromise their academic integrity. Innovative, authentic assessment that provides opportunities for students to evaluate their performance against negotiated criteria and offer timely, quality feedback goes a long way to combating the temptations of the internet's so called 'cheat-sites' and eBay.

The case studies show that good assessments centre on the process of learning and examine the extent to which an individual has increased skills and understanding. This process can be evidenced through, for example: oral examinations, vivas, debates, portfolios, skeleton drafts, reflective logs, teamwork projects and any other method that requires the student to account for the process of learning, the links and connections that prompted him or her to connect one piece of information in relation to his/her own experience. Accounting for how you learned and the rationale for choosing to site one particular source over another is very difficult if you are not the author or orator of the particular piece of work. Speech, in particular, is transparent to waffle and it is very difficult, even for the most practised orator to pass off the work of someone else as his/her own when faced with inquisitive peers ready to ask challenging questions. Jude Caroll, author of *A handbook for deterring plagiarism in higher education* (2002), suggests that in designing assessment tutors should ensure that tasks include reference to current affairs (not dated such that old essays can be recycled) and require students to access primary sources. The more the task involves the student conducting research or referring to recent references, the less opportunity there is for plagiarism. There are endless possibilities for the learner to demonstrate thinking and engagement with the task, all of which make learning and teaching more interesting and plagiarism more difficult. In developing a set of guiding principles for innovative assessment it may be useful to extend the definition of 'authentic' to include the verification and authentication of the ownership of the assessed work. In light of the debate about academics not being beyond passing off someone else's work as their own (*The Times Higher Education Supplement*, 15 April 2005), perhaps we should also consider building into any new framework of professional standards a concept of academic scholarship legitimated by data protection.

Innovations: leading by example

Modelling good practice

Robinson and Udall (Chapter 7) and Williams and Ryan (Chapter 15) highlight the value of self- and peer assessment in helping students learn. These case studies corroborate research (Sadler, 1998; Cowan, 1998; Boud, 1995; Hinett and Thomas, 1999; Hinett, 2002) illustrating how involving students in discussions about quality and standards provides them with better insight into the assessment process. However, until recently there has been little evidence that training students in self and peer methods benefits them in a range of studies. In a case study at the University of the West Indies, McDonald and Boud (2003) conducted one of the first experiments into the value of training students in self-assessment techniques. Using a control group of high-school students to map responses, McDonald trained students in constructing, validating, applying and evaluating criteria. Students were taught to make reasoned choices, assess responses to questions by applying criteria, evaluate their own work and make and use self-assessment activities (p. 213). The result was a marked improvement in all subject areas and those students who had received training in self-assessment methods outperforming their peers.

In the UK, Orsmond *et al.* (2002) have further developed their work on peer assessment by exploring the extent to which student evaluation can be improved through the provision of exemplars. Working in groups, biology students were first asked to develop criteria for the assessment of their posters and then asked to rate each other's posters against the criteria. Previous studies (ibid. 1997; 2000) indicated that students were less able to discriminate between marking criteria that they had constructed themselves compared to marking criteria that were provided for them. In the 2002 study students were provided with ungraded exemplar posters to illustrate different design styles and prompt discussion about appropriate criteria. The results indicate that the use of exemplars helped students demonstrate greater understanding of both marking criteria and subject standards. In addition, the exemplars helped to provide a focus for meaningful feedback (Orsmond *et al.*, 2002: 321).

These studies reveal that the real value of innovations such as self- and peer assessment is not in helping students 'play the assessment game' or become more adept at giving grades but in providing an opportunity for them to discuss and become engaged with the process of making judgements and understanding how quality work is defined. It is not enough for a student to receive feedback that says the criteria have been 'met' since this refers to a threshold but says little about the standards or quality of the work. Peer assessment as described by Orsmond *et al.* helps students understand what constitutes quality work, not just a developed sense of what the criterion requires. In Chapter 5, Nicol and Milligan make a similar case for the use of exemplars.

In a case study involving trainee school teachers, Royce Sadler (2002) recounts how giving weak students exemplars from more able students helped them appreciate how quality is determined. Royce Sadler argues (2002: 135):

> Exemplars convey messages that nothing else can . . . they illustrate by example what works and help students to understand abstract concepts and the relevance of theory. Quality is determined by how the specified – and the unspecified – criteria are invoked in practice, and how all the various qualities contribute together in concert.

As Gibbs highlights in Chapter 2, the value of using peer feedback and exemplars is that they provide prompt and efficient feedback to students. However, there is still a real need for students to develop a sense of ownership of their work and to see learning as a series of incremental steps facilitated by assessment tasks. One such example is the 'Collaborative Learning Project' headed by John Issitt at the University of York. The objective is to create a student-produced textbook in which students have major responsibility for individual chapters but have to edit each other's chapters through a series of iterations. The individual chapters are not essays as such but explanatory prose designed to lead the target audience – younger students (typically A-level) – through a particular issue of ideas relating to educational studies. Students have to know their topics and develop skills in teamworking. Importantly, this includes supporting other learners/peers and developing skills in giving and receiving feedback. Students provide ongoing feedback to their peers and edit drafts until they are happy with the final result. The students agree the assessment criteria between them, which count for 50 per cent of the project (calculated using an algorithmic formula). The remaining 50 per cent is allocated by traditional criteria. The exercise is designed to facilitate the development of pedagogic craft in writing, giving feedback and taking on the role of 'expert' in order to develop professional judgement. The result is a bound collection of essays that can be used by future students and a product which they can keep and use as an example of collaborative work for prospective employers. John Issitt hopes to extend the project to include contributions from students across Europe, creating a truly multicultural peer-assessed project.

In most subjects, especially those like education studies that are related to a profession, rules, theories and conventions are used to provide the foundation for the curriculum. However, in postgraduate research programmes such as the Ph.D. there is an expectation that the conventions will be questioned and that current thinking will be challenged. The same is true at masters-level courses in creative disciplines such as art and fashion where the emphasis on originality requires that boundaries are pushed. Very few traditional assessment modes lend themselves to judging what is inherently subjective. The testing of learning outcomes such as cognition and knowledge simply does not meet the demands of courses that celebrate originality and creativity.

Fostering creativity: assessing creatively

Fostering creativity is essential for students to be able to deal with the unknown, with situations not yet existing. Preparing students for the unknown is an avowed new requirement of UK higher education.

Much has been written on fostering creativity in education (see Craft, 2001, for an analysis of the literature), with a general shift in the discourse which recognises that the concept of creativity may not just be applicable to 'high flyers' but that it may encompass a whole continuum from replication to formulation to innovation to origination (Fennell, 1993). In other words, we are all capable of creative acts. Fennell's model widens the focus and shifts it away from the 'genius end' of creativity that used to be the main focal point for discussion.

Rather than being viewed as a 'dumbing down' of the concept of creativity, this model recognises and allows for a developmental approach to be taken, acknowledging that different types of creativity may occur at different times within an individual's educational and personal development. The novice or apprentice is likely, therefore, to display predominantly replication, while the 'master', one could reasonably assume, would be working more within the realms of innovation and origination.

A developmental approach to fostering creativity may usefully draw on research by Jeffrey and Craft (2001), whose discourse on the concept of creativity also encompasses: operating in the economic and political field; acting as a possible vehicle for individual empowerment in institutions; and being used to develop effective learning (p. 3).

It is particularly the third of these categories which concerns us in the design of innovative assessments which support learner self-regulation and which may be capable of assessing creative products and processes. Employing methods of assessment so that students are used to develop effective learning is central to many of the innovations in this volume and is at the root of Nicol and Milligan's seven principles of good feedback (Chapter 5). Assessing creativity or creative products requires that we view assessment differently and think of the process almost as an art form which seeks to make sense of, and make judgements about, the unknown. What is required here is the development of high-level professional judgement.

Professional judgement required to assess the unknown need not and should not imply tutor judgement of student work. It is a concept which requires training, education and acculturation resulting in professional 'connoisseurs', as advocated by Elton (Chapter 19). Developing professional judgement in this instance applies equally to both student and 'professional', who may then engage in a discourse about the creative process or product before agreeing upon a grade.

So how can professional judgement which recognises creativity meet the requirements of quality and standards frameworks? Assessment based on professional judgement is common between examiners in the field of art and design where there is a well-established assessment practice based on a system of expert peer review. An example of assessing creativity was developed at the Liverpool Institute for Performing Arts (LIPA) and has been described by Kleiman (2005). The system of 'negotiated assessment' for creative practical work at LIPA originated in the performance design curriculum, an area where traditionally examiners are well used to alternative methods of assessment as frequently they can have only a very general preconception of what to expect. It was later adopted across the whole curriculum at LIPA.

Six assessment fields were identified:

1　Presentation/production, i.e. the finished product presented to an audience.
2　Process, i.e. the journey that led to the product.
3　Idea, i.e. the ideas that informed both the process and the product.
4　Technical, i.e. the quality and utility of the technical features of the product and the skills with which they were assembled and/or operated.
5　Documentation, i.e. research, design, planning, evaluation, etc.
6　Interview, i.e. the student's ability to articulate their understanding, utilisation and application and use of any of the above.

Each field was divided into grade bands and through negotiation between the students and the tutor(s), the assessment weighting for each of the fields could be altered. This allowed the student who was consciously and determinedly 'taking a creative risk' (working at Fennell's 1993 'innovation' or 'origination' level) to have the assessment emphasis placed less on presentation/production and more on process, idea and documentation. It also allowed the student who was carrying out a specific task or working to a strictly defined brief – i.e., to make rather than design a particular artefact (working at Fennell's 'replication' or 'formulation' level) – to have more emphasis placed on the final product and technical features and less on idea and process. In the case of the latter there would still be a requirement for documentation, and in both cases students would still be required to undertake an assessment interview.

The interview would normally last between thirty and forty minutes. Students would bring evidence to support their 'case', and the interview would consist of the tutors turning the assessment criteria statements into questions. An important and essential feature of this process was that tutors would rigorously work their way up from a level that was clearly below that which was applicable to the student's work. This gave an opportunity to the students to demonstrate or argue that their work not only met a particular criterion in full, but exceeded it. (Sometimes the tutors had to persuade the student that their work was actually better than they conceived it to be.) During this process, professional judgement was being exercised by both tutor and student. Eventually a point would be reached where there were more negative than positive responses to the questions. That would indicate – to both the assessors *and* the student – that the assessment of the work had reached its maximal level.

As Kleiman points out, one unexpected benefit of this system was that student appeals against their grades virtually disappeared, as the process was transparent, explicit and mutually agreed. It also demonstrates a system capable of assessing creative processes and products in a way that was not only valid, fair and reliable but, importantly, was *perceived and experienced* to be so. It demonstrates that 'assessment' and 'creativity' are not and need not be mutually exclusive terms.

We cannot, however, be complacent. This sort of innovation runs against the flow of learning outcomes and other constraints outlined in Chapter 1. We need to be mindful that there are usually no quick fixes and that as innovators we constantly seek to find a balance between gains and losses of different modes of assessment. For example, do we go for quick and efficient feedback at the expense of enhancing deep learning? Further research in the development of creativity and professional judgement is needed so that innovative and creative assessment solutions may become common practice within the higher education community.

Where do we go from here?

As the contributors have illustrated throughout the book, modern society requires a fundamentally different conceptual discourse for assessment. This is similar to what Broadfoot (2002: 201) advocactes: 'What is urgently needed now is the beginnings of an active search for a more humanistic, even intuitive, approach to educational assessment which is more in keeping with the spirit and needs of the times.'

It is the privilege of having achieved economical stability that allows Western society to be concerned with information and for our educational concerns to be with helping learners discern between what knowledge is needed, how to look for it and how to use it with integrity. We need to enter into a discourse on the perceived 'expectation gap' between what students think is acceptable and the reality of what is required of our citizens.

What we are proposing is a move from techno-rationalism to a more sophis-ticated, intuitive concept of assessment that accepts and embraces the subjectivity of judgement. The chapters in this book have provided evidence to support the reconceptualisation of assessment as an instrument of liberation rather than one of measurement and limitation. The case studies illustrate ways in which a 'toolkit' of skills can be developed. Such a shift in attitude, away from the assessment discourse of league tables, statistics and accountability and towards a discourse of development, requires nothing short of what Boud (2000: 159) calls, 'a revolution in assessment thinking'.

As Gibbs highlights in Chapter 1, the culture around assessment is 'conservative and defensive rather than bold'. Gaining approval for innovative assessment can be difficult as university teaching committees are reluctant to validate pro-grammes of study that include novel assessment for fear of external scrutiny. It can only be hoped that a general move away from quality assurance towards quality enhancement in the UK may provide the confidence for HEIs to embrace change and challenge the pedagogic value of traditional assessment methods.

The case studies offered in this book form part of a growing evidence base of innovative practice (Schwartz and Webb, 2002) illustrating that assessment can serve both a political and an educational purpose.

This new assessment culture is defined by the following characteristics:

- active participation in authentic, real-life tasks that require the application of existing knowledge and skills;
- participation in a dialogue and conversation between learners (including tutors);
- engagement with and development of criteria and self-regulation of one's own work;
- employment of a range of diverse assessment modes and methods adapted from different subject disciplines;
- opportunity to develop and apply attributes such as reflection, resilience, resourcefulness and professional judgement and conduct in relation to problems;
- acceptance of the limitations of judgement and the value of dialogue in developing new ways of working.

The role of the tutor is being reconfigured in light of interventions and empirical evidence of good practice in feedback mechanisms. As such the power differential is being broken down between tutor and student as both aspire to become more efficient, professional individuals. This collection signals the emergence of a new assessment paradigm built on the evidence base of research into student learning. The contributors share a common belief that assessment and learning should be seen in tandem; each should contribute to the other. Collectively we have acknowledged that there are problems with existing assessment and that we are short-changing students by failing to provide them with the feedback they need to improve. The much-used feedback phrase 'could do better' applies to ourselves as practitioners, not just to our students. We believe that better is possible even with more students. By definition, to be 'innovative' means improving and advancing our academic practice. It does not signal an achieved state of excellence but a constant search for enhancement. We invite others to join us in our search for excellence and to take the moral high ground, stand up for what research tells us is right and commit to better assessment.

Note

1   The University of York provides programmes of professional development and skills training for Ph.D. students, postgraduate teaching assistants and contract research staff: <http://www.york.ac.uk/admin/pod/graduate/links.shtml> (accessed 19 October 2005).

References

Atkinson, T. and Claxton, G. (eds) (2000) *The intuitive practitioner – on the value of not always knowing what one is doing.* Buckingham: Open University Press.

226 *Karen Clegg and Cordelia Bryan*

Barnett, R. (1999) *Realising the university in an age of supercomplexity*, Philadelphia and Buckingham: SRHE/Open University Press.

Biggs, J. (1999) Teaching for quality learning at university. Buckingham: SRHE/Open University Press.

Birenbaum, M. and Dochy, F. (eds) (1996) *Alternatives in assessment of achievements, learning processes and prior knowledge*, Boston, MA: Kluwer Academic Publishers.

Birenbaum, M. (2003) in M. Segers, F. Dochy and E. Cascallar (eds) *Optimising new modes of assessment: in search of qualities and standards*, Dordrecht: Kluwer Academic Publishers.

Black, P. and Wiliam, D. (1998) 'Assessment and classroom learning', in *Assessment in Education: Policy, Principles and Practice*, vol. 5, pp. 1 7–74.

Black, P., Harrison, C., Lee, C., Marshall, B. and Wiliam, D. (2003) *Assessment for learning: putting it into practice*, Buckingham: Open University Press.

Boud, D. (1995) *Enhancing Learning through Self Assessment*, London: Kogan Page.

Boud, D. (2000) 'Sustainable assessment: rethinking assessment for the learning society', in *Studies in Continuing Education*, vol. 22, 2, pp.151–67.

Broadfoot, P. (2002) in P. Schwartz and G. Webb (eds), 'Assessment case studies: experience and practice from higher education', in *Case Studies of Teaching in Higher Education Series*, London: Kogan Page.

Cannon, D. (2002) 'Learning to fail: learning to recover', in M. Peelo and T. Wareham (eds), *Failing Students in Higher Education*, Buckingham: SRHE/Open University Press.

Carroll, J. (2002) *A Handbook for deterring plagiarism in higher education*, Oxford: Oxford Centre for Staff and Learning Development.

Clegg, K. (2004) *Playing safe: learning and teaching in undergraduate law*. Available at <http://www.ukcle.ac.uk/research/ncle.html> (accessed 14 April 2005).

Cowan, J. (1998) *On becoming an innovative university teacher: reflection in action*, Buckingham: SRHE/Open University Press.

Craft, A. (2001) *Creativity in education: an analysis of research and literature on creativity*. Report prepared for the Qualifications and Curriculum Authority.

Crooks, T. J. (1988) 'The impact of classroom assessment evaluation practices on students', in *Review of Educational Research*, vol. 58, 44: pp.438–81.

Cross, K.P. (1987) 'Teaching for Learning', *AAHE Bulletin*, 39, 8, pp. 3–7.

Dochy F., Gijbels, D. and Van de Watering, G. (2004) *Assessment engineering: aligning assessment, learning and instruction*. Keynote lecture, EARLI–Northumbria Assessment Conference, Bergen.

Dweck, C.S. (1999) Self-theories: their role in motivation, personality and development. Philadelphia, PA: Psychology Press.

Entwistle, N. and Ramsden, P. (1983) *Understanding Student Learning*, London, Croom Helm.

Fennell, E. (1993) 'Categorising Creativity', *Competence and Assessment*, 23: 7.

Gulikers, J., Bastianens, T. and Kirschner, P. (2004) *Perceptions of authentic assessment: five dimensions of authenticity*. Paper presented at the Northumbria–EARLI Assessment Conference, Bergen.

Hinett, K. (2002) in M. Peelo and T. Wareham (eds) 'Failing to assess, or assessing failure?' *Failing Students in Higher Education*, Buckingham: SRHE/OU Press.

Hinett, K. and Thomas, J. (1999) *Staff Guide to Self and Peer Assessment*, Oxford: Oxford Centre for Staff and Learning Development.

Jeffrey, B. and Craft, A. (2001) 'The universalization of creativity', in A. Craft, B. Jeffrey and M. Leibling (eds), *Creativity in education*, London: Continuum.

Kleiman, P. (2005) 'Beyond the tingle factor: creativity and assessment in higher education'. Unpublished paper (submitted to *Studies in Higher Education*, May 2005) based on presentation at PALATINE Shared Learning workshop, January 2004, York.

McDonald, B. and Boud, D. (2003) 'The impact of self-assessment on achievement: the effects of self-assessment training on performance in external examinations', in *Assessment in Education*, vol. 10, 2 pp. 209–20.

Royce Sadler, D. (2002) '"RAH! . . . so that's Quality!": making students aware of what constitutes "quality" on assignments or other assessment products they prepare,' in P. Schwartz and G. Webb (eds), *Assessment case studies, experience and practice from higher education*. London: Kogan Page.

Orsmond, P., Merry, S. and Reiling, K. (1997) 'A study in self assessment: tutor and students' perceptions of performance criteria', in *Assessment and Evaluation in Higher Education*, 22, 4, pp. 357–69.

Orsmond, P., Merry, S. and Reiling, K. (2000) 'The use of student-derived marking criteria in peer and self assessment', in *Assessment and Evaluation in Higher Education*, 25, 1, pp. 23–38.

Orsmond, P., Merry, S. and Reiling, K. (2002) 'The use of exemplars and formative feedback when using student derived marking criteria in self and peer assessment', *Assessment and Evaluation in Higher Education*, 27(4): 309–23.

Sadler, D.R. (1989) 'Formative Assessment and the Design of Instructional Systems', in *Instructional Science*, vol. 18, pp.119–44.

Sadler, D.R. (1998) 'Formative assessment: revisiting the territory', *Assessment in Education*, vol. 5, 1, pp.77–84.

Sambell, L., McDowell, L. and Brow, S. (1997) '"But is it fair?": an exploratory study of student perceptions of the consequential validity of assessment', *Studies in Educational Evaluation*, 23(4): 349–71.

Schwartz, P. and Webb, G. (2002) *Assessment case studies, experience and practice from higher education*. London: Kogan Page.

Yorke, M. (2002) 'Non-completing students', in M. Peelo and T. Wareham (eds), *Failing Students in Higher Education*, Buckingham: SRHE/Open University Press.

Index